Dazzy Vance

ALSO BY JOHN SKIPPER
AND FROM McFARLAND

---

*Wicked Curve: The Life and Troubled
Times of Grover Cleveland Alexander* (2006)

*The Cubs Win the Pennant: Charlie Grimm, the
Billy Goat Curse, and the 1945 World Series Run* (2004)

*A Biographical Dictionary of Major
League Baseball Managers* (2003)

*A Biographical Dictionary of the
Baseball Hall of Fame* (2000)

*Take Me Out to the Cubs Game: 35 Former
Ballplayers Speak of Losing at Wrigley* (2000)

*Umpires: Classic Baseball Stories from
the Men Who Made the Calls* (1997)

*Inside Pitch: A Closer Look at
Classic Baseball Moments* (1996)

Dazzy Vance

A Biography of the Brooklyn Dodger Hall of Famer

John C. Skipper

McFarland & Company, Inc., Publishers
Jefferson, North Carolina, and London

LIBRARY OF CONGRESS CATALOGUING-IN-PUBLICATION DATA

Skipper, John C., 1945–
    Dazzy Vance : a biography of the Brooklyn Dodger hall of
famer / John C. Skipper.
        p.   cm.
    Includes bibliographical references and index.

    ISBN 978-0-7864-2985-1
    (softcover : 50# alkaline paper) ∞

    1. Vance, Dazzy.   2. Baseball players—United States—
Biography.   I. Title.
GV865.V37D49   2007
796.357092 — dc22   2007001366

British Library cataloguing data are available

On the cover: Dazzy Vance (National Baseball Hall of Fame and Library,
Cooperstown, NY)

Manufactured in the United States of America

McFarland & Company, Inc., Publishers
    Box 611, Jefferson, North Carolina 28640
    www.mcfarlandpub.com

For Craig Farrar

Contents

Preface

Baseball has had its share of memorable teams over the years. Some have had individual seasons of glory:

The Hitless Wonders Chicago White Sox of 1906 who barely hit .200 as a team but managed to beat the Cubs in the World Series.

The Miracle Braves of 1914 who were in last place on the Fourth of July and then rallied to win the National League championship and defeat Connie Mack's stellar Philadelphia A's in the World Series.

The Amazing Mets of 1969 who staged a furious stretch drive to overtake the seemingly invincible Chicago Cubs to win the pennant and then defeat the Baltimore Orioles in the World Series.

Other teams have made a name for themselves for what they accomplished over a period of years:

The Murderers' Row Yankees of the 1920s and Bronx Bombers of the 1950s and '60s.

The Gashouse Gang of the St. Louis Cardinals in 1930s.

The Big Red Machine that dominated the National League in the 1970s.

All of these teams had something in common. They won championships.

In the 1920s, there was another group of athletes that made a name for themselves. The Daffiness Boys of the Brooklyn Dodgers were a unique breed of ballplayer. They sometimes ran the bases as if they were blindfolded and caught fly balls as if they had Ping-Pong paddles as gloves. They had a manager who had to try to make sense of it all and fans who loved to hate them and packed the ballpark every year to watch them play. These were not championship ballplayers. The record will show they usually finished sixth.

The undisputed leader of the Daffiness Boys was Charles Arthur Vance, a hard-throwing right-handed pitcher who, at his peak, was the highest paid pitcher in the National League. A decade before the Dean brothers, Dizzy and Daffy, came along and ruled the roost for the St. Louis Cardinals, a man nicknamed Dazzy Vance was the strikeout king of the National League for the Brooklyn Robins.

It's hard to pinpoint the exact date and time that the daffiness set in with the team, but it is well to point out that their leader, Charles "Dazzy" Vance, changed his name unofficially twice, and when asked by the Hall of Fame for the name he wanted on his plaque gave them one that was not the name he was given at birth.

Jack Fournier, the first baseman and bookie, eventually gave way to Babe Herman, a great hitter but atrocious fielder and base runner whose antics are part of Brooklyn lore. Burleigh Grimes was the last of the legal spitballers in the National League. Zack Wheat, an outfielder and a tremendous hitter, was manager of the club for a short while — a fact that every baseball record book has seemed to ignore.

The manager of the Daffiness Boys was Wilbert Robinson, a good ballplayer in his own day, and who won two pennants piloting the Brooklyn ball club — both before the daffiness took hold on the field. He was known around the league as "Uncle Robbie" and his team, during his tenure, was known not by their real name, the Dodgers, but as the Robins.

Dazzy Vance led the National League in strikeouts seven years in a row. He won 28 games in 1924 and beat out Rogers Hornsby for the Most Valuable Player award even though Hornsby hit .424, the all-time best batting average in modern baseball. In 1925, Vance pitched a one-hitter and followed it up with a no-hitter. He finished his career with 197 victories and was the first Brooklyn player elected to the Hall of Fame in 1955.

He was a fun-loving, easy-going boy who grew up in Iowa and Nebraska but somehow picked up a southern drawl that he never lost. He was a prankster who was the chief judge of the Robins' kangaroo court and who mesmerized opposing hitters with a blazing fastball, off-the-tabletop curve, a high leg kick and a sleeve on the undershirt of his pitching arm with slits cut into it that would flutter and distract batters as he delivered the pitch.

Dazzy Vance overcame a perpetually sore arm to get to the major leagues — and even his entry into the big time was a fluke. Brooklyn wanted a minor league catcher, Hank DeBerry, but DeBerry refused to come to Brooklyn unless Vance came with him. So Dazzy made it to major leagues — at the age of 31. The Robins didn't know it yet, but their new pitcher had off-season skills that would serve him well for many years. He held out for more money every off-season and usually accomplished a couple of things. He always seemed to win the hold-out battles and, if he stretched the negotiations out long enough, he'd miss some of spring training which was another one of his goals.

In the late 1920s, when Vance was making $25,000 a year, he started investing in Florida real estate when prices were deflated. Each year he bought a little more and eventually he owned thousands of acres at a time when land prices were soaring. He retired at the age of 44 without achieving his goal of winning 200 games but retreated to an extremely comfortable life he had set up for himself, his wife, Edyth, and daughter, Dorothy, on the west coast of Florida.

He was a great pitcher and a shrewd businessman but he had another quality that made him a biographer's best friend. Dazzy Vance was a great storyteller. He loved to sit in the lobby of the hotel he built in Homosassa Springs, Florida, and entertain guests with stories about his days on the diamond at Ebbets Field in Brooklyn and throughout the National League. Sometimes, he would laugh as he talked and his sides would shake and his ruddy complexion would get even redder.

The author is especially grateful to Gary Vance, great-nephew of Dazzy, for providing extensive details about the Vance family history and some wonderful recollections about his famous great-uncle. He also expresses his appreciation to Robyn Tomlin, executive editor of the *Ocala Star-Banner* in Ocala, Florida, and Charlie Brennan, editor of the *Citrus County Chronicle*, for their help in the research process. Thanks also to staffers at the Coastal Heritage Museum and the Citrus County Historical Society in Florida for their help in providing valuable resource and research materials.

The staff at the National Baseball Hall of Fame Library in Cooperstown, New York, was extremely helpful (as usual) as were the "silent" research assistants, Retrosheet, baseball-reference.com, baseballlibrary. com — all excellent Internet links — and ProQuest, a link made available through the Society for American Baseball Research.

The author wishes to pay special tribute to the late Martin Yoseloff, whose words of encouragement paid off too late for him to witness the results; to Ted Savas, who, thank goodness, never takes "no" for an answer and therefore created the runway for projects like this to take off; and for the many people — too many to single out individually — who created welcome encouragement and motivation.

A researcher would be remiss in not acknowledging the work of all of the writers preceding him who followed the life and career of Dazzy Vance and preserved it through their work so that others, like me, could learn about this remarkable man. My hope would be that this work would serve the same purpose for the next generation of writers, historians and fans.

Thanks to Dazzy Vance himself for having the gift of gab and sharing so many stories with so many people over the years. This book would not have been possible without you in more ways than one.

As always, until the day I die, my love and gratitude to my life partner, Sandi Skipper, who understands me well enough to know how important my work is to me and allows me the freedom to do it. None of this would be possible without that freedom.

All of that being said, it's time to play ball. Read and enjoy.

I

The Old Jeepers Creepers

Along Florida's Gulf Coast, the Fort Harrison Hotel stood as a symbol of good and gracious living. Built in 1926, it was Clearwater's first skyscraper. Eleven stories in height, its majestic outline could be seen for miles up and down the coast. Its balconied roof gardens overlooked the islands and waters of Clearwater Bay and the Gulf of Mexico. Below the rooftop, beautiful lobbies, palm gardens, terraces, and lounges graced spacious balconies. The hotel was the centerpiece of downtown Clearwater, a touristy mecca landscaped with citrus and pines and sunshine and water and an average daily temperature of 72 degrees.

The man standing in front of the hotel on April 5, 1939, was two years shy of 50 but he looked older. And he looked out of place. He was tall and too thin for the clothes he was wearing. A felt hat with wide brim flopped on top of a large head. A tanned, freckled face carried a faint smile below a bulbous red nose that protruded prominently. He wore an open neck shirt under a suit coat that was a size too big and hung on him as if someone had draped it over the rigid torso of a department store mannequin.

He was a man most comfortable near water now, especially with a fishing pole no more than an arm's length away. But today, he was a fisherman out of water so to speak, as he stood amid the hustle and bustle of the car-honking, people-shouting, whistle-blowing-cop noise of urban life at the intersection of Fort Harrison Avenue and Second Street. His presence was but a shadow hardly noticed by the throng of pedestrians and hotel patrons deeply engrossed in their own little pavement-pounding lives.

One man noticed.

"You missing somebody, brother?" The questioner was a younger man, dressed casually but in clothes that fit. His tone of voice was not

A photograph from an old advertising brochure shows Dazzy near his Homosassa Springs, Florida, home in the late 1930s with former Brooklyn outfielder Bernie Neis, the fishing guide for guests at Dazzy's hotel and lodge.

threatening as he got the old fisherman's attention. Their eyes met and they both smiled.

"It's a funny thing you'd ask me that today," said the fisherman, Mr. A.C. Vance of nearby Homosassa Springs, who recognized the man immediately. And with that, the two old friends struck up a conversation filled with zest and nostalgia.

About an hour earlier, both had watched as a large, white rectangular truck made its way out of downtown Clearwater, the start of a thousand-mile journey north. The lettering on the side of the truck was in blue script, identifying the famous owners of the cargo it carried. It said, "Brooklyn Dodgers." Clearwater, with all of its other glowing attributes, was also the spring training home of the Dodgers.

Not far from the hotel, the Brooklyn players had boarded a train and started barnstorming their way north, full of the hopes and dreams that every ball club had at this time of year. It was April in America, the Christmas Eve of baseball, when everyone focuses on what tomorrow will bring and has pride and confidence and, most of all, hope.

The fisherman knew all about that. He was Arthur Charles Vance, shriveled now from his former self because he was recovering from a near-fatal bout with pneumonia. The way he looked today would have deceived a stranger because he was not a man who was poor and weak and wanting. Vance was a successful real estate developer and entrepreneur in Homosassa Springs where he owned a hotel and lodge. But his business holdings were merely a means to an end, for Arthur Charles Vance would have been content to just hunt and fish — and talk baseball.

His friends called him Dazzy — heck, everybody called him Dazzy — and had since he was growing up on the plains of Nebraska at the turn of the 20th century. And it wasn't that long ago — four years to be exact — that Dazzy Vance was on that train heading north from Clearwater as a member of the Brooklyn Dodgers. Ten years before that, this fisherman was the best pitcher in the National League.

He had long arms — an 83-inch reach in his prime. Boxer Joe Louis had a reach of 76 inches. And Dazzy had a way of distracting batters that was legal when he started doing it but was later outlawed because he was doing it. He'd cut long slits in the sleeve of the right arm of his white long-sleeved undershirt. The cloth would flutter in the breeze as he wound up, kicked his leg up high and blazed fastball after fastball past National League batters. He led the league in strikeouts seven years in a row and in 1924, when he won 28 games, he won the league's Most Valuable Player award, beating out the Cardinals' Rogers Hornsby, who set a major league record that year with his .424 batting average.

The fan who found Dazzy on that Clearwater street corner was Bill Corum, a New York sportswriter, who was a crony from the old days. He had ridden many a Pullman with Dazzy and the boys, from Brooklyn halfway across the United States to New York City and Boston and Pittsburgh and Philadelphia and Cincinnati and Chicago and to the western edge of the baseball universe, St. Louis.

Corum had been part of the crowd on the nights when some of the boys would go "over the river" in Cincinnati in search of moonshine that they always seemed to find and to wolf down the best knackwurst sandwiches this side of the Mississippi.

Corum was short and portly (*Time* magazine once described him as "stump-shaped") and wrote 10,000 columns over a 50-year career, mostly with New York newspapers.[1] He had a way with words and therefore had his way with most of the athletes he covered over the years. When Grover Cleveland Alexander struck out Tony Lazzeri to end a Yankee threat in the 1926 World Series, Corum wrote, "There is no rest for the wicked curve." When he covered the Kentucky Derby, he called it "the run for the roses," which has become the marquee name for the famous horse race.

Corum's first byline story in the *New York Times* appeared on April 15, 1925, and started like this: "Vance, victory and visions of a pennant served to mellow the otherwise chilly opening of another baseball season in Brooklyn yesterday. Some 20,000 hopeful fans of Flatbush gathered at Ebbets Field to see the Robins beat the Phillies, 3–1.[2]

So Corum's first word in print under his byline was "Vance." That's how far back the two of them went. Corum knew from experience that Dazzy had another skill in which he was as proficient as pitching a baseball, and that was spinning a good story or two or three, and without much prompting. So when he saw Dazzy in Clearwater on that April morning, he knew what to do. Just as gangster Willie Sutton used to say he robbed banks "because that's where the money is," Corum hooked on with Dazzy because that's where the story was.

"When I see that truck go down the street with the big trunks marked 'Brooklyn Baseball Club,' I sort of lift the old souper and start remembering. Which doesn't do a man any good," said Dazzy.

He hesitated, collected himself and said, "Nice fishing weather, ain't it?"[3]

It was as if the truck carried with it the ghosts of the Dodgers of yesteryear, like Charlie Ebbets, the man who began his career as a ticket seller and rose to become the feisty, determined owner; like the superb Baltimore manager Ned Hanlon, who came over to Brooklyn and much of his ball club came with him, including Wee Willie Keeler, Hughie

Jennings and Joe Kelly; like Nap Rucker and Zack Wheat and Hi Myers. There was the zany Casey Stengel and Burleigh Grimes and of course, Wilbert Robinson—"Uncle Robbie"—who guided his troops not only to two National League championships but also through some of the craziest antics ever seen on a major league baseball diamond.

The 1939 Dodgers had some spunk—a cocky two-fisted, player-manager in Leo Durocher, the starting shortstop; a slugging first baseman in Dolph Camilli, the only true power hitter on the ball club; a journeyman catcher in Babe Phelps; Cookie Lavagetto, who, eight years later, would break up a World Series no-hitter in the ninth inning; a rising young star in Dixie Walker; an aging one in Tony Lazzeri; and pitching featuring Luke Hamlin, Hugh Casey, Whitlow Wyatt, Freddie Fitzsimmons, and Van Lingle Mungo, whose name would become famous in a popular baseball song 40 years later. Of the 1939 Dodgers, only Phelps and Mungo were holdovers from the 1935 club that was the last one Vance played on.

"I wish I could think better of this team," Vance told Corum. "But the best I can give it is maybe sixth. There are too many question marks."

Corum was just listening now, and taking notes. The fisherman was on a roll. He talked about how the Dodgers fans deserved a winning team and that sooner or later they'd get one. He reminisced about how the Brooklyn faithful would shout at him from the upper level of the stands and sometimes not be real nice about it. Yet they deserved a winner, he said. But it wouldn't be this year.[4]

Dazzy won 197 games in a major league career that did not start until he was 31 years old except for brief stints with the Pirates and Yankees. His career lasted parts of 16 seasons but only 12 full seasons. He won 20 or more games three times, including 28 in his MVP year of 1924, led the National League in wins twice, led the league in strikeouts seven straight years, 1922–1928, in shutouts four years and in complete games two years. He was the National League's earned run average leader in three different seasons.

Corum described Vance this way: He had a "high, hard one hot enough to fry an egg and a hook that used to kiss the boys good-bye all the way from Ebbets Field around the Horn."

No wonder that when he stood on the street corner after the Dodgers made their way out of Clearwater that day, Dazzy looked at Corum and said, "This is the one day in the year when I get those old jeepers-creepers."[5]

The fisherman's attitude picked up when he talked about his place in Homosassa Springs, where the fish are so thick, he said, that a man could walk from one side of the springs to the other with his feet only touching the backs of the fish. He also thought that Spanish explorer Ferdinand Ponce de Leon just missed his mark when he came to Florida looking for the Fountain of Youth in 1521. His expedition led him to an area not far from where Homosassa Springs was located. Homosassa Springs won't make you young again literally, said Vance, but it will rejuvenate you.

"Come over and have a drink with me some time and be convinced," he told Corum. "It won't cost a dime unless you want to buy a beer for the house, which I can't drink now — worst luck."[6]

Oh, the stories that flowed night after night from the lobby of that hotel in Homosassa Springs, and from the porch, and from the lounge chairs on the grounds surrounding it. Dazzy would talk in a southern drawl and nobody knew where he got it. It didn't come from his upbringing in Iowa and Nebraska, nor was it picked up in any minor league towns he played in — because he never played in any of them long enough — and yet it wasn't fake either. Nothing about Dazzy was fake.

New York sportswriter Frank Graham described him as a man of great character who was a great character who could get along fine if he had some clothes, a warm bed and pitcher of beer. "He got more out of life than almost anyone he met in his wanderings, envied no one, and if he had any regrets, which is doubtful, he kept them to himself."[7]

He'd sit back in his chair, whittling a piece of wood and clenching a burned-out cigar stub in his teeth or holding it between the index and forefinger of his right hand as he talked. And he'd spin the stories about "Uncle Robbie" — Wilbert Robinson — his manager most of the years he was in Brooklyn. One time, as a publicity stunt, Robbie, a former catcher, agreed to catch a baseball dropped several thousand feet from an airplane. As a joke, someone substituted a grapefruit. It hit Robbie's glove with such a thud that it exploded, spraying him with juice. Robbie literally did not know what hit him and at first mistook the juice for blood and thought he was mortally wounded.

Then there was Babe Herman, the hard-hitting outfielder who had a little trouble with the glove and who was angered by rumors that he once was beaned by a flyball he failed to catch. "Never happened," said Babe. "What about a ball hitting you on the shoulder?" a sportswriter asked. "That don't count," said the Babe.[8]

Vance said the secret to Herman's success as a hitter was that he didn't think when he was in the batter's box. "It's hard for a pitcher to outsmart a batter who doesn't think," said Dazzy.[9]

The collection of Dodgers goofballs in the 1920s became known around the league as the Daffiness Boys. Vance was a charter member and until the day he died was their chief raconteur. Their manager, "Uncle Robbie," fit right in. On one occasion, Robinson decided to institute a system in which players would be fined for making stupid plays on the field. On the day this new system started, Robinson turned in an incorrect batting order to the home plate umpire before the game, resulting in a Dodger batting out of turn. After the game, Robbie levied a fine against himself. Just another day in the wacky Dodgers clubhouse.[10]

The Brooklyn ball club waited a long time for the ultimate baseball success. The Dodgers won the National League pennant in 1920, two years before Vance joined the club, and didn't win another one until 1941, six years after he left. They didn't win a World Series until 1955.

Like the Dodgers, Dazzy Vance's story is one of perseverance. It is the story of a kid who had a great arm and almost ruined it by continuing to pitch in the minor leagues when he was hurt —"I had to make a living," he said — and of a journeyman who didn't come up to the major leagues for good until he was 31 years old. He made the most of it while he was there and retired just three shy of 200 wins. Vance was considered the Dodgers' greatest pitcher until the Drysdale-Koufax era more than 20 years after he retired.

On Sept. 26, 1967, Don Drysdale beat the Pittsburgh Pirates 3–1 at Dodger Stadium in Los Angeles. It was his 190th career win, tying Vance for the most wins in a Dodgers uniform at that time. Drysdale achieved the mark at the age of 31— the same age at which Vance won his first game!

In 1955, a few months before Brooklyn clinched its first World Series title, Dazzy Vance became the first Dodger in the history of that fabled franchise to be inducted into the National Baseball Hall of Fame.

The fisherman on the corner knew more about the Dodgers than most people in Clearwater on that spring day in 1939. But he wasn't much of a forecaster. The Dodgers got on the train in Florida, chugged their way north and six months later finished third in the National League, 12½ games behind the first place Reds, and a few notches higher than the sixth place finish Ol' Daz thought they might achieve. But for Vance, you could chalk it up to an educated guess. You couldn't blame him for picking the Dodgers no higher that sixth. After all, in the 12 seasons he spent with Brooklyn, the Dodgers finished sixth six times. The Dazzy era looked like this:

Year	Record	Finish	Pct.	Vance W–L	Vance Pct.
1922	76–78	Sixth	.494	18–12	.600
1923	76–78	Sixth	.494	18–15	.545
1924	92–62	Second	.597	28–6	.824
1925	68–85	Seventh	.444	22–9	.710
1926	71–82	Sixth	.464	9–10	.474
1927	65–88	Sixth	.425	16–15	.516
1928	77–76	Sixth	.503	22–10	.688
1929	70–83	Sixth	.458	14–13	.519
1930	86–68	Fourth	.558	17–15	.531
1931	79–73	Fourth	.520	11–13	.458
1932	81–73	Third	.526	12–11	.522
(1933–1934, Vance played for St. Louis and Cincinnati, returning to Brooklyn for part of the 1935 season)					
1935	70–83	Fifth	.458	3–2	.600

For eight straight years, Dazzy's winning percentage was higher than the team's— and when that string was broken in 1930, Vance had one of his greatest years, despite his 17–15 record. He had a 13-game stretch where he gave up more than two earned runs only once and finished the year with a 2.61 earned run average, easily the best in the National League. All of this at the age of 39. He lost twice by 3–1 scores, once 2–1 and once 1–0 in 10 innings.

After toiling so many years for the often hapless Dodgers, Vance made his only World Series appearance for St. Louis, getting into one game, in relief, in 1934. For the old fisherman, despite his many great years with the Dodgers, the National League pennant was always the big one that got away in Brooklyn.

The rapport he had with writers and broadcasters over the years, and the joy he found in telling his old baseball stories, allows today's historians to recapture much of his life and times through an extremely valuable resource — his own words.

II

"Ain't it a dazzy?"

There were only two ways to describe the dirt roads around the farmland in Orient, Iowa, including the one that went by the Albert Vance property, in March of 1891. They were either dusty or muddy and their condition was always a sign of whether winter had finally vanished and spring rains had arrived or were still beckoning.

Orient, with its few hundred inhabitants, had been settled 12 years earlier. George Peet erected a small elevator and began buying grain from Albert Vance and neighboring farmers. It wasn't long before Marcus Hennesy started a coal and grain business not far from the general store and the meat market. Frank Cobb opened the first hardware store in 1882. There were a few buggies but transportation was mostly by foot, horseback and horse-drawn wagons. It was a simple life but often a hard life for men and women who lived and died by what their land provided for them. Vegetables were raised and canned; meat came from livestock and was butchered and crudely processed. Eggs, cream, milk and butter were products that were often bartered for sugar, flour and tobacco.[1]

Albert Vance was a Midwesterner, born in Washington County, Indiana, in 1844. On Oct. 13, 1862, he enlisted with the 66th Indiana Infantry Regiment at Camp Noble, Indiana, but his service in the Civil War was short lived. He suffered from chronic dysentery, an illness that limited his usefulness as a soldier. Assigned to Company H, war records show him as "absent sick" at Columbus, Kentucky, as of Dec. 16, 1862, just two months after he enlisted, "absent without leave" as of Jan. 15, 1863, and "deserter — by permission of Medical Director" at Columbus, Kentucky, as of April 14, 1863. He was sent to a hospital for six months and then sent home.

Albert migrated to Schuyler, Illinois, where he married a local girl, Sarah Elizabeth Ritchey on Feb. 24, 1875. The couple had six children, four boys and two girls, all of whom were born in Iowa where the couple moved within a year of their marriage. The children ranged in age from William Boyd Vance, called "Boyd" most of his life, born in 1876, to Charles Arthur Vance, called "Dazzy" most of his life, who was the youngest child and 15 years younger than Boyd. In between were sisters Aure Belle and Mary Louise and brothers Henry Wallace and Fred Sumner Vance.

All were part of a rather illustrious heritage. Four Vance brothers, David, Samuel, Andrew and James came to America from England in about 1735 and settled in the Philadelphia area and in the Shenandoah Valley. Future generations moved up the valley into Tennessee and North Carolina to the south and into western Pennsylvania to the north. Among the North Carolina Vances were David and his wife, Sarah, who were to become the grandparents of Zebulon Vance, governor of North Carolina during the Civil War and later a U.S. senator for several terms. He became an attorney after the Civil War and defended a man named Thomas Duvy, who was accused of murdering his mistress. Vance was unsuccessful in saving Duvy, who was hanged for his offense. A local writer became so caught up in the case that he wrote a song about it. "Duvy" was changed to "Dooley" for the purposes of the song, and the lyric, "Hang down your head, Tom Dooley," re-emerged almost 100 years later as a hit folk song sung by the Kingston Trio.

Mary Vance, a niece of David and Sarah Vance, married into the Hatfield family and her son, Anse Hatfield, was one of the central figures in the famed Hatfield-McCoy feud of the late 1800s. Through various marriages, President Andrew Jackson, Mary Todd Lincoln (wife of Abraham Lincoln) and Aaron Burr (vice president who was once tried for treason and who killed Alexander Hamilton in a duel) are all cousins of one Vance or another on the sprawling family tree.

When the man who would come to be known as Dazzy Vance was born on March 4, 1891, the sixth child of Albert and Sarah, no first name was listed on the birth certificate. The certification of birth in the Division of Records and Statistics for the Iowa Department of Health lists the baby's name as "(Not Shown) Vance." It is believed the doctor delivered the baby and then went on his way, not waiting around to learn the name of the child. The Vance family Bible, listing the births of all of the children of Albert and Sarah Vance — in Sarah's flowing script handwriting — notes that "Charles Arthur Vance" was born on March 4, 1891, in Adair County, Iowa. Family members say Dazzy

```
DEPARTMENT OF HEALTH                                STATE OF IOWA
        DIVISION OF RECORDS AND STATISTICS
                Certification of Birth
        This is to Certify That According to Records on File in This Office, That
                    (NOT SHOWN) VANCE

    Sex MALE        was born    MARCH 4, 1891

    at     UNION TWP,      ADAIR COUNTY,              Iowa.

        State File No. 1-91-10      Date of Filing MARCH 19, 1891,
    In witness whereof, the seal of the Department of Health, State of Iowa, has

    been affixed hereto this  24TH   day of    APRIL          , 1979.

    FATHER: A. T. VANCE
    MOTHER: SARAH RITCHEY
        ( SEAL )                    Norman L. Pawlewski
                                         STATE REGISTRAR

                                     Don R. Coughenour
                                            CHIEF

    WARNING: This certificate is not valid if it has been altered
        in any way whatsoever or if it does not bear the         R & S #4
        raised seal of the Department of Health.                 CP43671 1/70
```

Dazzy Vance's birth certificate (refiled in 1979) shows no first name. It was not unusual for country doctors in those days to deliver babies and leave on their next call before learning the child's name. (Courtesy of Gary Vance.)

started going by "Arthur Charles Vance" at about the time he started playing minor league baseball in Nebraska in about 1912 but nobody seems to know why. Much later, as a major leaguer, he had a little fun with a sportswriter and told him his name was "Clarence." For many years after that, he was referred to as "Arthur Clarence Vance" and "Clarence Arthur Vance." The confusion was so great that when he was elected to the Hall of Fame in 1955, he received a telegram from the Hall asking how he should be identified on his plaque. He responded, "Name is Arthur Charles Vance."[2]

In 1897, the family moved to Cowles, Nebraska, where Albert built a large, two-story wooden house and continued to toil in the fields to make a living. Young Arthur helped with the chores and began his life-long love of the outdoors. He befriended a neighbor who liked to hunt and to show off some of his "trophies" which he kept in a shack on his property. As Vance told the story years later, the neighbor would occasionally invite him in to show him pelts of wild animals he had killed as well as his cowboy outfit, chaps, lariat and the like. From time to

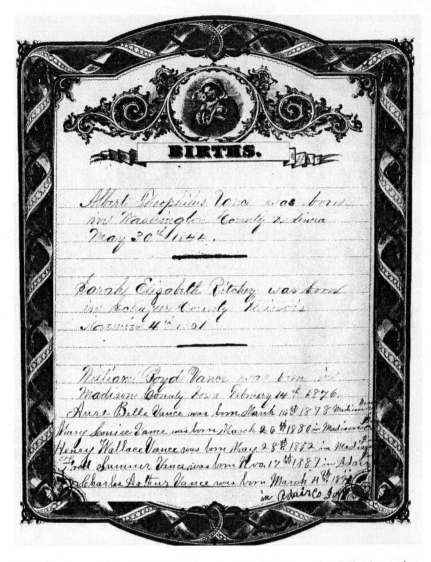

The last entry on this page in the Vance family Bible shows that "Charles Arthur Vance" was born on March 4, 1891, in Adair County. The handwriting is that of Vance's mother. Dazzy never went through the legal process of changing his name but went by "Arthur Charles Vance" most of his life and used "A.C. Vance" for his signature. (Courtesy of Gary Vance.)

time, he'd hold something up and say, "Ain't it a dazzy?" He meant daisy but he fractured the pronunciation. Dazzy started using the expression and soon it became his lifelong nickname.[3]

Nebraska was a state full of fields and plains and wide open spaces and was so flat that on a clear day in Omaha, it was said, if you turned to the west, you could see California. Major league baseball was something you heard about in Nebraska, but the closest major league teams were in St. Louis, 600 miles away. Despite its remote setting, the state produced some farm boys with strong arms who grew up to be some of the greatest pitchers in baseball history. About 90 miles up the road from Cowles, a young man named Grover Cleveland Alexander, who wowed spectators at county fairs with his blazing fastball and sharp-breaking curve, decided to give up his job as a telephone lineman and try to make a go of it in baseball. Today, his 373 victories are still the highest of any National League pitcher (tied with Christy Mathewson).

Dazzy Vance's climb to the big leagues was no less spectacular, particularly considering his introduction to baseball. He never even saw a ballgame until he was a teenager and playing baseball was a bit of a challenge on the farm. "My brother Fred and I lived on our father's farm near Hastings, Neb., and as we were the only boys in the neighborhood, we figured out a two-man baseball game. We built a backstop out of chicken wire and marked off the foul lines," said Dazzy in an interview about 20 years later. The year was 1907 when Detroit and Pittsburgh were baseball's best teams. Dazzy and Fred would take turns batting, with the other one pitching. When a fair ball was hit, the pitcher would get it and throw it toward home plate. If it came within 10 feet, Dazzy said, the batter was out. Otherwise, the batter was credited with a run scored. "I was a better pitcher than Fred but he was the best hitter so the scores were fairly even," said Dazzy. "We didn't have a great deal of time to play for there was plowing, hoeing, milking and other chores to be done, and sometimes a nine-inning game would last two or three days."

Dazzy said their equipment consisted of an old ball and a bat with a broken handle. They repaired the bat by nailing the handle and wrapping it with wire and tape. "We never went out to play without taking a needle and thread along to sew up the ball," he said. The two-man games continued until Fred left home and Dazzy figured out a way to play by himself. "Dad broke up my league after I had knocked half the siding off the house. After that, I confined my efforts to pitching to a milk can," he said.[4]

Dazzy had to walk three miles to the nearest elementary school, at Little Creek. In 1909, he enrolled at Hastings High School, up the road about 30 miles from Cowles, where he became a pitcher on the baseball team. A high school teammate recalled that Dazzy had the speed and power with his pitches to throw a ball through a fence. His problem was he was so wild, he often through the ball over the fence. In fact, the school put up an extra width of wire at the top of the fence to help keep Vance's pitches in the park.[5]

But he was good enough so that in the summer of 1909, he earned his first money from playing baseball — one dollar. He pitched for a local team called the Corn Crackers who took on the Blue Hill team. Vance struck out 22, the manager paid him a dollar, and the local newspaper compared him with Cy Young, the great major leaguer who once pitched for Red Cloud. When the press called him a young Cy Young, "that put the bee in my bonnet," said Dazzy. After his graduation from Hastings High in 1911, he returned to Cowles and organized a town team.

He wrote to the managers of teams in nearby towns and guaranteed to pay their expenses if they would bring their teams to Cowles for a game. "I'd pay their expenses and keep the rest of the gate receipts," Dazzy recalled years later. "Now and then I'd have to hire a man to pitch hay for one of my players who otherwise could not get away from his work," he said.

It was in this league that Vance ran into Clarence Mitchell, another Nebraska boy who was to make it to the major leagues. He was playing for Red Cloud in the Nebraska State League. Dazzy was a friend of Mitchell's cousin and the cousin arranged for Vance to have a tryout. He pitched five pretty good innings but got belted around in the sixth inning. He didn't make the team but the manager told him he'd pay his expenses so Dazzy gave him an itemized expense account:

Two meals	$.70
Rig rental	2.50
Telephone call	.05
Total	$3.25

During the fall of 1911, Vance hooked on with a semi-pro team in Superior, Neb., where he was spotted by the manager of the Superior team in the Nebraska State League, the same league that Mitchell was playing in. He was offered $75 a month but managed to negotiate the contract up to $100 a month. When he signed on to that, Dazzy Vance was officially a professional baseball player. But 1912 was not a good year for Superior or Dazzy. The team was awful and at one point lost 25 of 26 games. On Sept. 2, he pitched in the first game of a double header and was the winner as Superior beat Columbus 4–1. Then he pitched the first five innings of the second game, enough to be the winning pitcher in a 7–4 victory. Vance had an 11–15 record and did well enough to warrant a look by major league scouts. But he had an attack of appendicitis on the day a Washington Senators scout arrived and was out for the rest of the season.[6]

In the off-season, he spent the winter in Hastings and took up boxing and wrestling as ways of trying to stay in shape. While boxing one day, he got scratched on his arm. Vance didn't think much of it at the time but he developed blood poisoning and became deathly ill. As he recuperated, his weight dropped from 180 to 140 in 30 days, hardly what he had in mind for staying in shape. He reported to Superior and, after a slow start, he finished with an 11–14 record which was good in light of the fact he was performing for another sub-par team. He signed with Hastings for the 1914 season for $125 a month and had the best year of his professional career. He was 17–4 for Hastings and led the Nebraska State League in strikeouts with 194. On July 20, his contract was sold to St. Joseph, Mo., in the Western League. Vance joined the team in Wichita and in his first outing, he fanned 10 as St. Joseph beat Wichita 5–2. "I sat up all night writing postcards to my friends," he said.[7]

What was most remarkable about Dazzy's performance was that it was the first Class A ballgame he had ever seen — and he witnessed it from the pitcher's mound. When the Hastings ball club dealt him to St. Joe, he took the train from Hastings and, upon his arrival, learned right away that he wouldn't be idling away his time. St. Joseph was faced with back to back double headers and a depleted pitching staff. Vance tried to look confident — "intelligent" he would say later in describing the meeting, but the truth was he was nervous. To Dazzy, who a few years earlier was playing a makeshift game with a broken bat and a ball of yarn in the barnyard, this was the big time.

"When coming in on the train, I had been a little upset about by the thought of playing Class A ball," he said. "It looked like a jump to the majors to me. Besides, I was a little doubtful about myself. But I figured I'd have a few days to watch these fellows and learn the ropes. But when the manager began to spring that stuff about doubleheaders, I thought it was up to me to make an impression."

Vance told the manager he was willing to pitch one of the games in the upcoming double headers, and that's all his new boss needed to hear. Dazzy was the starting pitcher in the first game of the first double header against Wichita. He said when he sauntered out to the mound, his nerves started to get to him again. He thought, "These birds are great hitters" and he hoped he was up to the challenge. Like any pitcher on any given day, he wanted to throw the ball hard and get it over the plate.

"I cut loose.... The ball shot up over the batter's head," said Dazzy. "He lunged at it, and that brought me down to earth. 'Maybe these fellows are only human after all,' I thought, if they bite at that kind of thing. So I began to soak up confidence."[8]

He was 9–8 with St. Joseph, following his 17–4 stint with Hastings, giving him a 26–12 record for the year. He was starting to make his move to the big time, but the innings pitched and the toil on his right arm were starting to add up also. His statistics were good enough for the Pittsburgh Pirates to give him a look at the start of the 1915 season. When he took the mound for the Pirates against the Cincinnati Reds on April 16, it was the third major league game he had ever seen. On the bench that day and used as a pinch hitter was the great Honus Wagner. In left field was another future Hall of Famer, Max Carey. In the dugout was manager Fred Clarke, who also was destined for the Hall of Fame. His catcher was George Gibson. It was a picture-book setting, one that was ideal for the making of a future star. As it turned out, the only thing it lacked was a good performance. Vance lasted 2⅔ innings in his major league debut and was the losing pitcher as the Reds beat the Pirates 4–2. He had trouble getting the ball over the plate, walking five and hitting a batter. When he did get the ball over, the Reds clobbered it. They got three hits to go along with the five walks and one hit batsman. Vance was lucky to get out of there surrendering only three runs. With all of that, his major league debut left him with an earned run average of 10.12 and a severely battered ego.

April 16, 1915

Pittsburgh	AB	R	H		Cincinnati	AB	R	H
Carey, lf	3	1	0		Leach cf	2	1	1
Johnston 1b	1	0	0		Herzog ss	3	1	0
Viox 3b	2	0	0		Killifer lf	1	0	0
Hinchman rf	4	0	1		Griffith rf	4	0	2
Lejeune cf	3	0	0		Groh 3b	3	1	2
McCarthy 2b	4	0	0		Olson 2b	3	0	0
Gerber ss	2	1	0		Mollwitz 1b	3	0	1
Wagner (b)	1	0	0		Clarke c	3	0	1
Gibson c	1	0	0		Douglas p	3	1	0
Schang c	2	0	2		Dale p	0	0	0
Vance p	1	0	0		Totals	24	4	7

Pittsburgh	AB	R	H
Conzelman p	1	0	0
Kantlehner p	0	0	0
Costello (a)	1	0	0
Totals	26	2	3

(a) batted for Conzelman in 7th
(b) batted for Gerber in 9th

Pittsburgh	000	100	100 — 2
Cincinnati	003	001	00x — 4

Three base hit — Schang. Stolen base — Leach. Sacrifice hit — Olson. Double plays — Vance, McCarthy; Olson, Herzog, Mollwitz; Gerber, McCarthy; Groh, Mollwitz (2).

	IP	H	R	ER	BB	SO	
Vance	2⅔	3	3	3	5	0	(0–1)
Conzelman	3⅓	3	0	0	1	0	
Kantlehner	2	1	0	0	0	0	
Douglas	7⅓	3	2	2	7	4	(1–0)
Dale	1⅔	0	0	0	1	0	

Hit by pitcher — By Vance 1, by Conzelman 1. Umpires — Klem and Engle. Time — 1:47

On April 22, the Pirates announced what could not have come as a surprise. Vance was optioned to St. Joseph, Mo. But in his short stay with the big league club, he had made an impression on one observer who had a pretty good eye for talent — Honus Wagner. Two incidents in spring training caught the attention of the great shortstop, who talked about them a year later.

"We had a nervy big chap for a pitching experiment in the south last spring," Wagner wrote in a newspaper column. He mentioned that Vance hailed from Red Cloud, Neb., and that many of the guys kidded him about it, including one player who was also vying for a place on the opening day roster. As the rookie came to bat in the practice game, he yelled at Vance on the mound, "Say, is Red Cloud anywhere near Wahoo?"

Vance shouted back, "Taint very far but thar's an old native of Wahoo name o' Sam Crawford who might teach you how to hit a curve." He then struck the batter out. Wagner's assessment of Dazzy: "He's a bright prospect and a fine boy ... and if he does not take his place among stars ... then I will miss my guess."[9]

Wagner, one of the game's greatest base runners, was more directly involved in another story he related about Vance — the day Vance picked Wagner off first base.

Wagner said he seldom got picked off and when he did, it was usually by a lefthander with a quick move to first or by a catcher who nailed
him after a pitch-out. But he said he met his match in an exhibition game
in Arkansas when he was on first and Dazzy was pitching.

"I danced off first and drew five or six throws. He had thrown so
often that I took a longer lead. I sneaked off the bag only a few feet. His
snap throw caught me flat-footed and the game ended against us a few
seconds later."[10]

Dazzy had a good year at St. Joe, winning 17 and losing 15. He would
have won more but his wildness cost him. He walked 110 batters and hit
25–10 of them in the head, by his own admission. One in particular
scared him. He beaned Bert King of Topeka and described it this way:
"I hit him an awful belt to the head when he was at the bat. It knocked
him down and knocked his hat off. He picked up his hat, put it back on
his head and took his position once more in the batting box." Vance said
King's manager rushed out and told him to take first base.

But the umpire ruled that the ball had hit King's bat. "The manager yanked King's hat off his head and showed a big lump already beginning to swell where the ball hit him. So he took his base. I thought it
was queer but I didn't say anything," said Vance.

In King's next at-bat, he stood still while Dazzy fired three strikes
past him. King was the left fielder. Later in the game, someone hit a fly
ball to left. King ambled over, let the ball drop in front of him and then
lobbed it back into the infield. His teammates became concerned and,
between innings, gathered around him and discovered that King was
totally oblivious to what was going on. "The ball had stunned him and
he was only half conscious but he went through the motions of play.
Fortunately, he recovered ... but after that experience, it always gave me
the cold creeps to hit a batter anywhere around his cranium," said
Dazzy.[11]

On July 26, the Pirates sold Vance to the New York Yankees. The
Yankees were going through one of the periods in their history where
they were struggling on the field. They had Wally Pipp at first base, a
journeyman who would make history several years later when he had a
headache and couldn't play. He was replaced by Lou Gehrig who
remained at first base for the next 2,130 games. Another veteran was
shortstop Roger Peckinpaugh. Their best pitcher was Ray Caldwell, who
won 19 and lost 16. New York was to finish fifth with a record of 69–83.
At the end of the 1915 season, Vance was called up by the Yankees, but

once again he was not impressive in the big leagues. He started three games and lost them all — 3–1 to the St. Louis Browns on Sept. 10; 7–3 to the Chicago White Sox on Sept. 18; and 4–1 to the Cleveland Indians on Sept. 24. He also appeared in five games in relief. In 30⅔ innings, he allowed 50 base runners— 26 hits, 21 walks and 3 hit batsmen. The future Hall of Famer had this to show for his brief experience in the major leagues:

Year	Team	W–L	G	IP	H	R	BB	SO	HBP	ERA
1915	Pitt	0–1	1	2.2	3	3	5	0	1	10.12
	NY (A)	0–3	8	28	23	11	16	18	2	3.54
Totals		0–4	9	30.2	26	14	21	18	3	4.06

In the off-season, Dazzy went back to Nebraska and continued his conditioning routine which involved boxing. One day, as he punched and jabbed and danced around the ring with one of his brothers, he felt a pain in his arm. He had felt pain before, like all pitchers do on days when they have thrown one too many curve balls or their arm becomes weary from overwork. But this was different. Years later, he described it this way:

"I hurt my right elbow. I felt it sting but I kept on sparring around and never thought another thing about it. A week after I got to spring training in Macon, Ga., I couldn't throw to home plate, the arm was so sore."

The Yankees optioned him to Columbus, Ohio, and he struggled to pitch by soaking his elbow in ice water between innings. But his arm was shot. Dejectedly, he went home to Hastings, Neb. Dazzy said, "The old family doctor told me I'd damaged the gland that lubricates the elbow and that inflammation had set in." The doctor told him to take it easy for five years and then his arm would be "as good as new."[12]

When the Yankees started spring training in 1916, Vance was invited to join them in Macon but he was clearly among the third tier of players on the roster. *The New York Times* reported on Feb. 9 that Manager Bill Donovan would take the train along with Ray Keating, George Mogridge, Cy Fish, Pyus Schwart, Gilman Gay, Jim McGovern, Leslie Nunamaker, Coach Duke Farrell and Trainer Jimmy Duggan. "The players who will be picked up en route," according to the newspaper, "Ford Meadows, Cliff Markle, Allen Russell, George Finn and Scout Joe Kelley." Then, the third tier — those who would have to find their own way to Macon, were listed. "The players who will go direct from their homes to Macon are Tom Blodgett, William Piercy, Urban Shocker, Dan Tipple, Alfred Walters, Harold Cable, Walter Alexander, Neal Brady, E.H. Love, Samuel Ross, Dazzy Vance, Nick Cullop, Don Brown, Charles Mullen and Joe Gideon."[13]

The Yankees shipped Vance to Columbus in the American Association where he was used sparingly because there were days when he couldn't toss a ball across a room, let alone fire it by opposing batters. He was 2–2 at Columbus and his career, which had hardly started, was in jeopardy. Dazzy saw a number of specialists including the famed Bonesetter Reese in Youngstown, Ohio. Reese had treated many of the nation's greatest athletes and restored their sore and torn limbs to full mobility. But Vance's injury was different. It couldn't be fixed by manipulating the bones.

One thing was for certain. Dazzy knew he couldn't remain idle for five years waiting for his "salary arm," as he called it, to heal. For his life was changing off the field as well. In Nebraska, he had dated and fallen in love with Edythe Carmony and they were married on March 7, 1917. Dazzy had to keep pitching, as best he could, because, as he put it, "I had to make a living." He was a married man now, and within a year, he was a family man. A son, Donald Brewster Vance, was born at the end of 1917.

In the spring of 1917, he reported to the Yankees farm club at Toledo, with a bride, a sore arm and 20 cents in his pocket. He had the heart for the game but not the arm. He rode the bench much of the first half of the season, managing a record of 2–6. On July 6, he was traded to Memphis and made a spectacular debut with his new ball club on July 9, holding Birmingham hitless for the last six innings in a 3–0 Memphis victory. He struck out three and walked one. But, icing his sore elbow after every game, he continued a pattern of inconsistency, playing just well enough to stay on the roster. He struggled along to a 6–8 mark for the rest of the season.

The *New York Herald Tribune* described Dazzy's ordeal: "For an inning or two he was invincible; then came the dreadful shooting pain in that dry hinge of that vital elbow.... A week's rest and he was invincible for a game. This mystified the managers but it heartened Vance with the conviction that his home doctor was right.[14]

At season's end, Vance was broke as usual and couldn't afford to get back to Nebraska. He worked at a cotton gin in Memphis and looked forward to the 1918 season. He was convinced his arm was getting better and in fact, if he could have, he would have willed it well. Because he had to make a living and baseball was his life. These were times of incredible uncertainty where for Dazzy, it was not only important to have faith he would fully recover, but to have faith in the faith.

He had his best year since his arm went lame, going 8–6 for Memphis. On May 14, he had his best outing of the year, beating the Atlanta Crackers 3–0. *The Atlanta Constitution* recorded it this way: "Vance's work was the outstanding feature of a brilliantly and quickly played game. He held the Crackers to three widely scattered hits, fanned four batters and was seldom in danger of being scored upon."[15]

Two weeks later, the two teams met again in Memphis with similar results. Again, the *Atlanta Constitution*: "The Tribesmen gave Atlanta a further push into the cellar today when the second game ended in a 6–0 shutout against the visitors. Dazzy Vance was on the mound for the home club and … allowed the Crackers only three scattered hits and the best they could do was to reach second base once."[16]

Vance did well enough with Memphis that on June 21 the Yankees called him back up. He made two appearances, both in relief, and neither was pretty. On July 16, he came into a game against Detroit in the eighth inning after the Tigers had cuffed Ray Caldwell around and had a 7–1 lead. They continued the onslaught against Vance, plastering him for five runs on seven hits in an inning and a third. Another outing was not as bad as Dazzy pitched one inning and gave up two hits and two walks but escaped without a run being scored off him. Nonetheless, in this, his third time in the big time, he lacked the consistency and arm strength required of a big league pitcher. Within weeks he was dispatched to Rochester in the International League where he toiled to a 3–5 record.

In the off-season, Dazzy worked in a munitions plant and looked forward to one more attempt to conquer the arm problems and show what he could do when he was healthy. The Yankees offered him a contract for $250 a month but Sacramento of the Pacific Coast League offered him $300. He elected to sign with the minor league team because $50 a month more in pay was like a pot of gold to a career minor leaguer and besides, the Yankees had shown no confidence in him — not that he had given them any reason to do so.

At Sacramento, he had an up-and-down season and was on the verge of being fired several times, he said, but would come up with a good game just in time to save his job. The statistics weren't pretty —

10 wins and 18 losses—but he was starting to rack up some innings, something he hadn't been able to do for years. Prior to the 1920 season, he was shipped back to Memphis, familiar territory, and spent most of the season there. On Aug. 15, he was traded to New Orleans and finished the season with the Pelicans. It was his best season in the past five years. Though his combined record was 16–17 for the year, he pitched most of the season and with minimal pain compared to the recent past. And he had some fine games. In early May, while he was still with Memphis, he struck out 14 in a 10–0 victory over Atlanta, a team that seemed to be there at just the time that Dazzy needed a win. Newspaper accounts of the game hinted that Vance's arm might be returning to the condition it was in five years ago. "The Chickasaw hurler appeared to be going stronger in the ninth than when he started. He allowed, in all, five widely scattered hits and no bases on balls, and the precision with which he cut his fast breaking curves across the corners of the plate had the Cracker batsmen helpless."[17]

Dazzy went into the 1921 season with great optimism and on April 26, he threw a shutout against the Atlanta Crackers, a team he "owned" when he was with Memphis. This one did not come easily. Dazzy hit three batters, walked four and gave up three hits but managed to keep anyone from scoring in achieving the 4–0 victory. "The former Memphis moundsman was wilder than most Atlanta fans ever saw him," the *Atlanta Constitution* reported the next day.

But he settled down to have his greatest year in professional baseball, finishing the season with a 21–11 record. Vance was elated—and for the rest of his life, he told people that the old country doctor in Nebraska was right. The doc told him in 1916 it would take five years for his arm to heal, and he was right on.

One of the big benefits of his outstanding 1921 season was that major league teams were once again interested in him. Dazzy wasn't so sure he was interested in them. He hadn't done so well in three previous tries in the big leagues, one with Pittsburgh and two with the Yankees. He was 30 years old now and the Dodgers had expressed some interest. Nap Rucker, scouting for Brooklyn, had seen him pitch in New Orleans and liked what he saw. Dazzy thought it was a ruse. He suspected Brooklyn wanted to buy his contract for a cheap price to prevent him from being drafted by another ballclub. He had knocked around the minors for 10 years and figured as long as he had waited this long for his big chance, it wouldn't hurt to play the field. He said, "If it wasn't for an unexpected break at the end of spring training, I am sure I would have been sent back to New Orleans."[18]

But the break came and Dazzy Vance, the man who pitched in the first Class A ballgame he ever saw, the man who spent 10 years in the minor leagues, half of those with a sore arm, the man who had three mercifully short stays on big league teams, was about to get another chance with another major league team. He was just past his 31st birthday, an age at which many major league players were contemplating retirement.

His minor league statistics are testimony to persistence, patience, and the endeavors of a man who had to make a living the only way he knew how— throwing a baseball.

Year	Team	W–L
1912	Red Cloud	11–15
1913	Superior	11–14
1914	Hastings	17–4
	St. Joseph	9–8
1915	St. Joseph	17–15
1916	Columbus	2–2
1917	Toledo	2–6
	Memphis	6–8
1918	Memphis	8–6
	Rochester	3–5
1919	Sacramento	10–18
1920	Memphis/NO	16–17
1921	New Orleans	21–11
10 years		**133–129**

There is no question he had paid his dues, and he was wrong about being played for a stooge to keep him out of the draft. The strange career of Dazzy Vance was about to get stranger. He made it to the majors because the Dodgers wanted a catcher— and the only way they could get the catcher was to also take a pitcher they didn't really want— a rookie who, at age 31, was older than many of his teammates.

Charles Arthur Vance ... or Arthur Charles Vance ... or Clarence Arthur Vance— the big-beaked redhead simply known as Dazzy— was about to start his Hall of Fame big league career.

III

"I was just trying to think — but I give up"

In 1914, when Dazzy was 17–4 at Hastings and made the brief appearance with the Pittsburgh Pirates, the Brooklyn Dodgers made a move that later on would have a great impact on Vance and his future teammates. The Dodgers had not finished in the first division since 1902 when they were second, behind Fred Clarke's Pirates ball club. In the intervening years, they finished fifth, sixth, eighth, fifth, fifth, seventh, sixth, sixth, seventh, seventh and sixth. The ball club had four managers during that time, Ned Hanlon, Patsy Donovan, Harry Lumley and Bill Dahlen. Owner Charlie Ebbets was tired of losing and once again tried to turn the tide with a change in leadership. He chose as the next Dodgers manager Wilbert Robinson, a former catcher who played with Hanlon and John McGraw on the great Baltimore teams in the 1890s and then was one of McGraw's coaches with the New York Giants.

The portly, bespectacled Robinson looked more like a biology teacher than a baseball manager. He actually retired from baseball in 1902 and had opened a meat market. Six years later he got back into baseball, accepting a job as a coach for the Baltimore ball club and eventually joined McGraw with the Giants.

He and McGraw had been best friends when they were teammates on the great Oriole teams in the 1890s. Robinson, a catcher, played for the Philadelphia Athletics in the American Association for five years before joining the Orioles. In those days as in his managerial years, he was known as man who knew how to have a little fun. The Athletics had a Ladies Auxiliary, made up of women whose mission was apparently to keep the ballplayers loose and happy. Robinson, as a rookie, had the job of being the official measurer of the women's breasts—and met with little resistance from the ball club's unofficial cheerleaders.[1] By 1897, Robbie and McGraw had become such close friends that they decided to go into business together in Baltimore. In February, they bought a tavern and, spending about $15,000 collectively, turned it into a bowling alley and pool hall known as the Diamond Café. For years, the Diamond had two distinctions: it was co-owned by two legends of baseball — and it was the place where duckpin bowling originated.[2]

In 1909, McGraw hired his old buddy back and Robbie took on the task of handling the Giants' pitchers and catchers. It was in this time period that he developed a loyalty to older pitchers and an ability to get the most out of them. A little more than a decade later, he would show patience and have confidence in a 31-year-old rookie named Dazzy Vance. For the Giants in 1911, his project was Rube Marquard, a tall left-hander who had a record of 9–18 in three dismal seasons with the Giants. Under Robbie's guidance, Marquard won 24, 26 and 23 games in the next three years. When Robbie left the Giants after the 1913 season, Marquard slipped to 12–22 in 1914 and 11–10 in 1915. As manager of the Robins, Robbie got him for the 1916 season and he was 13–6 for the Brooklyn pennant winner.

In 1913, the Giants won the pennant but lost the World Series to Connie Mack's Athletics in five games. McGraw went ahead with a party he had planned as a reunion of the old Baltimore ball clubs in a New York bar. The drinks were flowing freely and so were the remarks. At one point McGraw told Robinson he hadn't done a good job of coaching in the World Series and in fact had made more mistakes in the series than any of his players. With that, he fired his old friend and ordered him to leave the party. Robinson complied, but not before dousing McGraw with his glass of beer. The two men, once inseparable friends and business partners, did not speak for 17 years.[3]

Ebbets had heard about the dispute and thought the timing was perfect to offer his job opening as manager of the Dodgers to Robinson. He accepted. It was his first managerial job. Thus, a great rivalry began between Robbie and McGraw that lasted nearly two decades.

In 1914, when all major league clubs found themselves competing with the new Federal League for players and fans, the Dodgers finished fifth, winning 75, ten more than they had the previous year. In 1915, the progress continued — Brooklyn finished third, winning 80 games. Clearly, the rebuilding process was working, and, just as important, the fans were ecstatic over their new manager, whom they called "Uncle Robbie." The team became known as the Robins. There was no official name change, but it didn't matter. Most everybody called them that. "Uncle Robbie" and his wife, who became known as "Ma," were among the most popular people in Brooklyn. A new era was well under way in Dodgers baseball.

Brooklyn was a unique baseball community. It didn't have the downtown flavor of the Giants and Yankees. It was less provincial, less aristocratic and more of a neighborhood. Indeed, in Brooklyn, the places where people lived were identified not so much by street address but by the church they attended. "Where ya from?" someone might ask. "Immaculate Conception," the response would be, and that was enough to identify the person. Charlie Ebbets built a cozy little ballpark in these environs, with seats close to the field, billboards on the outfield walls, a street corner entrance and a trolley nearby. The ball club had once been known as the Trolley Dodgers. Uncle Robbie often took the trolley to the ballpark and the fans loved it as they saw him emerge from the little train and head into Ebbets Field.

Robbie worked on developing a quality pitching staff and tabbed Otto Miller as the catcher who could help him do it. Robbie, the former catcher, and Miller, the present one, worked together for many years. Brooklyn won pennants in 1916 and 1920 with Robinson at the helm and Miller as his catcher. When Miller's days were just about up with Brooklyn, his imminent departure turned out to be a turning point in the career of Dazzy Vance.

Meanwhile, Robbie learned to deal with some eccentric ballplayers, something that would provide him with great experience for the Dodgers teams he would manage in the next decade. A young outfielder for Brooklyn by the name of Casey Stengel was a case in point. Stengel had a habit of scaring teammates and his manager by the way he circled under balls in right field. One day in 1914, when Stengel made a project out of catching a routine fly to end a game, Robbie glared at him in the clubhouse.

"What the hell were you staggering around for out there?" said Robbie.

"Well, I got it, didn't I?" replied Stengel.

"Yes, you got it, but you give me heart disease every time you go after a ball," said Robinson, adding, "Oh, well, with a rump and legs like that, you shouldn't be a ballplayer. You should be a ..."

"What should I be?" demanded Stengel.

"I was just trying to think — but I give up," said Robbie. Everyone, including Stengel and Robinson, laughed and the incident was over.[4]

Brooklyn won the pennant in 1916 and again in 1920, which must have given Robinson great satisfaction in overtaking McGraw's Giants.

In the 1920 World Series, with the Robins facing the Cleveland Indians, a play occurred that had not happened before and has not happened since — and was a precursor to the antics of the Daffiness Boys of several years later. In the fifth inning of the game on Oct. 10, 1920, a game eventually won by Cleveland 8–1, the Robins threatened to make a game of it by having Pete Kilduff on second and Miller on first with nobody out. Clarence Mitchell, the Robins pitcher, lined a shot

Wilbert "Uncle Robbie" Robinson was a Brooklyn institution. The Dodgers took on the unofficial nickname of the Robins under his tenure. He won two pennants, came close two other times and presided over a fun-loving group known as the Daffiness Boys. (Courtesy Baseball Hall of Fame.)

that was snared by Indians second baseman Bill Wambsganss. Wamby stepped on second to double up Kilduff and then tagged Miller who was steaming into second base — an unassisted triple play. Mitchell, who remains the only batter to hit into a triple play in the World Series, was the man who nine years earlier paved the way for Vance to pitch for Red Cloud.

The Robins slipped to fifth in 1921. Robbie wanted to make some changes in 1922 to get the team back on track. One of them was a delicate one. It was time to find a replacement for Miller, who had been behind the plate for Brooklyn since 1910 but who was nearing the end of the trail. Miller had always been one of Robbie's favorites as a fellow catcher and the man behind the plate in Robbie's two pennant-winning seasons. Ebbets had heard of a young catching prospect down in New Orleans, a fellow by the name of Hank DeBerry, who he thought might be ready to move up to the big club. He contacted his southern scout, Larry Sutton, to check out DeBerry. A few days later, Sutton reported back to Ebbets. He told him DeBerry looked ready and he was eager to come — but there was a catch. He wouldn't report unless his pitcher came with him, a career minor leaguer named Dazzy Vance.

Ebbets blew up. No deal, he told Sutton. He could have drafted Vance months ago if he wanted him. But he didn't want him. He instructed Sutton to call DeBerry's bluff, to tell New Orleans the deal was off. Sutton talked to the Pelicans and called Ebbets back. DeBerry was going nowhere without "his pitcher." No Vance, no DeBerry — that was the deal. Ebbets gave in.[5]

DeBerry was 28 and had 40 games of major league experience, 15 with Cleveland in 1916 and 25 with the Indians in 1917. For the next four years, he had knocked around the minor leagues and hooked up with Vance in New Orleans in 1921. He had a good year with the Pelicans but always claimed that Vance made him look like a better catcher than he actually was. He remained with the Dodgers for the next nine years. Miller played sparingly in 1922. He had talked about wanting to be a minor league manager when his playing days were over and he got his wish. With DeBerry settling in as the Dodgers catcher, Miller signed on to manage the Atlanta minor league ball club in 1923.

Vance arrived at the Robins' spring training camp on DeBerry's coattails. But the 31-year-old rookie saw a lot of people he knew and wound up introducing the young catcher to his new teammates. Dazzy once bragged, "I'll bet a hundred bucks that if I dropped in on every minor league club in the country — and I wouldn't care how small the league was— I would know at least three men on every one of them." Spoken like a man who pitched on 10 minor league teams in the past decade.[6]

The Robins had the makings of a good ball club and while Vance wasn't high on Ebbets' list, he fit right in to a pattern Robbie had developed for his teams— older pitchers who wouldn't rattle as easily as some of the younger guys. There was Jack Coombs, a 32-year-old veteran who had been pitching in the majors for 10 years and who had won 31, 28 and 21 games for Connie Mack's A's from 1910 through 1912. He won only one game in the next two years when Robbie picked him up for Brooklyn. He returned to form and won 15 in 1915 and was 13–8 for the 1916 pennant winner. Similarly, Richard "Rube" Marquard won 24, 26 and 23 games for McGraw's Giants in 1911–1913 and then fell to

Hank DeBerry, shown here when he played for the Giants, was the player Brooklyn wanted from the minor leagues in 1922. He refused to come unless Dazzy Vance came with him. The Robins reluctantly agreed because they wanted DeBerry. (Courtesy Baseball Hall of Fame.)

12–22 in 1914. Robbie picked him up mid-season in 1915 and old Rube was 13–6 for the pennant-winning 1916 ball club. Marquard was still around in 1920 and compiled a 10–7 record for that championship team.

The leader of the pitching staff in 1920 was Burleigh Grimes, who posted the first of his five 20-plus-win seasons with a record of 23–11. He was still the ace of the staff when Dazzy Vance came aboard. Grimes was the last of the legalized spitball pitchers, having been grandfathered in after the pitch was banned. He used it to great advantage, often faking that he was lathering up the ball just to keep hitters off guard. Grimes was known as a good guy off the field but a tenacious, fierce competitor on the mound. It was said that his idea of an intentional walk was four pitches at the batter's head. He never shaved on game day, accounting for his nickname of "Old Stubblebeard."

Another leader of the mound corps was Walter "Dutch" Ruether, 29, a big lefthander who gained fame with two other great ball clubs before and after he joined the Robins. Ruether was 19–6 with the 1919 Cincinnati Reds, the team that beat the Chicago White Sox in the World Series forever remembered for the "Black Sox" scandal. Several members of the White Sox conspired to throw the World Series. Nonetheless, Ruether lost a game to Chicago's Dickie Kerr, who was not involved in the fix and pitched well enough to overcome the shabby play of his conspirator teammates. Ruether also picked up a win in that World Series. Eight years later, he was 13–6 with the 1927 New York Yankees, considered one of the greatest ball clubs of all time, led by Babe Ruth, Lou Gehrig and others who made up Murderer's Row for opposing pitchers.

The other starting pitcher was Leon Cadore, a 32-year-old right-hander who was not nearly as colorful as the other three but had a claim to fame of his own. Hurling for Brooklyn on May 1, 1920, Cadore hooked up in a pitching duel with Joe Oeschger of Boston on a cold, rainy day at Braves Field. Each team scored a run but no more as the game headed for extra innings. From then on, inning after inning, Cadore and Oeschger matched zeros on the scoreboard. The game was called because of darkness at the end of 26 innings and the score still tied 1–1. Both pitchers went all the way. Cadore struck out seven, walked five and gave up 15 hits but just the one run.

The Robins' best ballplayer in 1922 was outfielder Zach Wheat, who happened to be their best ballplayer in 1921, 1920 and for many years before that. Wheat was a lefthanded batter who many thought could be awakened out of a sound sleep at 3 in the morning, and, given a bat, would start hitting line drives. He broke in with Brooklyn in 1909 after spending nearly three days on a train from Louisiana to get there. In the next 17 seasons, all with Brooklyn, he hit over .300 13 times. In 1918, he had a 26-game hitting streak. Wheat played more than half of his career in the deadball era and averaged five home runs a year from 1906 through 1919. From 1920 through 1925, when the ball became livelier, he averaged 12 home runs a season and hit .320 or above in each of those years. Robbie used him as his clean-up hitter most of the time so he was hardly ever called on to bunt. Part of Brooklyn folklore involves a game in which Wheat came to the plate with a runner on first in the late innings of a close game. He expected the bunt sign but Robbie, coaching at third, had forgotten what the sign was. So he just pantomimed a bunt for everyone in the ballpark to see — except Wheat, apparently. For the clean-up hitter swung away and hit the ball out of the ballpark. That was typical Robins' baseball.

Wheat's last homer in a Brooklyn uniform was a memorable one. It came in 1926 when, at age 38, aches and pains were starting to catch up with him. In late September, he was kept out of the lineup to nurse an aching heel when Robbie called on him to pinch hit. Wheat lunged at a pitch and lined it down the right field line and over the wall. As he limped around first base on the sore heel, he developed a charley horse in his other leg and was in agony. He sat down on second base, writhing in pain. Robbie came running out and time was called. After the umpires consulted with one another and Wheat's pain subsided, he was allowed to get up and try to make it the rest of the way around the bases. Sportswriters estimated it took five minutes from the time he hit the ball until the time he scored. Sixty-two years later, another Dodgers pinch hitter, Kirk Gibson, had a similar experience in the World Series, homering off of Oakland's Dennis Eckersley. Gibson didn't fall but his bum leg allowed him to only hobble around the bases.

Wheat's companions in the Robins' outfield were Hy Myers and Tommy Griffith. Myers was a speedster who played 12 years with Brooklyn and twice led the National League in triples, hitting 14 in 1919 and 22 in 1920. Griffith, the right fielder, had a rifle arm; he had more than 20 assists in three different seasons and was usually in double figures.

Second baseman Ivy Olson was the shortstop on the 1916 and 1920 pennant winners. Robbie often used him in the lead-off spot where he led the National League in at-bats in 1919 and 1921. He and Casey Stengel went to the same grade school in Kansas City and later were teammates at Brooklyn. Stengel said Olson was known as the bully at the grammar school and had a similar reputation in the major leagues. He said if a player came into second with his spikes high, Olson would warn him that if he did it again, he'd find the ball shoved down his throat.

Burleigh Grimes, the last legal spitball pitcher in the major leagues, provided the second half of Brooklyn's one-two punch (along with Vance) on the Robins' pitching staff. He had good years with several other ball clubs and, like Vance, is in the Hall of Fame. (Courtesy Baseball Hall of Fame.)

Shortstop Jimmy Johnston had a career similar to Dazzy's. He had poked around in the minor leagues, playing with seven teams in four leagues before coming up with Cincinnati in 1916. He too was comfortable as a leadoff man and was a good base stealer. On the corners of the infield were third baseman Andy High, called "Handy Andy" because of his slick fielding ability, and first baseman Ray Schmandt, who signed with Branch Rickey and the St. Louis Browns in 1916 and played five fairly nondescript seasons as first baseman for the Robins.

Out of this group, four eventually made it into the Hall of Fame in Cooperstown: Robinson; Grimes, the great pitcher who finished with 270 big league wins; Wheat, who still holds many Dodgers hitting records; and Vance, who was the first Dodger elected to the Hall of Fame.

Grimes was 23–11 with the championship team and followed up with a 22–13 record in 1921. But Ruether, 16–12 for the champs, slipped to 10–13. Cadore, 15–14 in 1920, was just 13–14 in 1921. Jeff Pfeffer, a fourth starter on the pennant winner and 16–9 for the season, started the 1921 season losing five of his first six decisions and was peddled to St. Louis (where he went 9–3 the rest of the way.) Clarence Mitchell was 11–9 as the fourth starter in 1921.

The trading of Pfeffer was curious. He was a 10-year veteran with the Dodgers, had seasons in which he was 23–12, 19–14, and 25–11 from 1914 through 1916 and had double-figure wins in six out of the past seven years, the only exception being the war year of 1918 when he was 1–0. He was traded for pitcher Ferdie Schupp, who was 16–13 the previous year for St. Louis and who was to win three games for the Robins before being peddled to Chicago before the start of the 1922 season, and Hal Janvrin, an infielder with a career batting average of below .230. Sportswriter Frank Graham suspected the trade was a "wake-up call" to the rest of the Robins—a warning to shape up or they too might be shipped out.[7]

Despite an 11-game winning streak early in the season and several spurts of good play, the Robins never elevated themselves to their 1920 pennant-winning form and finished in fifth place, 17 games behind McGraw's Giants. With their 77–75 record, they had 16 fewer wins than their 1920 championship club.

As the 1922 season approached, Brooklyn had a veritable mountain to climb to get back into serious contention for a league title. The Giants were still the team to beat, with three future Hall of Famers among their eight starting position players—and four if you count Casey Stengel, the ex-Robin who made it into the Hall as a manager but nonetheless hit .368 that year for New York. The Hall of Famers were second baseman Frankie Frisch, who hit .327; shortstop Dave Bancroft, who hit .321; and right fielder Ross Youngs, who hit .331.

Cincinnati had some punch with Jake Daubert, a 38-year-old first baseman who played his first nine years with the Robins and now was the Reds' leading hitter. Cincinnati also had Babe Pinelli at third, Bubbles Hargrave behind the plate and future Hall of Famer Ed Roush in the outfield. Lefthanded pitcher Eppa Rixey was to lead the league in innings pitched with 313 and wins with 25.

Pittsburgh had a good ball club as well with Pie Traynor and Rabbit Maranville on the left side of the infield, young Charlie Grimm at first base and Max Carey patrolling centerfield. The Cardinals had solid pitching, led by the ex-Robin Pfeffer but also featuring Bill Sherdel and Jess Haines. At second base, St. Louis had Rogers Hornsby, the best hitter in the National League, who in two years would hit .424, still the highest average ever for one season. The Cubs had few headline ballplayers, but had a pitching staff led by the great Grover Cleveland Alexander and veteran Vic Aldridge. The Phillies and Braves were destined to fight each other for the National League cellar with neither one of them winning 60 games.

The American League, the so-called junior circuit (because it was the youngest of the two leagues) was making some noise that would be heard for years to come. Babe Ruth hit 59 home runs for the New York

Zack Wheat was a star outfielder for the Robins and served several weeks as the team's manager when Wilbert Robinson was moved to the front office. When Uncle Robbie resumed his managerial duties, it caused some friction with Wheat, who never has been credited with managing the Robins. (Courtesy Hall of Fame.)

Yankees in 1921, more homers than five other teams in the league hit — and the same number that the Robins as a team hit in the National League. The Roaring '20s would produce Yankees teams that were dominant and powerful and, more important, drew attention away from the tarnished image caused by the Black Sox scandal of 1919 when eight

Chicago White Sox players were accused of fixing the World Series won by the Reds.

At the end of the season, Ruth and two teammates, Bob Meusel and Bill Piercy, went on a little barnstorming tour right after the World Series, ignoring an order from Judge Landis prohibiting players from participating in non-sanctioned exhibition games. Each of them was fined $3,362.26 — their World Series shares — and each was suspended from opening day through May 20, 1922. That suspension plus others he would receive for shenanigans during the next season most certainly cost Ruth the home run title in 1922. He hit 35 homers in 110 games. Ken Williams of the Browns won the home run crown, hitting 39 in 153 games.

Yankees management was frequently at odds with Ruth — and vice versa — but the ball club was smart enough to know who was bringing fans into the park. On March 6, 1922, Ruth signed a three-year contract for $52,000 a year. By contrast, three days later, Rogers Hornsby signed a three-year deal with the Cardinals for $18,500 a year, making him the highest paid player in National League history.

As the 1922 season beckoned, the Robins fielded a team that wasn't much different than the one that finished fifth the year before. One change for Uncle Robbie's troops was the addition of the catcher DeBerry, the guy brought up from New Orleans to replace Otto Miller, and the tag-along, Charles Arthur "Dazzy" Vance, the 31-year-old "career minor leaguer" with the perpetual sore arm, the guy Charlie Ebbets had to take in order to get DeBerry.

IV

"Here's where I came in"

Robbie went with Ruether on opening day at the Polo Grounds. His mound opponent was Art Nehf. The two hooked up in a pretty good pitching battle, but in the end, the Robins prevailed 4–3. It wouldn't last long, but for the moment at least, for 24 hours in fact, Brooklyn was in first place in the National League.

The next day, Robbie decided to trot out his rookie, Dazzy Vance, to go up against the Giants' Shufflin' Phil Douglas. The big Giants righthander was one of the best pitchers in the National League but had it not been for Grover Cleveland Alexander of the Cubs, he would have been the league's top drinker too. Douglas had defeated the Yankees twice in the 1921 World Series and was a key component if the Giants were to repeat in 1922. McGraw went to great lengths to keep his star pitcher on the straight and narrow but in the end, Douglas was his own worst enemy. By season's end, his career was over.

Vance had been around baseball long enough not to be intimidated by someone's reputation. He was a rookie but he was one of the old-timers in terms of age and could tell his teammates about the time he picked off Honus Wagner back in 1915. But he still hadn't proven himself as a major league pitcher. He wouldn't on this day either. *The New York Times* reported:

"Uncle Wilbert Robinson sent his pitcher to the well once too often yesterday. The pitcher in question is young Mr. Vance, late of New Orleans and once with the Yankees some five years back, and when the Giants finished with him in the second inning, the game was over and done with."[1]

Dazzy got through the first inning without a scratch. In the second inning, Emil "Irish" Meusel tagged a home run into the right field stands. Vance then walked George Kelly on four pitches and Ralph Shinners on five. Earl Smith then smashed a ground ball that handcuffed Schandt at

40

first base and he couldn't make a play. The bases were loaded without a ball being hit out of the infield—in fact, three men had reached base with only one fair ball being hit, and that about 90 feet. Douglas then fouled out to catcher DeBerry. But Dave Bancroft walked and when Johnny Rawlings followed with a two-run single, Vance was through for the day. His totals were not pretty:

IP	H	R	BB	SO	HBP
1⅓	3	4	4	0	1

Douglas, the winning pitcher, was also the winner in Dazzy's big league debut with Pittsburgh in 1915.

The Robins lost two more in a row, including a 17–10 pasting by the Giants on April 15 in which New York scored 11 runs in the first inning. Ruether got them back on the winning track when he beat the Phillies 10–2 on April 16. Vance, now 0–5 in his big league career, took the mound again on April 20 in a home game against the Giants. Once again, the mound opponent was Douglas; once again, the outcome wasn't good as New York battered the Robins 8–1; and once again the damage against Dazzy was done early. The Giants scored three in the first and three more in the second. Before Robbie could get Dazzy out of there, he had allowed six runs on seven hits and left the game without getting anybody out in the second inning. So the fellow Ebbets was forced to bring to Brooklyn was now 0–2 for the Robins, 0–6 in his major league career and looking like he belonged back in Hastings.

Meanwhile, in the American League, the St. Louis Browns were on top and Ken Williams was leading the league in home runs. On April 22, he became the first player in American League history to hit three home runs in one game as the Browns beat the White Sox 10–7.

Strange things were happening all over baseball. In a game in the Sally League on April 17, Charleston and Charlotte were in a 6–6 tie at the end of six innings in what was a fairly routine game. In the top of the seventh, Charleston scored 11 runs. Charlotte came back with 10 in the bottom of the seventh—21 runs in one inning for the two teams. Charleston won 17–16. On April 24, the Phillies, who often played like a minor league team, made eight errors in a 3–2 loss to the Giants. On April 29, the Giants beat the Braves 15–4 on the strength of four inside-the-park home runs—two by Kelly and one each by Youngs and Bancroft.

Vance notched his long-awaited first major league victory on April 26, beating Boston 8–1 at Braves Field. On April 30, back home at Ebbets Field, he tossed the first shutout of his career as the Robins downed the Phillies 4–0. With the win Brooklyn evened its record at 8–8, the first time in 17 days the Robins had been even with the league. The last time had been after the second game of the season when they were 1–1. As they entered May, Uncle Robbie's club was in fourth place, 4½ games behind the Giants.

Dazzy dazzled for the first time in his major league career and the *New York Times* took notice, saying he was "at all times the master of the situation." He got into a jam in the ninth inning but got out of it in spectacular form. The *Times* reported the final out this way: "To Leslie, Dazzy pitched one ball, and as he put the following three across for strikes, ending the battle, the crowd gave Vance a cheer which could be heard throughout Flatbush."[2]

On May 1, Robbie put Harry "Pop" Shriver out on the mound for his first major league start and he responded by becoming the first Brooklyn pitcher to throw a shutout in his big league debut. The Robins beat the Phillies 2–0. As for Shriver, he won three more games that year, lost six and never won another major league game after that. When Ruether beat the Braves 4–2 on May 6, Brooklyn had a four-game winning streak, its longest of the year, and had won five out of six on a homestand just completed. But the Giants seemed unstoppable. On May 7, Jesse Barnes threw a no-hitter as New York beat the Phillies 6–0. The Robins went on the road, hoping to keep their momentum going to gain some ground on the Giants. Instead, the roof fell in. Vance lost a tough one 4–3 to the Braves and the Robins lost five more in a row before stopping the skid with a 6–5 win over the Reds at Crosley Field. The Robins lost two more before Vance won his third game of the year in a 7–5 win over the Cardinals on May 18. On May 22, Dazzy tossed his second shutout of the year, a 3–0 win over the Cubs at Wrigley Field and followed that up with another shutout, this one a 7–0 win against the Phillies at Baker Bowl in the second game of a double header on May 26. Vance won his fourth straight game four days later, an 8–4 win over the Braves. On May 31, Pittsburgh beat Brooklyn 11–2. Ray Lutz, a third string catcher for the Robins (after DeBerry and Miller) got to bat once and hit a double. It turned out to be his only major league at-bat.

The Robins entered June with a 23–21 record but found themselves in fourth place, 4½ games behind McGraw's Giants.

Brooklyn was treading water, not getting anyone terribly excited. But Dazzy Vance appeared to have turned the corner. The more he pitched, the more confident he seemed. His fastball was buzzing and he had much better control of his pitches. Perhaps most important, he showed no signs of the sore arm that had plagued him for years. For the rest of his life, he would credit the diagnosis of an old country doctor in Nebraska who had predicted it would heal in five years.

Robbie knew enough to leave well enough alone. Vance was an unusual rookie. He was new and yet he had expe-

Dazzy was 31 years old when he came up from the minor leagues to Brooklyn as a throw-in in a deal for the player the Robins really wanted — catcher Hank DeBerry. (Courtesy Baseball Hall of Fame.)

rience. "Robbie was wise enough to let him go his own way and satisfied to let him pitch his own way, too. He pitched the way he lived, easily and untroubled, taking his time as he went along, and taking his fun, too."[3]

Dazzy lost to the Reds in his next start 6–2 on June 7, but came back four days later and threw another gem. Robbie took him out in the sixth inning to give him some rest because the Robins were up 12–0. They eventually won the game 13–0 over the Cubs. On June 12, it was the Cardinals' day to hit. The Redbirds got 10 straight hits in the sixth inning of a game against the Phillies, beating them 14–7. Two days later, Vance pitched against the hot-hitting Cardinals. He met up with Pffefer, the former Robin, and tossed his second straight shutout and fifth of the year as Brooklyn beat St. Louis. The Robins lost Vance's next three starts but he got back on track on Sunday, July 2, besting the Braves 8–6 at

Ebbets Field. On July 3, the Robins and Giants tied 5–5 in a game called after 14 innings to allow the Robins to catch a train.

With the end of play on July 4, McGraw's Giants found themselves in familiar territory—first place—at 44–24. The Cardinals were second at 41–32, 5½ games off the pace. Robbie's boys were third at 40–33, 6½ behind the Giants. Every other team in the league was under .500. Whatever chance or glimmer of hope the Robins had of catching the Giants evaporated quickly when they lost their next seven games, including five in a row to the Cardinals and two to Cincinnati. Counting a contest they had lost prior to the 5–5 tie, the losing streak was actually eight. Then they lost four out of their next six. At the start of play on July 20, the Robins were 42–44, 11 games behind the Giants. Meanwhile, the Cardinals were on a rampage, winning 23 of 29. They took over first place in the National League on July 22 but it would last only a day. But for that day, the Redbirds and Browns each held the top spot in their respective leagues—the first time that had ever happened in baseball history.

The Robins played pretty close to .500 baseball for the next two weeks. On Aug. 5, Dazzy tossed his fifth shutout of the season (counting the one in which Robbie took him out in the sixth inning with a 12–0 lead.) This one was a 5–0 victory over Cincinnati, and the next day, when Leon Cadore beat the Reds 3–2, Brooklyn was at .500 again at 50–50. But the Robins lost six out of their next seven. On Aug. 31, they found themselves in sixth place, 14 games behind the Giants who once again had taken control in the National League. Only the hapless Braves and Phillies trailed the Robins in the standings.

Since Aug. 8, the Giants had been playing without their star pitcher, Shufflin' Phil Douglas, who was 11–4 with a 2.63 earned run average, best in the National League. But Douglas's drinking caught up with him. He hated his manager, McGraw, because of McGraw's stern tactics in trying to keep his top starter sober. Douglas wrote a letter to an ex-teammate, Les Mann, who was now with the Cardinals, suggesting that Douglas would take it easy for the rest of the season if someone was to make it worth his while. Mann turned the letter over to Cards general manager Branch Rickey, who forwarded it to Commissioner Landis. While this was going on, Douglas had a change of heart, contacted Mann, and wanted his letter back. But it was too late. Landis, not too far removed from the Black Sox scandal of 1919, banned Douglas for life.

The Robins were 15–15 the rest of the way and finished in sixth place, 17 games behind the Giants. They could hardly have asked for more from their rookie Dazzy Vance. He won 18, lost 12, had four shutouts plus the partial shutout and had an earned run average of 3.70. In addition, he led the league in strikeouts with 134. Had there been a Rookie of the Year award in those days, it would have been hard to deny Dazzy the honor.

Among the starters, only Ruether had a better year. The lefty won 21 and lost 12 with an ERA of 3.53. Burleigh Grimes checked in with a 17–14 record. The problem for the Robins was the rest of the staff compiled a 20–40 record. Cadore, a starter who won 14, 15 and 13 games in the previous three seasons, fell to 8–15 in 1922. Zack Wheat had his typical good year, hitting .335 with 16 home runs and 112 runs batted in. But the rest of the lineup got on base but didn't score. Hy Myers hit .319 and drove in 89 runs and Andy High hit .283 with 65 RBIs. While three other starters hit over .300 — DeBerry (.301), Johnston (.319) and Griffith (.316) — no other Robin drove in more than 49 runs. The Giants scored 840 runs for the year. The Robins had 667.

The big hitter in the National League in 1922 was Rogers Hornsby of the Cardinals. He went 3 for 5 on the last day of the season to push his average up to .401. With 42 home runs and 152 runs batted in, he was a Triple Crown winner. In addition, his 250 hits were the most ever in the National League.

The Brooklyn brain trust went to work in the off-season to try to put more punch in the lineup. On Feb. 11, 1923, the Robins traded speedy outfielder Hi Myers and Ray Schmandt to the Cardinals for their slugging first baseman Jack Fournier. St. Louis had Jim Bottomly coming up and felt that Fournier was expendable. Fournier at first threatened to quit rather than report to the Dodgers but changed his mind and stayed in Brooklyn for several years, long enough to be a part of the Daffiness Boys who didn't win as many games as Robbie would have liked but won the hearts of the fans in Flatbush.

Like Vance, Fournier had kicked around several years in the minor leagues in the White Sox and Yankees organizations but made his mark with the Cardinals, hitting many balls over the right field pavilion in Sportsman's Park. The Robins expected him to do the same at Ebbets Field. Fournier was a bit of a character. The first time the Cardinals played at Ebbets Field in 1923, Fournier was at first base and the Robins had a rookie on the mound in the late innings of a ballgame when Rogers Hornsby strode to the plate. The young pitcher conferred with Fournier since Fournier had been a teammate of Hornsby's and probably could give good advice on how to pitch to the great righthanded batter. "Pitch him inside," said Fournier. The youngster threw a fastball inside and Hornsby jumped all over it, lining a double down the leftfield line. The pitcher looked perplexed. He said to Fournier, "I thought you said he couldn't hit inside pitches." Fournier replied, "I didn't say that. I told you to pitch him inside because I didn't want him to hit one of those line drives at me. I've got a wife and kids."[4]

In another move, the club traded aging pitcher Clarence Mitchell to the Phillies for George Smith. This was a curious trade and had "Robbie hunch" written all over it. Smith had won 4 and lost 20 games for the Phillies in 1921 and was 5–14 in 1922, but this was hardly a mark of incompetence, considering he played for a team that had trouble winning 50 games in either season. The rest of the Robins must have had mixed feelings about Smith coming over to Brooklyn. They had beaten him in 14 consecutive games.[5]

Even before the season started, the Robins, including their manager, showed signs that it promised to be a year full of surprises. In spring training one day, the Brooklyn players, coaches and managers boarded a bus in Clearwater and headed for Lakeland for an exhibition game with the Cleveland Indians. When they got there, they noticed manager Tris Speaker and many of his players lounging around in street clothes. Speaker approached Robbie and asked him what was going on. "We're here for the game," said Robbie, or words to that effect. "You're a day early," said Speaker. "The game's tomorrow."

As usual, the Giants were the team to beat as the 1923 season got under way. The Robins had a chance to get off to a quick start, opening up with four games against the lowly Phillies at Ebbets Field. The first game ended in a 5–5 tie after 14 innings, with Ruether going all the way for the Robins. Then Burleigh Grimes won the second game of the season 6–5, but the Robins lost the next two with Vance and Harry Shriver taking the losses. It was hardly the way they wanted to start the season because the Giants then came to town and swept a four game series, the first two by shutouts. With the season less than a week old, the Robins were 1–6, in eighth place and already six games behind the Giants. It would get worse. After a modest two-game winning streak, Brooklyn lost five more in a row and were 3–11 on May 2, the day Vance picked up his fourth loss of the year without a win. It was also the day, in the American League, that Walter Johnson of the Washington Senators threw his 100th career shutout.

Dazzy's loss was a heartbreaker. He struck out 15 Giants and had a 5–3 lead going into the ninth inning. New York scored three in the ninth to briefly take the lead before Brooklyn sent it to extra innings with a run in the bottom of the ninth. The Giants scored a run in the 11th to win it 7–6.

The *New York Times* was ecstatic. "It was the Robins' seventh straight setback at the Giants' hands and 10,000 were tickled pink with excitement and thrills....

"Attacks and counter attacks, rallies and then some more rallies, tense moments, nerve-racking situations and, over it all, the music of the Giant bats playing a dirge for Uncle Wilbert Robinson, who sat in the dugout and brooded bitterly on life."[6]

A loss is a loss but for the floundering Robins, Dazzy's performance gave hope at least that better days might lie ahead. And they did. By putting together winning streaks of two and three games, the Robins steadily climbed and on May 28, when Burleigh Grimes beat the Giants in a battle won by the Robins 8–7, Brooklyn was above .500 for the first time at 18–17. Vance continued to struggle after his 15-strikeout masterpiece and was 1–6. One of the losses, on May 13, was a 5–2 decision in which the winning pitcher for the Cubs was Grover Cleveland Alexander. It was Alex's sixth consecutive game without issuing a walk, a string that would end in his next start. Meanwhile, Dazzy won four out of his next five starts including the best game of his major league career, a one-hitter against Cincinnati on June 17. Ol' Daz struck out five and walked three but did not give up a hit until, with two out in the ninth inning, Cincy's Sam Bohne blooped a base hit into center field that Bernie Neis raced in for but could not get before it dropped in front of him.

BROOKLYN	AB	R	H		CINCINNATI	AB	R	H
Neis cf	5	1	0		Burns rf	4	0	0
Johnston ss	4	0	0		Daubert 1b	3	0	0
Wheat lf	4	1	2		Bohne 2b	4	0	1
Fournier 1b	4	1	2		Roush cf	3	0	0
Griffith rf	4	2	2		Duncan lf	4	0	0
DeBerry c	2	1	1		Pinelli 3b	3	0	0
McCarren 3b	4	1	0		Caveney ss	3	0	0
Olson 2b	2	1	0		Wingo c	3	0	0
Vance p	3	1	0		Donohue p	1	0	0
Totals	32	9	7		Couch p	1	0	0
					Totals	29	0	1

Brooklyn   0 1 0 4 0 0 3 1 0 — 9
Cincinnati   0 0 0 0 0 0 0 0 0 — 0

Errors— Brooklyn 2 (Wheat, Fournier). Cincinnati 2 (Caveney, Couch). Doubles— Griffith, DeBerry. Triples— Wheat, Griffith. Sacrifices— DeBerry (2), Olson. Left on base— Brooklyn 1, Cincinnati 5.

	IP	H	R	BB	SO
Vance	9	1	0	3	5
Donohue	3	5	5	1	1
Couch	6	2	4	1	1

Umpires: Moran, Hart and Finneran. Time: 1:26

Murray Robinson covered the game for the *New York Evening Mail*. He wrote a heart-wrenching account of how a bloop single deprived a young Brooklyn pitcher from reaching baseball immortality. Robinson said Vance read his account of the game and told him later, "I'm glad Bohne got the hit. A no-hitter would have prevented this fine literary effort."

Twelve days later, the Robins clobbered the Phillies 14–5 with Fournier leading the way. He was 6 for 6 and was at bat in the ninth inning with a chance to make it 7 for 7 when a bizarre play occurred. He came to bat with two out and a man on first. For whatever reason, the runner broke for second and was thrown out trying to steal to end the inning. Fournier stood at the plate, his chance for a seventh hit eliminated. What made the situation so strange was that a runner would try to steal with a nine-run lead and a man at the plate who was 6 for 6. One possible explanation: Robbie was the first base coach who sent the runner. Had Fournier gotten a hit, he would have tied the all-time record of 7 for 7 set by none other than Wilbert Robinson, playing for the Baltimore Orioles on June 10, 1892. Fournier went to his grave thinking Robinson purposely sent the runner to prevent his record from being tied.[7]

On July 4, Brooklyn beat the Braves in a double header with Vance winning the first game 4–1, bringing his record to 7–9. When Burleigh Grimes won the nightcap, the Robins were 36–31, the most they had been above .500 all year and were riding a three-game winning streak. They were in fourth place, 10 games behind the Giants.

Meanwhile, Dazzy hit a streak that turned his season around. From June 30 through Aug. 2 he was unbeatable — literally — winning 10 straight games. The streak began on June 30 when Vance beat the Phillies in the first game of a double header 10–4 with Wheat and Johnston hitting home runs and Dazzy allowing just three hits. On July 5, Vance and the Robins beat the Braves 4–1 with Boston "submitting quietly" according to the *New York Times.* On July 9, Dazzy was wild, walking five, but Brooklyn beat St. Louis 5–3 for Vance's third straight win. Number four in a row came at Pittsburgh with Dazzy winning a pitching duel over Earl Cooper 2–1. On July 19, Vance hooked up in another classic. The Robins managed a run in the second inning and Dazzy did the rest as Brooklyn beat Cincinnati 1–0. He beat the Reds again 6–3 on July 25. His seventh straight win came against the Cardinals in St. Louis and was the first one in the streak where Dazzy needed some big help. Trailing 5–1 going into the ninth inning, Vance was lifted for a pinch hitter. The Robins scored five runs and relief pitcher Arthur Decatur held the Cardinals in check in the bottom of the ninth to save the victory for Vance.

On Aug. 4, Vance beat the Cubs 7–3 in a game in which the *Chicago Tribune* reported "Vance had the Bears in hand." The ninth straight win came Aug. 8 at Pittsburgh with the Robins winning 9–2. Five days later, the two teams met in Brooklyn with Vance notching his 10th straight victory 11–2. Dazzy struck out 10 and walked one. The streak came to an end on Aug. 17 but it took 11 innings to do it. St. Louis catcher Eddie Ainsmith doubled with the bases loaded to give the Cardinals the 8–5 victory.

Just about coinciding with Vance's streak ending, the Robins hit the skids in August when they lost 10 in a row between Aug. 17 and Aug. 30. Vance suffered three of the 10 losses and had a record of 14–12 going into September. The Robins had fallen 20½ games behind the Giants and were destined for their familiar spot, sixth place in the standings. Vance had a good September and finished the year with an 18–15 mark and led the league in strikeouts for the second year in a row with 197. He went home to Omaha where he operated a cigar store in the off-season, a great place for the locals to stop in, light up and talk a little baseball.

Grimes won 21 but he lost 18. Dutch Ruether finished at 15–14. Fournier, the big first baseman, fulfilled expectations with his .351 average, 22 home runs and 102 RBIs. Wheat hit .375 but injuries limited him to just 98 games and 65 runs batted in. Johnston had 60 RBIs. No one else could get as many as 50. It was the same old story for the Robins. They scored 753 runs, 101 fewer than the Giants.

New York had a lineup that featured future Hall of Famers Frisch, Bancroft and Youngs, veterans Stengel, Kelly and Heinie Groh and pitching staff featuring five starters who won in double figures: Jack Scott (16–7), Wilfred "Rosy" Ryan (16–5), Hugh McQuillan (15–14), Art Nehf (13–10), and John Needles Bentley (13–8).

Fournier's numbers for the year were impressive. He was second in the league in home runs with 22, behind the Phillies' Cy Williams who hit 41, most of them in the Baker Bowl bandbox. In RBIs, he was fifth with 102. Three out of the top four were Giants—Muesel with 125, Frisch with 111 and Kelly with 103 (Williams of the Phillies was second, tallying 114). He was third in batting (.351), behind Hornsby's .384 and Bottomley's .371. He finished second in slugging (.588), behind Hornsby's .627. Fournier was third in total bases (303) with Frisch (311) and Williams (308) finishing first and second. For the most part, Fournier finished behind Frisch, Williams and the heart of the Giants' lineup.

Sportswriter Frank Graham summed up the season this way in the *New York Times*: "Except for the change of a name or a date or a place here and there, the season of 1923, so far as the Robins were concerned, was so like that of 1922 that a fan who had slept through the winter and awakened in the middle of the 1923 season would have said: Here's where I came in."

V

"You couldn't hit him on a Monday"

The off-season produced little excitement in the way of trades or major changes on any of the big league clubs. On Feb. 9, Washington Senators owner Clark Griffith announced that his shortstop and team captain, Bucky Harris, was his new manager. Three days later, the National League announced it would join the American League practice of awarding $1,000 to whatever player was named the league's most valuable player at the end of the season. A committee of sportswriters would make the selection. On Feb. 17, Frank Chance, who had been named Chicago White Sox manager three months earlier, resigned because of illness. Coach Johnny Evers was named acting manager. Twenty years earlier, Chance and Evers had been two-thirds of the Cubs' famous double play combination of "Tinker to Evers to Chance"—famous more because of a poem about them than any record-setting performances on the field.

John McGraw of the Giants caused a stir at the start of spring training in 1924 when he prohibited his players from playing golf, effective immediately and through the end of the season. McGraw predicted that before long, all managers would ban golf during the baseball season. "Golf is a great game, and I'm for it," he said, "but it can be overdone. In fact, golf is too good, for it sometimes grips a ballplayer so tightly … I don't want any of my players sitting around talking nothing but golf in the heat of a pennant race."

McGraw said other factors played into his decision. Baseball swings and golf swings are radically different, he said, and shouldn't be mixed. Also, he said, too much golf in spring training can provide too much exercise, making players tired on the ball field. "Some of my players, especially the youngsters, are out there on the links getting a game in

51

between the morning and afternoon practices and in late afternoon. They get too much exercise and not enough rest and are likely to go stale," he said.[1]

While McGraw was extolling the vices of golf, sportswriters were writing off the Robins. Frank Smith in the *Chicago Tribune* called Uncle Robbie's charges "the surplus circle in New York's three-ring baseball circus" and concluded that "with the most liberal treatment it can be classed only a step ahead of the misfit Phillies."

As the season progressed, the strangest thing about it was that the Brooklyn Robins suddenly got good. It happens in every sport every so often — when a team that has been mediocre for years and has not made any vast roster changes somehow manages to put it all together in one season. But there's another part to the equation — you better win it when "it's your year" because it may be a long time before the pendulum swings back your way. The Miracle Braves did it in 1914 — rising from last place on the Fourth of July to not only win the National League pennant but the World Series as well. But they didn't win the pennant again until the "Spahn and Sain and pray for rain" championship club of 1948!

Robbie opened spring training as optimistic as ever. "Give me three fellows who can pitch that ball and four that can hit it and I'll win the pennant," he said. It is not recorded whether McGraw snickered when he read that. His Giants had won the pennant three years in a row and showed no signs of faltering. The Robins had made no major changes from their sixth-place roster of the year before. One writer described their pitching staff as "Grimes, Ruether, Vance and a lot of guys named Joe."

The Robins opened the season well with Ruether outdueling Rosy Ryan of the Giants, the result being a 3–2 Brooklyn win at the Polo Grounds before 45,000 fans, the biggest opening day crowd anywhere. Elsewhere, Rogers Hornsby went 2 for 5 against Vic Aldredge and the Cubs. What made that significant is that he hit higher than that for the rest of the year, finishing with a .424 average. In the American League, it was business as usual for Walter Johnson, starting the season by hurling a shutout. George Sisler, out all of the 1923 season with vision problems, returned to the St. Louis Browns lineup and rapped out two hits as St. Louis beat the White Sox 7–3.

In the Robins' second game of the season, Grimes got hammered and the Giants evened the series with a 7–1 victory. Vance got the call in the rubber game and lost a tough 3–2 10-inning decision, losing to

Wayland Dean in his major league debut. The *New York Times* called Dean a "blushing debutante" and went on to say, "Anyone who can beat the Vance of yesterday is flinging great baseball — and that was Dean — tall, loose, rangy, cool as the breeze that was blowing into the park."[2]

By the end of April, it was difficult to differentiate this Robins team from those of the previous few years, if the standings were any indication. Robbie's boys were 5–7 and in their familiar territory — sixth place in the National League standings. Vance, after having lost his first start, came back to win a 3–2 decision over the Giants and young Dean on April 25. *The New York Times* was not nearly as giddy about Dean in his second matchup with Ol' Daz. "History does not always repeat itself," the newspaper reported. Vance also won his next start, besting the Braves 6–4 on April 30. Zack Wheat had three hits for the Robins and was second in the National League to Hornsby of the Cardinals who was well on his way to a .400 season.

The Robins weren't the best baseball team around, but they did lead the league in having fun. On an early season road trip, they discovered they were on the same train as the Boston Braves, both heading for Boston, in fact, where they were to play each other the next day. Someone came up with the idea of giving the Braves a good scare. Dazzy, Fournier, Grimes and a few others found a scissors. They cut eye-holes in pillow cases and put the cloth masks over their heads to cover their faces. Then they raided the Braves' Pullman car, screaming and pulling some of the Boston players out of their sleeping berths and onto the floor. They hovered over Boston catcher Mickey O'Neill and threatened him within an inch of his life if he didn't divulge the Braves' signals during games. They may not have been the greatest, but the Robins were the loosest team in the league.[3]

On May 1, Brooklyn beat the Phillies 10–4 at Ebbets Field, but the big news of the day occurred in the American League where White Sox shortstop Bill Barrett stole home twice in Chicago's 13–7 win over the Cleveland Indians. The Robins had a pretty good May, winning 15 out of 25 with Dazzy beating the Braves 7–3 on May 4 and defeating the Cubs by the same score on May 12. The Cubs gave Dazzy some unexpected help by committing four errors. Irving Vaughn in the *Chicago Tribune* told his readers, "a mere glimpse of the skillful Dazzy Vance apparently was enough to give the Cubs a severe case of the jimmies." When Cincinnati beat the Phillies 4–3, coupled with the Giants' 5–3 loss to St. Louis, the Reds snuck into first place. The Giants and Reds went back and forth between first and second place for a little over a month. On June 13, the Cubs beat the Braves 5–1, giving Chicago temporary custody of first place. Before the season was over, Pittsburgh would also have a short stay at the top. No one gave a thought to the Robins climbing that high.

Vance beat the Cardinals 4–3 on May 17 and then won his sixth straight game, downing the Pirates 4–2 on May 22. No pitcher in baseball was as hot as Dazzy, but Walter Johnson was creating headlines of his own in the American League. On May 23, he struck out 14, including six straight batters, as the Senators beat the White Sox 4–0. It was Johnson's fifth shutout of the year and 103rd of his career.

Vance's latest win streak ended when the Robins dropped a 6–5 decision to the Giants on May 29. He headed into June with a 6–2 record. The Robins treaded water for a while in June. After starting the month with their fourth straight win, they hit a stretch where they lost two, won one, then lost two more and won one, then lost, then won two — never quite hitting their stride. By June 30, they had a 35–29 record, good for third place, eight games behind the Giants. They would have been further behind except that Dazzy was putting together the best year of his life — he was 11–3 and was running away with the National League strikeout title.

Rube Bressler, an outfielder and first baseman for the Cincinnati Reds, who later would room with Vance for four years with the Robins, described why Dazzy was so hard to hit. He said Dazzy had a fastball you couldn't see and a curve that was like "an apple rolling off a crooked table."

"You couldn't hit him on a Monday. He'd cut the sleeve of his undershirt to the elbow…. Then he'd pitch overhand, out of the apartment houses in the background at Ebbets Field. Between the bleached sleeve waving and the Monday wash hanging out to dry — you lost the ball entirely."[4]

The Robins played 33 games in July — winning 16, losing 17 — with Vance winning five of his six starts that month. With two months to play, Uncle Robbie's boys were mired in fourth place, 10½ games behind McGraw's Giants, with Chicago and Pittsburgh also ahead of them in the standings. But Dazzy was putting together his best year. He was 16–4. The rest of the pitching staff was 35–46.

New York's George Kelly had a torrid July including a stretch in which he homered in six consecutive games — an achievement not even Babe Ruth in the American League had accomplished. Another highlight of the month occurred on July 17 when Jesse Haines of the Cardinals tossed a no-hitter against the Braves, the first no-hitter ever thrown in St. Louis. It was Haines' first shutout in two years. Two days later, a Cardinals rookie pitcher, Herman Bell, nearly outdid Haines. He held the Braves hitless into the eighth inning of the first game of a double header. Then he did the same thing in the second game. St. Louis and Bell won both games 6–1 and 2–1. Bell gave up six hits in the two games. A Cardinals pitcher was involved in yet a third oddity on July 30. Lefty Bill Sherdel came out of the bullpen to face Phillies pinch hitter Johnny Mokan with runners on first and second and nobody out. On Sherdel's first pitch, Mokan bunted. The ball popped off his bat into the air. Cardinals first baseman Jim Bottomley, charging in from first, caught the ball. He threw it to shortstop Johnny Cooney who stepped on second to double up one runner. Cooney then threw to first where Rogers Hornsby was covering, nailing the runner on first before he could get back. The result was a triple play—on one pitch from Sherdel. It was a critical play in the game as the Cardinals won 9–8.

On Aug. 1, Vance pitched the best game of his major league career on a day he didn't feel good. When he arrived at Ebbets Field, he told Robbie he wasn't feeling his best but it was his turn to pitch and that he would give it a try. Robbie started having relief pitchers warm up in the early innings in case Dazzy got physically ill during the game. He didn't. He shut out the Cubs 4–0 and struck out 14, including seven in a row in one stretch. He fanned Gabby Hartnett to end the first inning and then mowed down each of the next six Cubs in order in the second and third innings—Barney Friberg, Denver Grigsby, Cliff Heathcote, Bill Barrett, Vic Aldridge and Jigger Statz. The streak ended when Dazzy walked Hollocher to start the fourth inning. The seven consecutive strikeouts tied the major league record. Hod Eller accomplished the feat with Cincinnati in 1919. The 14 strikeouts for the game equaled Vance's own personal record which he set in 1923. Aldridge, pitching well for the Cubs, had a shutout for six innings as the teams were locked in a scoreless tie. The Robins broke the game open with two runs in the seventh and two more in the eighth.

The next day, Brooklyn beat the Cubs again 9–7, but then lost three in a row to the Pirates. Dazzy got them back on track on Aug. 6 with a 5–3 win over Pittsburgh. He was now 18–4 but his team was still treading water, trailing the Giants, Pirates and Cubs. It was Vance's ninth straight win over the Pirates, dating back to 1922.

Something started to happen in August — one of those hard-to-explain things that happens in baseball — because suddenly, the Robins started to win in bunches. They hadn't made any blockbuster trades that gave them a new superstar and Uncle Robbie hadn't changed the lineup or given any hellfire and brimstone locker room talks to turn the team around. They just jelled and in so doing threw a scare into McGraw's Giants and every other team in the National League.

Between Aug. 6 and Aug. 8, they won three in a row; between Aug. 10 and Aug. 14, they won four in a row; between Aug. 17 and Aug. 21, they won six in a row. That streak ended on Aug. 22 with a 7–2 loss to the Cubs. The next day, Dazzy bested the Bruins 6–5 for his 10th consecutive victory. He struck out 15, one shy of the National League record held by Rube Waddell of the Philadelphia A's in 1908. Irving Vaughan in the *Chicago Tribune* described Dazzy this way: "Phenomenal speed and a curve that breaks so sharply that even the umpires get dizzy trying to call em have made strikeouts a commonplace item for the big fellow who bends back and lets go with a sweep that would shame a windmill."

Vance was now 22–4 and the Robins were on the move, in third place, behind the Giants and Pirates, but were now 15 games above .500 at 67–52. And the best was yet to come.

Brooklyn ended August with a five-game winning streak, including a three-game sweep of the Giants at Ebbets Field. Bill Doak, Burleigh Grimes and Vance picked up the victories. For Dazzy, the 3–1 victory was his 23rd win of the season, his 11th in succession — and his eight strikeouts brought his season total to 202, far and away the best in the National League. The Robins won 21 of 29 games in August and went into the final month of the season in third place, four games behind the Giants and two behind the second place Pirates. But Brooklyn had a tough schedule — four double headers in four days, the first three against the Phillies at Baker Bowl.

On Sept. 1, the Robins won the first two 7–2 and 6–3. The next day, Vance pitched the opener and had his worst outing of the year. He hit a batter, and then gave up a single and back-to-back home runs. He gave up four runs on five hits and was out of the game after one inning — but the Robins rallied to win the game 12–9 and won the second game 4–3, a contest called at the end of six innings because of a rainstorm. The Robins had now won nine in a row and were just two games behind McGraw's Giants. On Wednesday, Sept. 3, Burleigh Grimes and Bill Doak were the winning pitchers in the Robins' third double header sweep in three days.

That night, they took the train from Philly to Boston where the Robins took on the Braves in yet another double header, their fourth in four days. Vance pitched the opener and was back in his usual form, winning 5–1. When Ruether was a 9–1 winner in the nightcap, the Robins were sitting on a 13-game winning streak and were just 1½ games behind the Giants. When they beat the Braves two more times, on Sept. 5–6, they crept to within one game of McGraw's crew and extended their winning streak to 15. The 15th win was 1–0 in the first game of a double header but the streak came to an end when Boston won the nightcap, 5–4. The Robins now headed home to Ebbets Field for a two-game set with the Giants and a chance to take over first place in the National League.

If there was a baseball city more excited than Brooklyn and its high-flying Robins, it was Washington, the nation's capital, where Bucky Harris's Senators were atop the American League and were on their way to the World Series. The *Washington Post* gave notice to what was happening in the National League when it compared the modern-day Robins to ancient warriors. "It is to be doubted if there has been a triumvirate since the days of old Rome more formidable than the Brooklyn three—Vance, Wheat and Fournier," reported the *Post*. It pointed out Wheat was in his prime 10 years ago, Vance was struggling in the minors with a sore arm at about that time and Fournier had been a 12-year minor leaguer who, like Vance, couldn't make it with an American League team. Yet, said the *Post*, "their work has lifted Brooklyn to heights where the club can fight for the flag."

A summary of the Robins' 15-game winning streak:

Aug. 25—defeated St. Louis 5–3; Aug. 26—defeated St. Louis 7–4; Aug. 29—defeated New York 3–1; Aug. 30—defeated New York 8–5; Aug. 31—defeated New York 3–2; Sept. 1—defeated Philadelphia 7–2 and 6–3; Sept. 2—defeated Philadelphia 12–9 and 4–3; Sept. 3—defeated Philadelphia 7–6 and 7–0; Sept. 4—defeated Boston 5–1 and 9–1; Sept. 5—defeated Boston 4–0 Sept. 6—defeated Boston 1–0.

The Giants came into Ebbets Field on Sunday, Sept. 7, with something to prove. They were the defending National League champions for each of the past three years. But the upstart Robins were poised to catch them. In an unusual series, the two teams would square off at Ebbets

Field on one day and travel to the Polo Grounds the next day. In the first game, at Ebbets Field, Clarence Mitchell took the mound for the Giants against Bill Doak but neither had their best stuff and the Giants won a free-swinging battle 8–7. They now had a two-game lead and were assured of ending the series in first place. The Robins, on the other hand, fresh off their 15-game winning streak, had now lost two in a row and had to face the Giants at the Polo Grounds. Uncle Robbie sent Dazzy Vance to the mound. Art Nehf took the hill for the Giants.

Forty thousand screaming fans saw the Giants take the lead with a run in the third inning. The Robins tied it with a run in the fourth but the Giants recaptured the lead with a run of their own in the bottom of the fourth. DeBerry hit a two-run homer for Brooklyn in the fifth and that was enough for Dazzy to notch his 13th consecutive win. The Robins added two in the seventh and one each in the eighth and ninth innings in posting a 7–2 victory. Vance was now 25–4 — and DeBerry was the hitting hero of the game. So the two guys who came up from New Orleans three years ago — the wily catcher and the wild throw-in that Ebbets didn't want but had to take — were paying big dividends for him now.

In the American League, Walter Johnson won his 20th game as the Senators beat the Athletics and maintained a two-game lead over the Yankees. The Nats were having a sensational year under rookie manager Bucky Harris.

On Monday, the Robins had an off day and got ready for a 15-game homestand to end the season. If they were to win the National League pennant, they would need some help, for they had no more games against the Giants. They opened the homestand with a two-game sweep of the Phillies, then lost to the Reds 6–5. On Sunday, Sept. 14, two future Hall of Famers matched up when Dazzy took the mound for the Robins against Eppa Rixey of the Reds. The game was scoreless for the first three innings. The Robins pushed across a run in the fourth on a sacrifice fly. In the eighth, Vance helped his own cause with an RBI single. He also struck out nine and tossed a shutout as the Robins won 2–0 and were within 1½ games of New York with 17 to play.

Brooklyn took two out of three from St. Louis but then lost two in a row to the Pirates, including a 5–4 defeat in 11 innings on Sept. 20, a game in which Vance went all the way and took the loss, snapping his personal winning streak at 15. More important, Pittsburgh snuck ahead of the Robins in the standings. Brooklyn was in third place, though just two games behind New York. With just six games to play—and none with the Giants—Uncle Robbie's upstarts would now need a miracle to overtake them. McGraw's crew could have eliminated the Robins the next day but while Brooklyn lost 5–4 in 11 innings, the Giants also lost in extra innings. The Cubs beat them 7–3 as Grover Cleveland Alexander won his 300th game.

Chicago proved it did not play favorites in being a spoiler in the pennant race. On Sept. 23, the Cubs beat the Robins 5–4 in 10 innings—the second straight extra-inning loss for Dazzy Vance in the fourth straight extra-inning game for the weary Robins. Gabby Hartnett's homer in the 10th was the deciding factor, only the third hit off of Dazzy up to that point. The next day, Alexander hooked up with Burleigh Grimes, and this time the Robins prevailed 6–5. Brooklyn was hanging on by a thread, 1½ games out with two to play. The final curtain went down on the pennant race on Saturday, Sept. 27, when the Robins lost to the Boston Braves 3–2 while the Giants were winning two. That put New York ahead by three with one game remaining. Vance closed out the season with a 5–1 victory over the Braves, giving him a record of 28–6. The win pushed the Robins into second place, their best finish in four years. Their record was 92–62, two games behind the Giants.

Dazzy led the league in wins with 28, in strikeouts with 262 and in earned run average, 2.16. He was second best in winning percentage with a mark of .824. Only Emil Yde of the Pirates had a higher percentage, .842, a product of his 16–3 record. In addition to the 15-game winning streak, Vance had eight games in which he struck out 10 or more batters. Here is how he fared against every other team in the National League:

Team	Games	IP	SO	Record
New York	7	61	45	4–3
Boston	5	46	40	4–1
Chicago	6	55	60	5–1
St. Louis	4	35	36	4–0
Pittsburgh	6	56	34	5–1
Cincinnati	5	45	37	5–0
Philadelphia	2	10	9	1–0
Totals	**35**	**308**	**261**	**28–6**

Vance's season was topped off with being named as the National League's most valuable player, complete with the $1,000 prize that owners had approved at the start of the season. Dazzy beat out Rogers

Hornsby, the St. Louis second baseman who hit .424, still the highest batting average achieved in modern major league baseball. The MVP is selected by writers. Dazzy was a darling of the sportswriters with his quick wit and his penchant for providing good copy with the way he pitched and the stories he told in the clubhouse before and after he pitched. By contrast, Hornsby wasn't interested in getting along with anybody. In three years, Cardinals owner Sam Breadon would trade him, even though Hornsby, as manager of the ball club, had led the team to the pennant. In the voting for most valuable player, in which writers were allowed to fill in 10 names, one writer omitted Hornsby's name altogether.

Selection committee members—one writer from each National League city—explained their choice this way: "The committee argued that Vance lifted a pretty good club up to a pennant contender clear up to the last week, while Hornsby could not lift a pretty good club out of the second division. Therefore, based on raw and finished values, Vance's claim is undisputed."[5]

Dazzy was the darling of baseball and the stories about him filled the sports pages. *The Atlanta Constitution* caught up with a fellow by the name of Adam Breede, who was a catcher for the Hastings ball club in the Nebraska State League when Vance was a hard-throwing, wild young pitcher.

Breede, a game hunter, told the newspaper he would rather shoot at a rhinoceros with a pea shooter than catch Dazzy Vance. Breede said, "When you're working out on a petulant rhino—and I might remark that the rhino can be extremely petulant at times—you have always got a chance to do something to him to offset what he is trying to do to you."

Not so when you're catching Dazzy Vance, he said. "You can only squat there and take it." Breede said he played first base for the Hastings ball club and prayed that Dazzy wouldn't throw over to him with a runner on first because he threw the ball so hard and all over the place. Breede switched to catcher so he'd have a bigger mitt. Even with that, he said he hoped the batters would hit the ball somewhere so he wouldn't have to catch so many pitches.

Also, said Breede, Dazzy was so wild in those days that every once in a while he would throw the ball over the backstop behind the plate. "Dazzy was just the least bit wilder than the wild Irish rose," he said.[6]

The *Los Angeles Times* reported that Vance was a man of many talents, including pistol shooting. The writer claimed Dazzy once hit a

Rogers Hornsby hit .424 for the St. Louis Cardinals in 1924 but did not win the Most Valuable Player award. That distinction went to Dazzy Vance who won 28 games for Brooklyn. (Courtesy Hall of Fame.)

dime three times in succession from a distance of 45 feet, cut a business card in two, edgewise, from the same distance, and blew the bottom out of a beer bottle by shooting through the neck, not breaking any of the glass in between.[7]

As great a year as Vance had, the Robins would not have been in the pennant chase had it not been for another Brooklyn ace, Burleigh Grimes, whose pitching would have been the talk of the league had it not been for the year his teammate was having. Grimes won 22 games, second in the league to Vance, and won many big games for the Robins as they chased the Giants in the great pennant drive.

"There is no truer test of real greatness in all this world than to play second fiddle to an extraordinary star in your own home orchestra," the *Washington Post* pontificated. The *Post* went on to say that though Grimes did not get the headlines like Vance did, and did not get the credit he deserved because of the great year Dazzy was having, "if it had not been for the cunning and courage of Burleigh Grimes, Brooklyn would not have been within many games of that final pennant grapple."[8]

Grimes represented what Wilbert Robinson wanted on all of his ball clubs: a veteran who had been through the wars many times. Uncle Robbie, the old catcher, had resurrected many a pitching career through his knowledge and teaching. He didn't have to do that with Grimes. He simply relied on the veteran to come through and he did. Robbie had picked him up from the Pirates in 1918. He was 23–11 with the Robins' 1920 pennant winner, the start of a string in which he won 20 or more games in four out of the next five years.

By contrast, Dutch Ruether, the lefthander who had been a consistent winner for the Cincinnati Reds—including a 19–6 mark in their 1919 pennant season—and who had won 21 games for Robbie in 1922 and 15 in 1923, inexplicably slipped to 8–13 in 1924. Pitching for the Washington Senators in 1925, Ruether returned to form winning 18 and losing only 7. He closed out his career with the Yankees, going 14–9 in 1926 splitting time between Washington and New York and then 13–6 with the 1927 New York pennant winner. The only aberration in an otherwise stellar career was his 1924 season.

The Robins were not quite out of the headlines for the year. Fournier, the big first baseman who hit .340, went with several teammates on a barnstorming trip to the Pacific Northwest not long after the season ended. Players from other teams also made the trip. On Oct. 27, in Wenatchee, Wash., a scuffle broke out in a hotel room occupied by one of the players. In the melee, a bellhop was beaten because he reportedly was too slow in delivering ice water to the room. When police arrived and sorted everything out, Eddie Brown, Milt Stock, Bernie Neis and Clarence Mitchell were arrested and taken to jail where they were obliged to spend the night. As the players told the story years later, without mentioning any names, three of the "inmates" remained unruly, banging on the cell door, demanding to be bailed out. The fourth calmly took off his coat, folded it in such a way that it could be used as a pillow on his bunk, then took off the rest of his clothes, all the way down to his underwear, and laid on the bed sedately, as if ready to go to sleep. One of his teammates saw him, stopped banging for a moment, and said, "You ain't foolin' me. You've been in jail before."[9]

VI

"The best pitch is the unexpected pitch"

The first big surprise of the fall came on Oct. 10 when Washington won the World Series, beating the New York Giants. The winning run was scored in the 12th inning in a way that John McGraw hated. Muddy Ruel hit a pop-up that catcher Hank Gowdy went after. But he stepped on his mask and could not shake it off his foot. Meanwhile, the ball hit the ground in foul territory. Given another chance, Ruel doubled. Walter Johnson, who had pitched 12 innings and was batting for himself, bounced a ground ball that shortstop Travis Jackson booted. Then Earl McNeely hit a seemingly harmless ground ball that took a bad hop over Freddy Lindstrom's head. Ruel jogged home with the winning run.

On Oct. 27, the Pirates and the Cubs, two teams that hovered near the top of the standings for part of 1924, made a major deal. The Cubs sent pitcher Vic Aldridge, infielder George Grantham and first baseman Al Niehaus to the Pirates in exchange for first baseman Charlie Grimm, shortstop Rabbit Maranville and pitcher Wilbur Cooper. Two years later, Pittsburgh won the pennant with Grantham fitting into a lineup that already had three Hall of Famers, Pie Traynor and the Waner brothers, Lloyd and Paul. Aldridge won 15 games for the Pirates. The deal had a more long-term impact on the Cubs. Grimm played 11 years for Chicago and eventually became their manager, winning pennants in 1935 and 1945 and sharing duties with Gabby Hartnett in 1938 when the Cubs also won the National League championship.

Brooklyn, euphoric over its second place finish in 1924, made a few moves during the winter months. The Robins, disappointed in Ruether's decline, sold him to the Washington Senators where he experienced a revival, putting up an 18–7 record in 1925. The next year, he went to the Yankees and was the fourth starter on the 1927 championship team. In another deal, the Robins traded Vance's fishing buddy, Bernie Neis, to the Braves for outfielder Cotton Tierney. But 1925 would be remembered in Brooklyn history as much for events that occurred off the field as what happened between the white lines.

As the Robins reported for spring training, five players, including Dazzy Vance, remained unsigned. The others were Grimes, Bill Doak, Zack Taylor and Dutch Henry. Vance was the most important one, not only because he was the best pitcher in the National League but also because Charlie Ebbets and Uncle Robbie were convinced that once Dazzy signed, the others would fall into line. Doak was another important piece to the puzzle. Coming over from the Cardinals in 1924, the veteran hurler was 13–6 and helped keep the Robins in the pennant race. Now he was threatening to retire to spend more time on his real estate business in Bradenton, Fla. With Ruether already gone and Doak talking about quitting, the Robins' season was in danger of falling apart before it even began.

Vance, who earned $9,000 in 1924, was holding out for $22,000 a year. Ebbets bluntly refused. When Dazzy reported for spring training in Clearwater without a signed contract, Robbie told him he could not suit up. On March 7, Ebbets went public about the contract dispute, telling reporters he had offered Vance a three-year deal worth $47,500 that Dazzy had agreed to in their discussions but then refused to sign the contract.

"First he wanted $22,000 for one year, $37,500 for two and $50,000 for three," said Ebbets. "I was willing to pay him $45,000 for three. We compromised at $47,500."

But Ebbets said he did not have a blank contract with him when he negotiated with Vance so Dazzy signed a statement saying he agreed to sign the contract. When the contract was drawn up, he then refused to sign it, according to Ebbets.

The sticking points for Dazzy were clauses that gave Brooklyn the right to trade him, suspend him or release him — standard fare in contracts of that era. Ebbets said he would be glad to give Vance a contract without that language but to do so, he said, "would violate the laws of baseball." On March 11, Dazzy signed for the $47,500, including the clauses he didn't like but had to accept. To sweeten the deal, Ebbets provided a $5,000 advance on his salary.[1]

Dazzy had his own take on his discussions with Ebbets. "I pointed out to the Squire that if Hornsby was worth so much money to the Cardinals as the most valuable player in 1923, I ought to be worth about as much as the most valuable player in 1924," said Vance. But Ebbets pointed out that Hornsby played every day and Dazzy played only once every four days.

The give and take continued. Vance told Ebbets if Hornsby was taken out and replaced with a high school kid, the Cardinals would still win most of the time. "Take a pitcher out of the game and put a high school boy in his place and I'll bet they wouldn't win any," Dazzy said he told his boss.

He then reminded Ebbets that Connie Mack and other managers rated pitching as being 70 percent of a ball club's strength. If a pitcher works once every four games, that's 17½ percent of that 70 percent. "Taking the strength of a ballclub as a full 100 percent, the other eight players, giving them the benefit of the figures, individually only represent 12½ percent of the club's strength. That gives the pitcher an edge of 5 percent, doesn't it?" asked Dazzy.

It was classic Dazzy Vance — ballplayer, businessman, storyteller and, in the end, deal maker. It is not recorded whether Ebbets was convinced by Dazzy's logic or simply bowled over by the rambling rhetoric.

Grimes eventually signed, but Doak followed through on his threat to retire, leaving the pitching staff, in Robbie's words, "shot to pieces."

Abe Yager, sports editor of the *Brooklyn Eagle*, wrote on April 1 that only two were left of the "Big 4" on the pitching staff of 1924 and that the outlook for the season was one of shattered hopes. Yager said the loss of Doak would be severely felt but was not unexpected. He had been talking about retirement ever since the end of the previous season. But Yager thought the Robins may have made a mistake in giving up on Ruether.

He wrote, "His failure to live up to his previous record [is] being blamed for the loss of the pennant to Brooklyn. Dutch is still a great twirler and his change of environment should bring out his latent strength. He has left a big hole in the Dodger pitching offense."[2]

The Robins ended spring training with two games in the last week against the Yankees. The first, in Birmingham, Ala., was labeled "The Babe Ruth and Dazzy Vance Combined Shows." The 10,000 fans who showed up got their money's worth. Vance did not pitch but Ruth played and did not disappoint the masses. His grand-slam home run was the difference in an 11–8 Yankees victory.

A week later, the two teams met up again in Knoxville, Tenn., the seventh time they had played each other this spring, with the series tied at three games apiece. The *New York Times* had this to say: "Knoxville saw what perhaps no other city will see this year — a battle between the greatest hitter and one of the greatest pitchers of all time. It was a meeting which was calculated to thrill, and it did."

In his first at-bat against Dazzy, Ruth grounded into a force play at second. In his next at-bat, Vance took his time, shuffling dirt around the pitcher's mound. Then he fired three straight strikes past the Bambino, who didn't take the bat off his shoulder. In the fifth inning, which was to be Dazzy's last, Ruth was in the on-deck circle when Earl Combs hit a slow roller to short and beat it out for a hit on a close play at first. Some said if the shortstop had been quicker at fielding it, Combs would have been easily out at first. But he wasn't, and that gave the Babe his third chance against Dazzy. The first two pitches were wide of the plate. The next one was a sizzler that Vance tried to whiz by Ruth. The Babe swung, and, as the *Times* reported the next day, "the sound of the ensuing crash still lingers in Vance's ears. The nice white ball left the bat as if it had been shot from a cannon, cleared the left centerfield wall by 30 feet and knocked a limb off a dead tree."[3]

About a month after Ebbets got the signed contracts from Vance and Grimes, he took ill and was confined to his bed in his suite at the Waldorf-Astoria Hotel in New York. Ebbets was a robust, active man who had fended off serious illnesses in the past and had bragged that he survived ailments that would have killed ten men. This one he could not shake off. On the morning of April 18, Charles Ebbets died at the age of 66.

The Robins were scheduled to play the arch-rival Giants that afternoon. After much deliberation between officials of both teams and the National League office, it was decided to play the game. It was what Charlie would have wanted, the Robins said, and therefore there was no need to disrupt the schedule. The Robins wore black armbands and the ballpark flags were flown at half-staff. The Giants won 7–1.

Ebbets had owned the team in partnership with two businessmen, Ed and Steve McKeever, who were brothers. It was decided that Ed McKeever would be acting president until the board of directors could meet to elect a permanent president. Ebbets' funeral took place on a cold, windy day. When Ed McKeever returned home from the cemetery, he went to bed complaining of having caught a cold at the funeral. It was

more than a cold. It was pneumonia and McKeever never recovered. His
death came less than a week after Ebbets passed away.

The stunned directors of the Brooklyn organization met to choose
a new president. After lengthy deliberations, they chose Robbie, the man
who had led them on the field for 12 years and had more baseball savvy
than anyone else in the organization. Robbie named Zack Wheat, the
great outfielder and longtime Brooklyn player, to be acting manager so
that Robbie could spend as much time as possible learning the rigors of
the front office.

Wheat took over on June 14 but the Robins game with Cincinnati
was rained out. The next day, he made his managerial debut and, as Bill
Corum put it in the *New York Times*, "mid the thunder of base hits,
under a shower of pop bottles and the groans of 20,000, Zack Wheat,
the Missouri dirt farmer was officially installed as the manager of the
Brooklyn baseball team today." The Robins beat the Reds 12–3, ending
Cincinnati's eight-game winning streak in a game that featured a fight
in the stands that became downright ugly when a police officer made an
arrest. The crowd, sweating under a hot sun and perhaps including a
few inebriated souls, turned on the officer and began pelting him with
bottles. On the field, Wheat played his usual position in left field, got
one hit in three at-bats and scored two runs. Vance got the victory.

That turned out to be one of the few highlights of Wheat's managerial career. The Robins lost 10 of their next 15 and Brooklyn's board
of directors, fairly new to their own jobs, became uneasy with having
a brand new man in the front office and a brand new man in the
dugout. Robbie watched the games from the box seats and tried to
divorce himself from managing the team. But as time went on, and with
the urging of the other higher-ups, Robbie returned to the dugout as
sort of an adviser or assistant manager to the acting manager although
he had no official title. The arrangement was a disaster and caused a
rift in his relationship with Wheat that never healed. At one point,
Wheat confronted Robbie and said, "Nobody knows where I stand,
including me. Who's running the ballclub on the field, anyway?" he
asked. Robbie is said to have responded, "You are. And, hell, you're
right. We don't need two managers." Robbie resumed his watch from
the box seats.[4]

But only temporarily. When the Robins continued to falter, on Aug.
6 he returned to the dugout as manager. When Wheat took over on June
14, the Robins were 28–23. They were 20–24 under his direction. Wheat

never again managed in the major leagues and his tenure as manager of the Robins is not mentioned in official record books.[5]

While all of this was going on, the Robins were playing baseball and were losing more than they were winning, no matter who was managing. They opened the season with two straight wins over the Phillies at Ebbets Field, with Dazzy winning the opener 3–1. In that one, Jack Fournier, the Robins' slugging first baseman, was ejected along with Phillies coach Benny Myers after Fournier punched him and Myers retaliated with a flurry of blows. Players from both teams as well as umpires separated the two men as order was restored. Fournier said the fight started when Myers insulted Vance.

The Robins then lost their next five, including four in a row immediately after Ebbets' death. They got back on track with a 10–8 win over the Phillies on April 24. Vance was the winning pitcher though he was hammered for 15 hits. The Robins were 3–5; Vance was 2–0. On May 3, Uncle Robbie's troops made their first venture of the year into the Polo Grounds. "With the mingling of the Robins and the Giants, baseball broke out like a rash," wrote Harry Cross in the *New York Times*. The Giants beat the Robins and Vance 7–5. Three days later, Dazzy shut out the Braves in Boston in a 10–0 laugher. Brooklyn edged its way back to the .500 mark on May 9 when Burleigh Grimes beat the Reds 5–3 at Ebbets Field. On May 14, the Robins took an unusual step. A letter signed by every player was sent to Doak, the retired pitcher, in Bradenton, urging him to come back and help the ball club for the rest of the season. With all the front office turmoil and the loss of Ruether and Doak, the players were obviously aware of their team's shortcomings and how Doak could help. He was flattered but he chose to stay with his real estate business in Florida. The Robins trudged on. On May 26, Robbie formally took over as club president while retaining, at least for now, his position as manager. Brooklyn beat the lowly Phillies in a double header with Vance and Grimes picking up the victories. At the end of May, the Robins seemed to be turning it around. A victory over the Braves in the first game of a double header on May 30 put them at 23–15, their high point of the year.

Just as Ruether had struggled in 1924, Grimes was having trouble winning in 1925. The difference was that the Robins no longer had anyone to fall back on like they had in previous years. The Big Four had become the Big Two and was becoming the Big One — Dazzy Vance. Entering June, the Robins were still very much in the race, in second place, 5½ games behind the Giants, but they weren't firing on all cylinders and would need a second-half surge if they were to create the excitement they did in 1924. They ended May with a tough 2–0 loss to the Giants in which Jack Scott outdueled Dazzy Vance at Ebbets Field. Vance struck out 13 Giants in the loss.

On June 4, the Robins got enough clutch hits to support Dazzy in a 7–6 win over the Cubs in a game that featured an unusual triple play. In the seventh inning, Hod Ford, the Robins' shortstop singled. Third baseman Jimmy Johnston bunted. Charlie Grimm, the Cubs' first baseman, picked up the ball and tagged Johnston coming down the line. But the umpire ruled that Grimm missed the tag. Grimm was incensed. He claimed that not only did he tag Johnston but that Johnston had run out of the baseline trying to avoid the tag. In the heat of the moment, Grimm tossed his glove in the air after which he was tossed from the game. Bernie Friberg took over at first base. On the next pitch, Wheat hit a scorching line drive right at Friberg who stepped on first to double up Johnston and then fired to second where Maranville stepped on the bag before Ford could get back. So Friberg participated in a triple play on the first pitch after he had entered the game.

Meanwhile, some interesting things were happening in the American League, where the Yankees hoped to return to championship form. Young Lou Gehrig pinch-hit for shortstop Paul Wanninger in a game on June 1 in which the Senators beat the Yankees 5–3 at Yankee Stadium. The next day, New York's regular first baseman, Wally Pipp, asked to be taken out of the lineup because of what turned out to be one of the most famous headaches in baseball history. Manager Miller Huggins inserted Gehrig into the lineup and, counting his pinch-hitting performance the day before, remained there for 2,130 consecutive games.

On June 18, Dazzy and the Robins clipped Pittsburgh 6–2. Bill Corum in the *New York Times* described his performance this way: "Vance had all his vaunted speed and a dizzy curve which looped the loop, twisted and twirled and cut capers like a toy balloon in a Kansas cyclone…. Seven of the enemy fanned furiously at the ozone." Two days later, the Robins played an exhibition game against the St. Louis Browns and lost 6–5 at Ebbets Field. Corum wrote it off, telling his readers the Robins proved they could lose in any league.

A week after that, while the Robins were losing to the Phillies 10–6, Dazzy was telling sportswriters how he got his nickname. As happened with so many Vance recollections over the years, the story changed a little. Dazzy said as a child he mispronounced the word "daisy" for "dazzy" as in "ain't it a dazzy." That part of the story hadn't changed over the years. But now, Dazzy told the writers that when he was pitching for Hastings, way back when, he came across a situation where Hastings was up by one run, but the opponent had the bases loaded with two out in the ninth inning. Dazzy ran the count to 3 and 2 on the batter and then fired a fastball that the batter swung and missed. Vance said he shouted, "Whoopee. Wasn't that a dazzy?" And the nickname stuck.[6]

The Robins won a July 4th double header against the Giants at Ebbets Field by scores of 10–2 and 5–3 with Vance getting his fifth straight win in the second game, bringing his season record to 11–5. Sportswriter Corum told his readers about a fan in the stands who rated the Robins' two managers in 1926. When Wheat ran up against the wall to pull in a long fly ball off the bat of Bill Terry, the fan said, "That settles it. Zack is a better manager. Robbie would have never caught that ball."

On July 9, two of the greatest pitchers in National League history matched up when Dazzy went up against the Cubs and Grover Cleveland Alexander in Brooklyn. Vance won his sixth straight, 4–2, and drove in three of the four runs with a single and a home run. Going into the game, Dazzy had a total of two hits all season. His season record was 12–5, winning almost one-third of his team's 39 victories. The Robins were two games above .500 in third place, 7½ games behind the Pirates.

They had a chance to gain some ground when Pittsburgh came to Ebbets Field for a four-game series but it didn't work out that way. The Robins lost three out of four, and when Vance took the loss in an 8–5 decision on July 14, his personal winning streak ended at six and Brooklyn was once again a .500 ball club at 40–40. After the game, manager Wheat told the press that both Dazzy and Jess Petty had sore arms and might miss their next starts.

The Cardinals wished it had panned out that way, at least with respect to Vance. On July 20, Dazzy struck out 17 Redbirds and got three hits, including a home run, in a 4–3 victory over St. Louis. The game went 10 innings and Vance's single in the 10th drove in the winning run. But what fans and historians remember about that game is Dazzy's mastery over the Cardinals batters. Richard Vidmer, reporting for the *New York Times*, wrote: "The great Brooklyn righthander fanned 17 alleged hitters, including the league-leading Mr. Hornsby three times and the bustling Mr. Bottomley as many." The 17 strikeouts was a record for a

10-inning game. Dazzy had 15 strikeouts after nine innings, tying the high mark most recently achieved by Rube Waddell.

BROOKLYN	*AB*	*R*	*H*		*ST. LOUIS*	*AB*	*R*	*H*
Ford, ss	3	1	0		Flack, rf	3	0	2
Stock, 2b	4	0	1		Shinners, cf	3	0	0
Wheat, lf	4	0	1		Hornsby, 2b	5	0	1
Fournier, 1b	4	0	1		Bottomley, 1b	5	1	1
Cox, rf	4	0	0		Hafey, rf	5	1	2
Brown, cf	4	0	1		Toporcer, ss	2	1	1
Tierney, 3b	4	0	0		Bell, 3b	5	0	2
DeBerry, c	4	1	1		O'Farrell, c	3	0	0
Mitchell (a)	0	1	0		Mails, p	3	0	0
Vance, p	4	1	3		Totals	34	3	9
Totals	35	4	8					

(a) Ran for DeBerry in 10th

Brooklyn   0 0 0 0 2 0 0 1 0 1 — 4
St. Louis   0 0 0 2 0 0 0 0 0 0 — 3

Errors: Mails. Doubles: Stock, Fournier, DeBerry. Triples: Toporcer. Home runs: Vance. Stolen base: Hafey. Sacrifices: Shinners, Toporcer, Mails. Double play: Bell and Bottomley. Left on base: St. Louis 10, Brooklyn 5

	IP	*H*	*R*	*BB*	*SO*
Vance	10	9	3	6	17
Mails	10	8	4	1	3

Umpires: McLaughlin, Quigley and Rigler. Time: 2:10

Dazzy's 17th strikeout victim that day was Bottomley and he took particular pride in it. As he recalled years later, he had struck out everyone in the Cardinals' lineup that day except Toporcer, a pesky slap hitter who didn't have much power but was a tough out. With the game in the balance, Robbie, the "co-manager," flashed the sign to walk the power-hitting Bottomley and pitch to Toporcer. This would put the winning run on base with much less of a power hitter at the plate. Dazzy said he shook his head in disagreement because he thought he could handle the free-swinging Bottomley and wouldn't have to face the little punch hitter.

"Robbie finally swept out his hands in a downward motion. That was his favorite sign," said Dazzy. "OK, use your own judgment." So Dazzy faced Bottomley, hitting .367, instead of Toporcer, hitting .284 and struck out Sunny Jim.

Vance revealed one of the secrets to his pitching success by telling of an encounter he had with Lefty O'Doul of the Giants. Dazzy said he saw O'Doul before the game and told him about a vision he had. Vance said he'd probably be called in from the bullpen with the bases loaded and O'Doul at the plate. He said he would get two strikes on him and then strike him out with a pitch right down the middle of the plate. The fates of baseball were hard at work that day and, sure enough, Dazzy was summoned from the bullpen with the bases loaded and O'Doul at the plate. Dazzy unloaded two of his jug-handle curveballs and O'Doul got out in front of each of them and pulled them long and foul. Then Dazzy fired a fastball over the heart of the plate and Lefty couldn't pull the trigger. Strike three. He said he told O'Doul afterwards that he knew Lefty, one of the best fastball hitters in all of baseball, would never believe he would get a fastball right down the middle.

When slugger Wally Berger broke in with the Boston Braves, Vance struck him out on three curveballs his first time up. His next time up, Vance struck him out with three fastballs. "What gives?" Berger asked Vance after the game. "You strike me out on curve balls and then my next time up, I don't see a curve ball."

Dazzy had the same answer for Berger that he had for O'Doul and it capsulized his philosophy of pitching. "The best pitch," he said, "is the unexpected pitch."[7]

MacLean Kennedy of the *Atlanta Constitution* did some research and determined that Vance was one of 14 who had struck out 17 men or more in the history of the major leagues— but most of those occurred prior to 1893 when the pitcher's mound was 50 feet from the plate and pitchers could do just about anything they wanted to do in their motions to distract the batters, Kennedy's list:

Charlie Sweeney, Providence, 19 strikeouts against Boston, June 7, 1884; Hugh Daly, Chicago, 19 strikeouts against Boston, July 7, 1884.; Henry Porter, Milwaukee, 18 strikeouts against Boston, Oct. 2, 1884; Fred Shaw, Boston, 18 strikeouts against St. Louis, June 24, 1884; Charlie Buffinton, Boston, 17 strikeouts against Cleveland, Sept. 12, 1884; Guy Hacker, Louisville, 17 strikeouts against Columbus, Aug. 30, 1884; Tom Ramsey, Louisville, 17 strikeouts against Metropolitan, August 1886; Tom Ramsey, Louisville, 17 strikeouts against Cleveland, June 21, 1887; Rube Waddell, St. Louis Browns, 17 strikeouts against Philadelphia (10 innings), Sept. 20, 1908; Rube Waddell, Philadelphia Athletics, 17 strikeouts against Boston (13 innings), Sept. 5, 1905; Arthur Vance, Brooklyn Dodgers, 17 strikeouts against St. Louis, (10 innings) July 20, 1925; J. Whitney, Boston, 18 strikeouts against Providence (15 innings), June 14, 1884; Jack Combs, Philadelphia Athletics, 18 strikeouts against Boston (24 innings), Sept. 1, 1906.[8]

After the 17-strikeout performance, Dazzy was 13–6 for the year but the Robins were at 43–43 in third place, 8½ games behind Pittsburgh. Brooklyn made some roster moves but none of the blockbuster variety that might turn their fortunes around. The Robins placed infielder Andy High on waivers and he was snatched up by the Boston Braves. They brought up two minor league pitchers, Jim Elliott and Lee Ellenberg. Of the two, Elliott was the brightest prospect. The lefthander had an 18–3 record at Terre Haute in the Three-I League. Known as "Jumbo Jim" Elliot, he appeared in three games for the Robins, gave up 17 hits and 9 walks in 11 innings of work and had an 0–2 record to show for it. He pitched parts of four more years with Brooklyn and won 26 games in that span before being shipped off to the Phillies, where he spent most of the rest of his career. Ellenberg never made it to the major leagues.

Vance followed up on his 17-K outing with a shutout of the Giants 3–0 at Ebbets Field on July 26, striking out eight, and then beating the Cardinals 3–1 on Aug. 1, striking out eight again and raising his season record to 15–6. The press noted that in Dazzy's 17-strikeout game against St. Louis, Specs Toporcer was the only Redbird who didn't fan. In this, the next game in which the two faced each other, Toporcer was Vance's first strikeout victim.

On Aug. 5, an off day, the Robins announced that Uncle Robbie would return to the dugout to "relieve Zack Wheat of his temporary command" of the Brooklyn ball club. The decision was made in part because of pressure from National League club owners who believed Robinson was a drawing card and that his absence from the field was hurting attendance at the Robins' road games. Wheat was not happy with the demotion and said he might be traded to the Cubs where a managerial opportunity might be coming.[9]

The Pirates spoiled Robbie's return to the dugout by beating his troops 5–1 with Dazzy taking the loss, his second to the Pirates in the past 11 games. His record now was 15–7 but the team as a whole was 48–48, in fourth place, 10 games behind the Pirates and in a three-game losing streak When they lost three more to Pittsburgh, they just about buried their pennant hopes—13 games out with 55 to play. In the second game of the four game series with Pittsburgh, Burleigh Grimes, suffering through his worst season in years, let out his frustration in a way that nearly started a riot. In the seventh inning, with the Robins winning 5–4, the Pirates staged a rally. At one point, speedster Max Carey found himself in a rundown between second and third. Grimes, who had been knocked down by a line drive that started the play, had by now righted himself and was in the baseline between second and third. Carey ran into him going toward third. As he headed back toward second in the rundown, he shoved Grimes to try to get him out of the baseline. When Grimes shoved him back, Burleigh landed a right hook to Max's jaw and he went down in a heap. That brought players from both benches and bullpens scurrying onto the field and they were joined by batboys and at least one spectator. The press covering the game said the only uniformed person not on the field was Uncle Robbie, who sat quietly in the dugout as the umpires tried to restore order. Grimes and Carey were ejected and the Pirates went on to win the game 10–9.[10]

Brooklyn got back on the winning track the way most teams did in the National League in 1925 — by playing the Cincinnati Reds. The Robins took a double header from Cincy on Aug. 10 with Tiny Osborne and Dazzy picking up the victories. For Vance, it was his 16th win of the year — and another 20-win season was clearly in sight. While he was having another great year, hitters throughout both leagues were putting up big numbers, as they had in the past few years. When Dazzy was asked why this was happening, he said, "The constant substitution of new balls for ones slightly used and the rules that forbid a pitcher to tamper with the ball in any way are the real reasons for the revolution of the game in the past few years." In fact, said Vance, "it is impossible for the pitcher to do more than just throw the ball."[11]

Dazzy won three more games in August to up his record to 19–7. On Aug. 23, he set down the Cubs 6–0 in the first game of a double header at Ebbets Field. He was so masterful that many fans left the ballpark thinking they had witnessed a no-hitter. But the official scorer gave the Cubs two hits, one a ground ball from Pinky Pittinger that took a bad hop and which Jimmy Johnston couldn't handle, the other a pop fly off the bat of Mandy Brooks that Hod Ford got a glove on but couldn't grab. In his next outing, Dazzy lost a 3–2 decision to Cincinnati on Aug. 29.

His 20th victory came on Sept. 5, a 5–3 win over Boston in the first game of a double header at Braves Field. Vance gave up eight hits and struck out nine and kept both his catcher and the home plate umpire on their toes. *The New York Times* reported, "Vance's fast ball gave Hank DeBerry and umpire Sweeney, who was behind the bat in the first game, a lot of trouble. Both were nicked several times in vital spots."

By now, the pennant races had been pretty well decided and for the first time in a long time did not involve any New York teams. The Giants, winners of four straight pennants, were mired in second place, 7½ games behind the Pirates. The Robins were fourth, 18 back of the pack. In the American League, the Yankees were in the process of chasing the Washington Senators. For all three teams, September would be a month of evaluating talent for future trades and bringing up youngsters from the minor leagues to take a look at them with an eye toward next year. The Robins brought up their top prospect, Charlie Corgan from Wichita of the Western League. Although no such honors were given in those days, Corgan was thought by many to be the most valuable player in the minor leagues. He was a switch hitter who batted .308 and hit 18 home runs. He was also fast on the base paths, filling a big weakness on the Robins' roster, and was a good fielding shortstop. He came up to the Robins on Sept. 1, got into 14 games and hit .170.[12]

Uncle Robbie, the old catcher, always believed the key to a good ball club was solid pitching and he thought the nucleus was still there with Vance, Grimes, Tiny Osborne, Rube Ehrhardt and Jesse Petty. No telling what would have happened if Grimes had had his typical year, if Doak hadn't retired and if the Robins had held on to Ruether, who was becoming a bona fide star in the American League.

So, it was with an atmosphere of "wait till next year" that the Robins entertained the lowly Philadelphia Phillies in a double header on Sept. 8. Because of tight scheduling, Vance pitched the first game on two days' rest, instead of his usual four, and Grimes was on the mound for game two. As it turned out, Burleigh won a 10-inning thriller 4–3 in which he survived to get the win though he struck out two and walked eight — but hardly anyone in the crowd remembered that game. Because in the opener, Dazzy Vance missed perfection by inches and had one of the best pitching performances in baseball history.

He shut out the Phillies 1–0 on a one-hitter. The one hit was a bloop by Nelson "Chicken" Hawks that just got by the outstretched glove of second baseman Milt Stock and dropped into short right field. One batter later, Hawks was gunned down trying to steal. No one else reached base as Dazzy faced the minimum 27 batters.

Vidmer in the *New York Times* reached journalistic euphoria in describing Vance's mastery of the Phillies:

"With blinding speed, deceptive curves and a baffling change of pace, Vance majestically swept the Phillies aside three at a time," he wrote. "His great right arm moved backward and forward with rhythmic motion ... his right wrist snapped ... his tattered sleeve flapped in derision and batters were mowed down as ripe wheat falls before the sweep of a scythe."

On a metaphoric journey, Vidmer unabashedly compared the effectiveness of Vance's right arm to weapons throughout world history—the "slingshots of the Phoenicians, the Grecian javelin, the crossbows of the Romans, the flintlocks of the Colonials and the Big Berthas of the Germans."[13]

September 8, 1925

BROOKLYN	AB	R	H		PHILADELPHIA	AB	R	H
Mitchell, ss	4	0	1		Sand, ss	3	0	0
Stock, 2b	4	1	2		Leach, cf	3	0	0
Wheat, lf	1	0	0		Williams, rf	3	0	0
Fournier, 1b	3	0	1		Harper, lf	3	0	0
Cox, rf	3	0	0		Hawks, 1b	3	0	1
Brown, cf	3	0	1		Wrightstone, 3b	3	0	0
Tierney, 3b	3	0	0		Fonseca, 2b	3	0	0
Taylor, c	3	0	1		Wendell, c	3	0	0
Vance, p	3	0	0		Pierce, p	2	0	0
Totals	27	1	6		Wilson (a)	1	0	0
					Totals	27	0	1

(a) batted for Pierce in 9th

Philadelphia 0 0 0 0 0 0 0 0 0 — 0
Brooklyn   0 0 0 1 0 0 0 0 0 — 1

Doubles: Brown, Taylor. Stolen base: Stock. Sacrifice hit: Wheat. Double plays: Harper and Hawks; Pierce, Sand and Hawks. Left on base: Brooklyn 4

	IP	H	R	BB	SO
Vance	9	1	0	0	6
Pierce	9	6	1	1	0

Umpires: McCormick and Klem. Time: 1:20

Had writer Vidmer known what was to happen next, he might have held back on some of the flowery rhetoric—for the best was yet to come. On Sept. 13, Dazzy once again took the mound for the Robins, once again against the Phillies, once again in the first game of a double header with Grimes pitching the nightcap, and once again pitching a master-piece.

Only this time, he did himself one better — he threw a no-hitter in a game the Robins won 10–1. Dazzy walked Heinie Sand, the first bat-ter he faced, and allowed only one other base runner. Again, it was Chicken Hawks who lofted a fly ball to left field. Jimmy Johnston, play-ing in place of Wheat, got a bad angle on it under a scorching sun and then allowed the ball to drop out of his glove as he attempted to catch it. It was rightfully ruled an error on Johnston. He immediately com-pounded his problems by throwing wildly back into the infield. Hawks wound up on third and scored on a sacrifice fly. The Robins had scored four in the first, added four in the fourth and single runs in the sixth and seventh to ease the way for Dazzy.

The crowd was noisy and expectant as the Phillies took their turn in the ninth inning. Lew Fonseca led off, batting for Huck Betts, the Philadelphia pitcher. Fonseca took two called strikes and then hit a pop foul along the first base line. Charlie Hargreaves, filling in at first base for Fournier, dropped the ball for an error. More important, it gave the dangerous Fonseca another chance at the plate with the no-hitter at stake. Dazzy threw him a knee-buckling curve that Fonseca watched for strike three. Then Wally Kimmick came up to pinch-hit for shortstop Lenny Metz. He went down on three straight strikes. The next batter, Freddy Leach, didn't waste any time or pitches. He lined Dazzy's first pitch into left field. Johnston, who had blown the play in the second inning, got a good jump on this one and hauled it in to secure the no-hitter. As the crowd roared and players stampeded toward Vance, he walked off the mound toward the dugout, his uniform dripping with sweat and his face bearing the countenance, not of a hero or someone who had just climbed the highest mountain, but of someone who had completed his work for the day. "His face was calm but in his heart, there must have been a great glow of happiness," wrote Vidmer.

Coupled with his one-hitter against the Phillies in his previous start, Dazzy had tossed 16 consecutive innings of no-hit baseball. The no-hitter and one-hitter in consecutive starts equaled a record set by Sam Jones, pitching for the Boston Red Sox, in 1923. The 16 consecutive hit-less innings against one team was a new major league record.[14]

Later, in recounting the one-hitter, Dazzy said he ran into Phillies coach Art Fletcher as he was leaving the field. "You lucky stiff," said Fletcher. Dazzy said he replied, "I'll do better against you the next time."

To which Fletcher responded, "If you do, I'll kiss your foot in Macy's window." That night, according to Dazzy, he saw Fletcher's wife in Penn Station. "I said to her, 'You tell your husband the old Dazzler got tired today but the next time I pitch against him, I'll do better.'"

The "next time" turned out to be four days later. Dazzy said it was about the eighth inning when he realized he had a no-hitter going. He said he hollered at Fletcher, "Hey, Fletch, what time will I meet you at Macy's." He then mowed down the rest of the Phillies to complete the no-hitter. Fletcher didn't follow through with the Macy's offer, but the two men chuckled about it for years.[15]

The Washington Post put it all in perspective when it surmised that baseball is the most "statisticalized" of all the sports. Therefore, it was easy to point out that Vance's no-hitter was the first of the season in the major leagues, the first for a Brooklyn pitcher since Nap Rucker turned the trick against the Braves on Sept. 5, 1908, and that it was Vance's 22nd victory of the year and that in striking out nine, he brought his season strikeout total to 213.

These kinds of statistics, said the *Post*, are "a living, breathing part of a great national game." It concluded, "More people in the United States knew yesterday, without the papers telling them, that this was the first no-hit game of the season than know who is the Secretary of the Interior."[16]

September 13, 1925

BROOKLYN	AB	R	H		PHILADELPHIA	AB	R	H
J. Mitchell, ss	5	2	3		Sand, ss	1	0	0
Stock, 2b	4	3	2		Metz, ss	0	0	0
Johnston, lf	4	2	3		Leach, cf	4	0	0
Cox, rf	5	1	4		Williams, rf	3	0	0
Brown, cf	4	0	0		Harper lf	3	0	0
Hargreave 1b	4	1	1		Hawks, 1b	3	1	0
Tierney 3b	3	0	1		Huber, 3b	3	0	0
DeBerry, c	3	1	1		Friberg, 2b	2	0	0
Vance, p	4	0	0		Wilson, c	2	0	0
Totals	36	10	15		Wandell, c	1	0	0
					C. Mitchell, p	1	0	0
					Decatur, p	1	0	0
					Betts, p	1	0	0
					Totals	27	1	0

PHILADELPHIA   0 1 0 0 0 0 0 0 0 — 1
BROOKLYN   4 0 0 4 0 1 1 0 X — 10

Doubles: J. Mitchell, Cox. Triples: Johnston. Stolen bases: J. Mitchell, Stock, Cox, Johnston, Hargreaves.

	IP	H	R	BB	SO
Vance	9	0	0	1	9
Mitchell	0	4	4	0	0
Decatur	4	7	4	2	0
Betts	5	5	2	1	4

Umpires: Pfirman, Wilson and O'Day. Time: 1:45

On the same day as Vance's no-hitter, major league baseball released its latest statistics for the season. Dazzy's 22 wins led all of baseball. Eddie Rommel of the Philadelphia A's led the American League with 20 wins while Walter Johnson of the Senators had 19. Lee Meadows of the Pirates was closest to Vance in the National League with 18 victories. Leading hitters were Rogers Hornsby of the Cardinals in the National League with a .390 mark. Tris Speaker of Cleveland led American League hitters with a .377 average. Hornsby led the National League in home runs with 36. Fournier, the Robins' top slugger, was a distant second with 21. Cy Williams of the St. Louis Browns topped American League home run hitters with 25. Babe Ruth, plagued by problems with management on and off the field, had 18.

On Sept. 18, Dazzy took the mound against the Cardinals at Sportsman's Park. If he wasn't thinking about it, he was probably the only one in the ballpark who wasn't wondering how long his hitless inning streak would continue. As it turned out, the suspense ended quickly when Hornsby, the third batter he faced, doubled in the first inning. The Robins took a 4–2 lead into the eighth inning when the roof caved in on Vance. St. Louis scored seven runs and by the time Robbie came to get him with two out in the eighth, he had surrendered 12 hits for the game and all of the Cardinals' nine runs in a 9–5 loss. It was his last outing of the year.

They were not through playing in unusual games, however. On Sept. 22, Burleigh Grimes lost a 3–2 heartbreaker to the Cubs in 12 innings. He had a good day on the mound but a horrible one at the plate. He hit into two double plays and a triple play. No one had ever done that before — and no one has done it since.[17]

On Sept. 25, in a game against the Reds, Cincinnati's Curt Walker and Rube Bressler each hit bases-loaded triples in the same game — the first time that had occurred in baseball history. The Reds beat the Robins 18–7 before a "crowd" of 534 fans in Cincinnati.

Vance's string of 16 hitless innings was one of the big highlights of the year for National League pitchers. He was the only one in the league to pitch a no-hitter, one of three to pitch a one-hitter and the only man to throw a two-hitter (the game against the Cubs on Aug. 23 in which Chicago got two scratch hits). Dazzy had three four-hitters. He led the league in wins for the second straight year with 22 and in strikeouts for the third straight year with 221. The problem for the Robins was that Dazzy's 22 wins represented just about one-third of the club's 68 victories. Dazzy was 22–9. The rest of the staff was 46–76. It had been a year of front office shuffling, confusion over leadership in the dugout, personnel changes through retirements and ill-advised transactions and some key players having some off years.

The result was all too familiar. The Robins finished sixth in the National League.

VII

"Three Men on Base.
Which Base?"

In Dazzy Vance's first four years with the Robins, he was 18–12, 18–15, 28–6 and 22–9 for teams that finished sixth, tied for sixth, second and sixth. He led the league in strikeouts all four years, and in wins and shutouts two of those years. He was not only the ace of the staff; he was the ace of the league. But his supporting cast, except for the 1924 season, was not good enough to keep the Robins in the pennant race for much more than the first month or so of the season. But the Robins were a loose, entertaining bunch and their woes in the standings didn't stop the faithful fans from coming to Ebbets Field to see what antics the boys would pull from one day to the next.

Otto Miller, the old Robins catcher who went off to manage the Atlanta Crackers, was back in the Brooklyn spring training camp as a coach in 1926. As he was strolling on the field one day, he saw a young player he recognized — Floyd Caves Herman, whom everyone called "Babe." Herman was a first baseman when Miller had him in Atlanta in 1923 and had a well-earned reputation for being a great hitter but a lousy fielder.

"If I put him in the line up every day, he can hit .400 if he puts his mind to it. But he'll lose the club 2–3 games a week with his glove," said Miller.

The Robins already had a first baseman in their slugger Jack Fournier so it was decided to put young Herman in the outfield where he wouldn't be involved in bang-bang plays and could be taught the fundamentals of catching fly balls, fielding ground balls, hitting the cut-off man and throwing to the right base.

The problem was that Babe Herman wasn't terribly teachable. In Atlanta, he had a tendency of allowing throws to come to him at first base instead of stretching for them or extending his arm and leg in the direction of the throw. Miller told him to reach out more, to help the infielders get those outs. Instead of taking the advice to heart, Herman scoffed at his manager and told him if he didn't like the way he played first base, he knew what he could do. "Go to hell is the way I interpreted it," said Miller. In most cases, an attitude like that was a sure ticket back to the minor leagues. But as one of the Robins' scouts concluded, "He's kind of funny in the field, but when I see a guy go 6-for-6, I've got to go for him."[1]

The Robins were confident that Burleigh Grimes would snap back to form after his 12–19 year in 1925. In addition, lefthander Jesse Petty was 9–9 for a team that finished 17 games below .500 and youngsters Doug McWeeny and Bob McGraw looked like they were ready to compete for spots in the starting rotation. Fournier still supplied most of the power on the club, coming off a season in which he hit 22 home runs and drove in 130 runs with a .350 batting average. Wheat was returning with another great year behind him — .359 average, 14 home runs, 103 runs batted in.

Uncle Robbie, never a big fan of young, untested pitchers, raved about McWeeny in spring training. "He's the best looking young pitcher I have ever seen in training camp," said Robinson. "When he was with the White Sox [organization], he had everything but control and good judgment. Now he has plenty of both."[2]

Westbrook Pegler, the veteran writer with the caustic pen, looked over the Robins in spring training and was not impressed. They were more than old, said Pegler. They were "elderly." And they were just as offbeat in their antics and habits off the field as they were between the white lines. Pegler said "it is probably true that they eat off the kitchen table, don't use napkins and sleep in their underwear." Pegler said when he last covered the Robins in spring training two years earlier, he came to their hotel and asked for a room with a bath. When he returned to the same hotel this year, he said, the room clerk said, "Har, har, har — here comes the guy who wanted a room with a bath."[3]

As spring training moved along, Robbie got more and more excited about his ball club, especially his pitching staff. He predicted Vance would win between 20 and 30 games, Grimes would return to his old form and win more than 20, Jess Barnes would be one of the toughest pitchers in the league, that McWeeny (nicknamed "Buzz" because he was "busy as a bee" on the mound) was the "find" of spring and that

Petty would have a great year. "We don't admit that any staff in the major leagues is our superior," said Uncle Robbie.[4]

Spring training is the Christmas Eve of baseball where all teams have high hopes for tomorrow. Robinson could not have anticipated that Petty, the lefthander who was 9–9 the year before, would win his first five starts of 1926 on his way to a 17-win season or that young McGraw would win four in the first month and that by mid–May the rest of the league would be chasing the Robins. But seasons are long and full of surprises, so no one would have anticipated in April that by October Petty's 17 wins would lead the club and that at 17–17 he would be the only starting pitcher to be at the .500 level. Needless to say, in April, no one would have believed that Dazzy Vance, averaging 22 wins a season for the past four years, would not get his first victory until June and would have the worst year of his major league career.

The Robins opened the season against the Giants at the Polo Grounds on April 13. The night before, New York was buzzing with reports that Vance was suffering from boils and might not be the opening day pitcher. *The New York Times* told its readers not to be too concerned. "These night-before-the-game rumors, however, may be taken with a grain of salt, and unless the Vance boil is one of enormous proportions, the chances are that Dazzy will be in there burning them over so fast that the Giants will be blinking."

But the next day, Dazzy couldn't answer the call. Petty pitched instead and nearly created some baseball history. The Robins beat the Giants 3–0 and Petty gave up just one hit, a sixth-inning double by Frankie Frisch that was a pop fly that dropped just out of reach of Fournier, Cox and Stock, all of whom were chasing it down. There had never been an opening day no-hitter.[5]

Dazzy didn't start until April 22, the home opener for the Robins, but he didn't last long. He departed in the fifth inning after giving up six runs on nine hits. While Vance was struggling, most of the rest of the Robins were off to a good start. Between April 25 and April 30, they put together a six-game winning streak with the victories going to Hugh McQuillan, McGraw, McWeeny, Petty and Grimes. On May 1, Brooklyn, with a record of 9–5, found itself in sole possession of first place for the first time since September of 1924.

But Vance continued to struggle. The winning streak was snapped when Dazzy and the Robins lost to the Phillies 4–2 on May 1, then Brooklyn won three in a row — increasing their hot streak to 9 out of 10 —

before Vance lost again, a 3–1 decision to the Cardinals on May 6. He had gotten rocked in his first start but had given up a total of seven runs in his next two while his teammates came up with only three runs in his support. Whatever the reasons, Vance was 0–3 for the first time in his career — and it would get worse. In the 3–1 loss to the Cardinals, Dazzy gave up all the runs in the first inning and suffered the indignity of being lifted for a pinch hitter in the second inning, creating his earliest exit while in a Robins uniform. While he was struggling on the field, he had matters to contend with off the field as well. The *Chicago Tribune* reported on May 12 that Dazzy had left the team to go home to Hastings, Nebraska, because of illness in the family. He would miss his next start.

The Robins continued to roll. Fournier was spiked in a game against Boston and had to be sidelined. Herman replaced him at first base and rapped out three hits in the last two games of a series with the Cubs at Wrigley Field. Brooklyn won both of them, the latter being a complete game shutout for McWeeny, the rookie so highly touted by Robbie before the season started. He was now 3–0 and had a string of 19 scoreless innings.

Vance rejoined the team but was clobbered in his next start. In addition, he was in Uncle Robbie's doghouse for the first time in his career. The Reds pasted him for 11 runs on 13 hits, leading Richard Vidmer in the *New York Times* to surmise, "It looks as if Dazzy Vance will never be able to win again." He pointed out that Dazzy was 0–4 and had been knocked out of two games "and it would have been three times if Uncle Robbie hadn't been disgusted this afternoon."[6]

The old Dazzler, in the second year of his $47,500 three-year contract, had not won a game since his no-hitter against the Phillies in September of 1925, was battling nuisance injuries such as boils for the first time in his career, had distractions off the field such as family illnesses, and was, at least for the time being, not the shining light on the pitching staff in the eyes of his manager. And the Robins desperately needed him to get on track. On May 15, Johnny Morrison of the Pirates outpitched McGraw in a 2–0 thriller in which the Robins dropped out of first place for the first time since April 30. It was the start of a six-game losing streak that concluded with Vance's ugly performance against the Reds. They didn't know it at the time, but when they dropped one game out of first on May 15, that was the closest they would be to the top for the rest of the season.

Dazzy didn't pick up his first win until June 4 when the Robins gave him some run support, too, in a 10–1 victory over the Giants. He struck out 10, walked only one and showed signs of returning to the form that earned him the big bucks and the big reputation. The most unusual aspect of the game was not Vance's pitching but the fellow behind the plate receiving the pitches. Charlie Hargreaves did the catching, the first time in Vance's career that Hank DeBerry, who came to the majors in 1922 with Vance as a tag-along, wasn't behind the plate when Dazzy was on the mound.

Five days later, Vance pitched the first nine innings but did not get the decision when the Robins beat the Reds 4–3 in a 10-inning thriller. The score was tied 1–1 after eight innings. Cincinnati touched Dazzy for two runs in the ninth but Brooklyn rallied to tie the score with two of their own in the bottom of the ninth. When the Robins pushed the winning run over in the 10th, Vance had given way to McGraw, who got the win in relief. Dazzy didn't pitch badly in his next outing, against the Cardinals; he just didn't pitch well enough to win as St. Louis got him for a run in the first and two in the sixth. He was in the showers when the Cardinals scored their final run in a 4–0 victory.

Vance's record fell to 1–5. For the first time in his career, he was not among the league leaders when the two major leagues released statistics covering about the first third of the season. Flint Rhem, the hard drinking, hard throwing pitcher for the St. Louis Cardinals, led all National League pitchers with a 10–1 record and the Redbirds' Vic Keen was 8–2. The hottest hurler in the league was the well-traveled Lee Meadows, who had won his first seven starts with the Pittsburgh Pirates. In the American League, the New York Yankees had a one-two-three punch on their pitching staff that was literally hard to beat. Both Herb Pennock and Waite Hoyt were 10–3 and Urban Shocker was 9–3. The Yankees, of course, had a formidable lineup of hitters and Babe Ruth was leading the pack with a .380 batting average and 22 home runs. KiKi Cuyler led National League hitters with a .379 mark while Hack Wilson was the top home run hitter with nine.

Hardly noticed in the sea of statistics and the list of big-name ballplayers was the year that Floyd Caves "Babe" Herman was having for the Robins. The rookie was getting playing time in both the outfield and at first base, where Fournier had been hampered with injuries. Herman had about 80 fewer at-bats than Cuyler, who played every day, but was second in the league in hitting with a .370 average. As his playing time increased, his batting average dropped and he wound up hitting .319 in 137 games.

His hitting made up for some of his baserunning miscues and his adventures chasing fly balls became part of the legend of the Robins. Babe Herman, more than any one player, symbolized this group of Brooklyn athletes that would come to be known in baseball lore as the Daffiness Boys.

Fournier was an important part of the group because he was the team bookie. He figured why should guys have to go to all the trouble of going to the track when they could just place their bets through him. Vance was the head of the 4-for-0 Club, the name being simply a backward way of saying "0-for-4" and was in keeping with the club's purpose of recognizing backward antics on the field.

Vance said the club had one rule: "Raise all the hell you want, but don't get caught." One night Jess Petty got caught coming in after curfew to the hotel where the club was staying. Robbie caught him and fined him. But worse, from Petty's standpoint, Vance kicked him out of the 4-for-0 Club. After all, he had broken the only rule.

The only way he could get back in to the club was to write a letter of apology. With the help of a New York sportswriter, Petty got the letter written. He was summoned to Vance's hotel room the next night for a hearing. When he arrived, he was greeted by Vance, Fournier, Rube Ehrhardt and Rabbit Maranville (who had joined the team earlier in the year), all draped in sheets with bath towels around their heads. They chided Petty for using words in his letter that were way beyond his level of comprehension or spelling ability. Everyone except Petty had a good laugh out of it.

Sportswriter Murray Robinson said he once wrote about the antics of the "0-for-4" bunch, saying they were "more ale than hearty." Vance read the article and invited Robinson to his hotel room. One of the walls looked like a speakeasy, said the writer. "Why do you write stuff like that?" asked Dazzy. "It ain't right to show up us athletic heroes like that." The room erupted in laughter and Dazzy offered Robinson a drink.

But nobody could top Herman for zaniness. He once did an interview with newspaperman Joe Gordon of the *New York Journal American* where he pleaded with Gordon to quit making fun of him in print. He said he could take a joke, just like the next guy, but people were starting not to take him seriously as a ballplayer. Gordon agreed to try to take it easy on him. When the interview was over, Babe pulled a cigar out of his shirt pocket. Gordon started to offer him a match to light it but watched in amazement as Herman put the cigar in his mouth, puffed on it a couple of times, and went on his way. Only Babe Herman, the man who wanted the press to lighten up on him, would think nothing of putting a lit cigar in his pocket.

Babe chafed when people kidded him about his fielding and especially when writers said they were worried he would one day get beaned by a fly ball hit to him. Herman told Tom Meany of the *New York World Telegram* that if that ever happened, he would quit baseball. "How about if you get hit on the shoulder?" asked Meany. "Oh, no, the shoulder don't count," said Herman.

The daffiness was not confined to just the players. Uncle Robbie, trying to put some semblance of order and discipline to this dysfunctional family of ballplayers, instituted a system where a player would be fined anytime Robbie thought he made a bonehead play on the field. That afternoon, before a game with the Pirates, Robinson made a mistake in the batting order he submitted to the umpires. After the game, as his first official act as head of the Bonehead Club, he fined himself.[7]

The shenanigans off the field were a diversion from the tension that was mounting on the field as the Robins continued to disappoint. Vance was having his worst year in the majors and Robbie asked him to go to the bullpen and be ready to come in for short stints if needed. Dazzy, the highest paid pitcher in baseball, refused. He told his manager flatly that he was a starting pitcher.

Joe Vila, sports editor of the *New York Sun*, learned about Vance's attitude and wrote a column criticizing Dazzy. Feg Murray, the newspaper's artist, drew a cartoon to accompany the column. Robinson saw it and blew up the next afternoon when he saw Eddie Murphy, the writer who covered the Robins for the *Sun*. He thought the column was an indirect slam at him. The next day, he called Keats Speed, the paper's managing editor, to complain. Speed told Robinson he agreed with his writer's opinion. Robinson blew up again, telling him his opinion didn't mean anything because he didn't know anything about baseball. Speed hung up from Uncle Robbie and immediately called Vila, his sports editor. He was to return all passes issued to the newspaper by the ball club; Murphy was to make his own travel arrangements to cover the games but was prohibited from taking the same train or stay in the same hotel as the ball club and, from now on, Wilbert Robinson's name would not grace the pages of the newspaper and the team was no longer to be referred to as the Robins.

Steve McKeever, now principal owner of the club, learned of the situation and called Robbie on the carpet. The two men exchanged heated words and Robbie left McKeever's office with the owner shaking his cane at him. The two hardly spoke to each other after that.

The Robins weren't the only team having problems with a star pitcher or a dual manager situation in 1926. In Chicago, Joe McCarthy, a rookie manager got tired of 300-game winner Grover Cleveland Alexander breaking training rules and suspended him. Within days he was a member of the St. Louis Cardinals. In Pittsburgh, Bill McKechnie was manager of the Pirates but was often joined in the dugout by former manager Fred Clarke, now a vice president of the club. When some of the players objected to Clarke's interference, owner Barney Dreyfuss responded by releasing two of the players, Babe Adams and Carson Bigbee, and asking for waivers on his team captain, Max Carey. When the dust settled, Uncle Robbie plucked Carey from the waiver list and put him in the Robins outfield.

Dazzy lost to the Giants 5–2 on July 3, bringing his won-loss record for the year to 1–6. His record wasn't the only thing that was hurting. For the first time in 10 years, Vance had arm problems. He attributed his sore arm to neuritis and didn't want to pitch against the Giants. Robbie told him he had to and would be fined or suspended if he didn't. Further, Robinson told the press Vance was 20 pounds overweight and that he had not seriously tried to get into shape. Dazzy said none of that was true and that his ailments, more than anything else, accounted for his poor showing on the mound this year.[8]

Vance won his next two starts: on July 7, a 5–1 decision over the Boston Braves, and on July 12, a 4–0 win over the Cubs. In the Cubs game, Dazzy's string of misfortune continued when he was struck on the arm by a line drive in the fifth inning and was unable to continue. As for his two straight wins, Vidmer in the *New York Times* said, "Evidently Uncle Robbie's threat of an operation which would cause the amputation of several hundred dollars from Dazzy's salary had the desired effect."[9]

Vance missed one start because of a bruised elbow but came back strong to beat the Pirates 6–2 at Forbes Field with both Pittsburgh runs scoring with two out in the ninth inning. He was now 4–6 with a three-game winning streak. The Robins were 47–43, in fourth place, five games behind Cincinnati. At the start of August, Dazzy missed yet another start after coming to the ballpark with a fever. On Aug. 7, he was the losing pitcher in an ugly game with St. Louis in which Dazzy walked six batters and was victimized by two infield throwing errors and fielding so inept in left field by Babe Herman that Robbie lifted him in the second inning before he got killed by a batted ball that he clearly couldn't catch. He circled under one fly ball and it dropped behind him for a double. The next batter hit a fly ball in his direction that he misjudged badly and it fell in front of him for a single. Final score: St. Louis 6, Brooklyn 3. That was the first game of a double header. In the nightcap, Grover Cleveland Alexander, newly acquired from the Cubs, tossed a four-hit shutout, beating the Robins 3–0. On Aug. 11, Dazzy pitched well enough to win, but almost didn't. The Robins scored four in the eighth to beat Pittsburgh 4–2 and snap a nine-game Robins losing streak. He was 5–7, trying to salvage what was left of a bad season both for him and his team.

On Aug. 15, Brooklyn beat the Boston Braves in a double header at Ebbets Field that is long remembered for a classic baserunning gaffe. Naturally, Herman was a key player in it. Vance was locked in a pitching duel with Johnny Wertz. As the Robins came to bat in the bottom of the seventh, Boston led 1–0. Johnny Butler singled and scored on a double by DeBerry. When Vance followed with a single, DeBerry held up at third. Then Fewster was hit with a pitched ball to load the bases. Merwin Jacobson popped out for the first out of the inning. Up to the plate stepped Herman. Babe hit a rocket that bounded off the right field wall, scoring DeBerry easily. Vance hesitated at first, thinking Braves right fielder Jimmy Welsh might catch the ball. Dazzy then took off, rounded third with the thought of scoring but then suddenly thought better of it and ran back to third. Meanwhile, Fewster chugged around second and made it to third just about the time Vance was retreating back to third. Herman put his head down and started running hard as soon as he hit the ball. He didn't look up until he too wound up on third base. When Herman discovered he had way too much company on third base, he turned and started to head back to second. Boston third baseman Eddie Taylor, who had taken the relay throw, tagged Vance and Fewster and then threw to Doc Gautreau, the Boston second baseman, who tagged Herman. It was left up to umpire Beans Reardon to sort it all out.

Reardon ruled the base belonged to Vance — though it was his hesitation that started all the confusion. Fewster was out for, in effect, passing the base runner. The tagging of Herman was just a bonus because

Floyd Caves "Babe" Herman was a great hitter but had his problems defensively and on the bases. He once was part of a trio of Brooklyn base runners who all were on third base at the same time. (Courtesy Baseball Hall of Fame.)

only two outs were needed to end the inning. Vidmer in the *New York Times* said, "Herman was tagged out but tagging was too good for him." There was enough blame to go around — Vance couldn't score from second on what could have been a triple; Fewster and Herman were inattentive and inept in their base running. Uncle Robbie shook his head and said it was the first time all year his team had been together on anything.

The base-running blunder led to a joke that haunted Brooklyn for years:

"Did you hear the Dodgers have three men on base?

"Oh yeah? Which base?

Vidmer told his readers the base-running blunders brought back memories of other baseball farces, such as the time when John Anderson "stole third" — except the bases were already loaded; or when the Giants' Fred Merkle, who was a runner on first, left the field without touching second when a teammate singled home the winning run, thereby being a force-out victim when the Cubs' Johnny Evers retrieved the ball and touched second; or when Heinie Zimmerman chased Eddie Collins across the plate for the winning run in a 1910 World Series game.

The two-run seventh inning gave the Robins a 2–1 lead and they scored two more in the eighth to put the game away, a 4–1 victory. Vance improved his record to 6–7 but the statistic Herman wanted everyone to remember is that he drove in what turned out to be the winning run — when he doubled into a double play.

The Robins meandered their way through the rest of the season and finished in their customary position — sixth place — where they had landed three out of the last four years, this time with a 71–82 record. In his last start, he struck out 15 Chicago Cubs in a 3–1 Brooklyn victory in which, according to Irving Vaughan in the *Chicago Tribune*, both teams were just going through the paces without much effort from either club. He wrote, "With the horseplay usually reserved for such occasions, the Cubs and Robins interred their share of the National League corpse today."

Vance, who had boils at the start of the season, neuritis in mid-season, was hit by a line drive on his pitching arm forcing him to miss a start, and was out two other times because of illness in the family and his own illness, could muster only a 9–10 record for the year, by far his worst showing in the National League. Still, his winning percentage was better than his team's and only Jess Petty among the starters could come up with a .500 record at 17–17. Remarkably, with all the problems he had, Dazzy still managed to lead the National League in strikeouts for the fifth straight year, finishing with 140. Charlie Root of the Cubs was second with 116.

The Robins were in shambles. They were entertaining enough to have a lively, loyal fan base, but a golden rule that applies to all of sports was closing in on them: Sooner or later, you have to win to keep the customers coming through the turnstiles— and the Robins had pretty well established themselves as a sixth place ball club.

A shakeup was brewing, and rumors were that it might start at the top.

VIII

"Ain't it awful?"

As the Robins prepared for the 1927 season, the natives were restless both on and off the field. In the front office, principal owner Steve McKeever and president-manager Wilbert Robinson were not on speaking terms, a situation made all the more difficult by the fact that Uncle Robbie had to go by McKeever's office to get to his own. One thing both of them agreed on: The Robins needed to make some big changes on the field if they were to move up in the standings.

Within a month after the season ended, the Robins made it known that nobody's job was safe, including that of Dazzy Vance. The *Los Angeles Times* reported, "The big blow-off is due at the National League meeting in December, at which time Robbie may ask for bids on Vance, his star pitcher. Dazzy's tactics last season antagonized Robbie and he is ready to get rid of him if he can get a first-class pitcher in return."[1]

Vance had a couple of things in his favor, despite the difference he had with his manager. First, he had another year to go on his $47,500 three-year contract. Considering he was coming off his worst season in the big leagues, it would have been unlikely any other team would have wanted to assume the third year of that contract. Second, most observers expected him to bounce back to have another great year. He was still the strikeout king of the National League five years running and was still the best arm on the Brooklyn staff.

The rebuilding began on Nov. 5 when the Robins sold their slugging first baseman and resident bookie, Jack Fournier, to the Boston Braves. The fact that they settled for cash and got no players in return was a sure sign the Robins meant business about unloading and reloading. Fournier played four years for the Robins—and three of them were great. In 1923, he hit .351 with 22 home runs and 102 runs batted in. The next year, he batted .334 with 27 homers and 116 RBIs. In 1925, he was back up to .350 with 22 home runs and 130 runs batted in. But in an injury-riddled 1926 season, Fournier slumped to .284 with 11 homers in 48 RBIs, playing in just 86 games.

On Jan. 1, the Robins released Zack Wheat, the greatest player in franchise history. He had played 18 years with Brooklyn and had been a star on their 1916 and 1920 championship clubs. As a Robin, he had 2,804 hits and a lifetime batting average of .317. But age was catching up with him. His last home run with Brooklyn was a memorable one. He hit the ball out of the park and started to trot around the bases. As he rounded first base, he developed a charley horse, fell to the ground as he touched second base and could not get up. As he writhed in pain, Robbie huddled with the umpires. When his pain subsided, he was allowed to get up and limp the rest of the way to home plate. It took about five minutes. Wheat played sparingly for the Philadelphia A's in 1927 and then retired. He still holds Dodgers records for most games, 2,322; hits, 2,804; doubles, 476; and triples, 172.

The Brooklyn broom continued to clean house on Jan. 9, 1927, when the Robins traded Burleigh Grimes to the New York Giants as part of a three-way trade with the Philadelphia Phillies. The main player Brooklyn got in return was catcher Butch Henline. What they gave up was a veteran hurler who had played second-fiddle to Vance for five of his nine years with Brooklyn. He won 148 games for the Robins, an average of 16 a year and had been part of the 1920 championship team.

Some great stars of the past had left but Robbie felt confident that Max Carey, whom he had picked up in the Pittsburgh Pirates fray the year before, would do well in Wheat's stead, and the Robins had managed to coax Bill Doak out of retirement in Florida to return to the mound. Two youngsters coming up from the minor leagues, Jimmy Partridge from Nashville and Bobby Barrett from Memphis, would be given a shot at second and third base, respectively, replacing Chick Fewster and Bob Marriott. Jigger Statz would join Carey and Gus Felix in the outfield. Vance, Felix, shortstop Johnny Butler, Babe Herman and Hank DeBerry (Vance's catcher) were the only regulars to survive the great shuffle of the winter of 1926.

As spring training opened in Clearwater, John Drebinger of the *New York Times* noticed several differences in 1927 from previous preseasons. One was the absence of so many veterans and the presence of so many newcomers. There was also the advent of two-a-days, drills in both the morning and afternoon, something Robbie hadn't done in the past and an indication of his desire to whip this team into shape as quickly as possible. Drebinger also made mention of the presence of Dazzy Vance on opening day of spring training, beginning the third year of his three-year contract and coming off a bad year. Vance now owned property in Clearwater and spent the winter there. He was at the train station to greet his manager when Uncle Robbie arrived and displayed what Drebinger described as "an astonishingly reduced waist line."[2]

On March 11, the Robins played an exhibition game against the University of Florida that was also a celebration of their fifth anniversary of making their spring training home in Clearwater. The Scarlet Guard marching band performed in a parade in the morning, Mayor Hamden Baskin blew a whistle at noon signaling the end of the workday and the Chamber of Commerce encouraged everyone to come to the ballpark. About 1,000 people did. They saw the mayor throw out the first pitch and the Robins took over from there, putting on quite a show. Vance pitched two scoreless innings, Babe Herman hit for the cycle and Brooklyn put a 12–0 thumping on the collegians.

But two weeks later, the Robins were sputtering, Robbie was saying exhibition games didn't count and fans were wondering whether this would yet be another year when the Robins would put their usual stranglehold on sixth place in the National League standings. John Kieran, a *New York Times* columnist, said the Robins infield was a weakness because neither Partridge nor Barrett were world-beaters defensively at second and third and they were getting no help from Herman at first base. "Babe has been trying to catch baseballs with his elbows and ankles this sprightly spring, a method which has never been particularly successful in any league," wrote Kieran.[3]

Babe's base-running exploits were becoming legendary and the stories about them made their way throughout the league. Like Yogi Berra stories 50 years later, it was often difficult to separate fact from fiction because any of them could have been true and Herman denied most all of them. One of the best, although there is no documentation to back it up, has Babe batting with a runner on first. Herman hit a screaming line drive to right field. The runner on first broke for second and then, thinking the ball was caught, turned and headed back to first. Meanwhile, the Babe ran as fast as he could with his head down, certain that he had at least a double. The two runners passed each other, going in opposite directions, on the base path. Obviously, some things about the Robins did not change from one year to the next.[4]

The Robins opened the 1927 season on the road on April 12 and Jess

Petty, 17-game winner from the previous year, got them off to a good start as Brooklyn won 6–2. Little could the Robins have realized that the night of April 12 and morning of April 13 would be the only time all year they would occupy first place. The Braves took the next two games, beating Jess Barnes and Vance. The Robins then went to Philadelphia where they suffered back-to-back losses to the lowly Phillies. Bill Doak made his first start out of retirement in the Robins' home opener April 17, but they lost to the Braves again, this time by a score of 7–2. When McWeeny and Vance each came out on the short end in the next two games, the Robins had lost seven in a row, had a 1–7 record for the season and were already in seventh place, five games out of first place. Dazzy lost his third straight game on April 24 when the Phillies, aided by four Robins errors, won 5–1.

The season wasn't a month old yet and the Robins were in trouble. Everyone knew it. The fans knew it. The rest of the league knew it. Uncle Robbie knew it. "Sure I'd like to make some trades," he told the press. "But every time I think up a deal that might benefit the Robins, someone remembers I still have Dazzy Vance and Jess Petty. They're about all I've got now." Robbie said he was close to a trade for George Kelly of Cincinnati but the Reds wanted Vance or nothing — and they got the latter.[5]

On Sunday, May 1, Dazzy hooked up with Freddie Fitzsimmons of the Giants before a full house at Ebbets Field. The Giants got to Vance early but by the fifth inning Dazzy was in total control, though he was losing 3–2. In the bottom of the ninth, Herman led off with a base hit. Felix attempted to sacrifice but forced Herman at second. There was one out, but the Robins had a much better base runner on first. When Barrett singled to left, Felix scampered all the way to third, representing the tying run. Robbie sent Max Carey, the aging but cagey veteran, in to run for Barrett. Johnny Butler got his third hit of the game, a single to left, to tie the score and when the ball was juggled momentarily in left, Carey took off for third and made it safely in a cloud of dust. Butler took second as the Giants tried to nail Carey. McGraw then ordered DeBerry to be intentionally walked to load the bases and set up a possible double play.

Uncle Robbie had his old nemesis, McGraw, on the ropes and he decided to see if he could fluster any of the rest of the Giants. He called time, barked some instructions, and suddenly, Robins were running all over the field. Some ran down to the bullpen. Some went to the runners on base, as if delivering messages from the bench. One ran up to the batter's box to say something to Merwin Jacobson, who was sent up to pinch hit for Vance. As Dazzy went back to the dugout, Chick Fewster came out of the dugout to pinch run for DeBerry. It looked like chaos with players going every which way but it was all orchestrated by Wilbert Robinson.

When play resumed, Fitzsimmons fired the first pitch to Jacobson and it nearly went over the catcher's head. On the next pitch, Jacobson blooped a pop up to center that Ed Roush caught easily. Carey took everyone by surprise by tagging up and chugging home, narrowly beating the throw to the plate and scoring the winning run. Vance got the win, his first of the season. He struck out seven and retired the last 15 batters he faced after giving up three runs on five hits and walking five batters in the first four innings. In the last five innings, Vance was the Dazzler of old — invincible.

It was a classic Robins-Giants matchup and a thrilling victory for Uncle Robbie and his charges, but more important, it was Brooklyn's third straight win and two more would come before the streak was over. Then they lost two, including a 4–1 spanking to the Giants in which Burleigh Grimes was the winning pitcher. Vance's next start was May 7 and he picked up his second win, a 3–0 shutout against St. Louis.

Vance's first five starts were an indication of how tough it was going to be for both him and his teammates to win. Dazzy gave up 17 runs in the five games. The Robins scored nine runs in his behalf — and seven of those were in two games, the games he won by scores of 4–3 and 3–0. In his three losses, Brooklyn scored two runs. In the May 7 3–0 shutout of the Cardinals, Dazzy picked up the victory but the Robins managed only three hits. Uncle Robbie had been on the money earlier in the year when he talked of the difficulty in making a trade to get some hitting. The Robins could offer little in return for a good hitter because they didn't have much to offer beyond Vance, Petty and possibly Doak, and Robinson was not about to give up any of them.

So the Robins trudged on. They finally showed some life in their bats on May 12, pounding out 14 hits in beating the Reds 6–3. Vance picked up his third straight win. He got four hits and allowed four hits as the Robins won for the eighth time in their last 11 games. But their slow start kept them well behind most of the rest of the pack and they remained in seventh place, behind Pittsburgh and everyone else besides Cincinnati.

John Kieran told his readers in the *New York Times* that Robbie was feeling better, but it had nothing to do with hitting. "His infielders are beginning to stop a few ground balls," he wrote. In an interview with Kieran, Robbie recalled other years when times were bad. He said he remembered a game when Burleigh Grimes had been hit hard. He said he remembered thinking, "There they go knocking Burleigh off. Vance has a sore arm. Wheat's legs are gone. Fournier is laid up and Butler is sick. Don't know what to do about tomorrow. Guess we better not show up."[6]

Five days later, Vance won his fourth straight, a 2–1 decision over the Pirates in which Partridge homered and Dazzy drove in the deciding run with a sacrifice fly. The Robins continued their weak support of their ace pitcher by getting only three hits. But they were uncharacteristically awesome on May 22 when they pounded out 22 hits and beat the Phillies 20–4 with Dazzy winning again. Vance walked the first three Phillies batters in the game and gave up two runs in the first inning. But the Robins scored three in the bottom of the first, then four in the second on their way to the easy victory. Herman had five hits, Statz and Felix each had four and Partridge had three. Dazzy got his sixth straight win in his last start in May when the Robins beat the Giants in a double header with Petty winning the second game. Vance was now 6–3 for a team that was 16–22, in sixth place, eight games behind the Pirates. His winning streak ended on June 4 when Flint Rhem and the Cardinals beat the Robins 4–0 at Sportsman's Park, ending a Brooklyn five-game winning streak that had the Robins edging closer to .500.

In Vance's three losses, the Robins had scored a total of four runs, having been shut out once and gotten one run and three runs in the other defeats. He was carrying the team but the load continued to be heavy and, except for Herman, pretty much punchless. He was the only pitcher with a winning record and none of the batters were close to hitting .300. The Robins found themselves in familiar territory—sixth place.

Amid the struggles on the field, the daffiness continued. In one game, Fewster watched from the dugout, vigorously banging his bat on the top step to try to unnerve the opposing pitcher. Robbie motioned to him to stop. "You might wake up Jess," he said, pointing to Petty who was asleep in a corner of the dugout. In a game against Pittsburgh, a Pirates player hit a ball into the left field corner, just out of the view of Robinson in the Brooklyn dugout. Herman was sitting on the other side of the dugout, presumably with a clear view of the ball. "What happened?" shouted Robbie. "I don't know," said Herman. "I was reading the newspaper."

When the Robins were home, Herman often brought his son to the ballpark and Uncle Robbie took a liking to the boy. Sometimes, when players were practicing, the youngster would sit on the manager's lap in the dugout. One day, when Herman was in one of his rare batting slumps, his son bounded into the dugout looking for some attention from Robinson. When Robbie seemed to ignore the child, the boy was puzzled. "What's the matter, Uncle Robbie?" he asked. Robinson looked at the boy and said sternly, "Go ask your old man why he ain't hitting."[7]

Dazzy lost a tough one to the Cubs on June 8 when he gave up only five hits but two of them were home runs, by Earl Webb and Hack Wilson. The final score was 3–2. Three days later, the Robins hooked up in a wild one with the Pittsburgh Pirates at Forbes Field. Doak and Lee Meadows were the starting pitchers but both got clobbered. Brooklyn staked Doak to a 3–0 lead after their first at-bat but the Pirates' runs in the first second and third innings, added four in the fourth and another one in the fifth to take an 8–3 lead. The Robins chased Meadows with four in the sixth and when they added four more in the ninth, Brooklyn had an 11–8 lead. By this time, Jess Petty was pitching for the Robins. With one out, Petty gave up a walk, a double, to Pie Traynor, putting runners on second and third. Robbie, anxious to win — or not to blow — this comeback victory, went to the bullpen one more time — this time calling on the Ole Dazzler to put out the fire.

Drebinger, in the *New York Times*, described it this way: "Then came the most dramatic moment of the afternoon. Uncle Wilbert Robinson, in desperate straits to win this game at all costs, called on Dazzy Vance to save the day. In the end he did, but before he accomplished the feat, he had the crowd close to hysterics."[8]

Dazzy lost his next start but then beat Eppa Rixey and the Reds 2–1 on June 15 and won his last two starts in June, a 7–3 decision over the Phillies on June 21 and a 7–1 win over the Giants on June 26 to give him a 9–5 record for a team that was 31–34, in fifth place, 9½ games behind the Pirates. Only six games separated the first four teams in the National League — Pittsburgh, St. Louis, Chicago and New York, with even the fourth place Giants winning more than they were losing (32–30). The Robins, chiefly because of the pitching of Vance, were eight games ahead of the sixth place Boston Braves with Philadelphia and Cincinnati even further back.

Dazzy continued to be good copy for writers all over the country. Feg Murray with the Metropolitan Newspaper Service was a feature writer and cartoonist. He depicted the Dazzler in a drawing showing him about to go into his wind-up with a caption that read: "Here he is: Realtor, marksman, golfer, comedian. Dazzy Vance. Strike out king of the Dodgers. Will he ever again regain the form that made him the league's leading pitcher in 1924?" Murray then seemed to answer his own question in the text that accompanies the drawing. He pointed out the disappointment that hundreds of baseball fans had in 1924 when the Robins just missed going to the World Series because that series would have featured baseball's two best pitchers— Dazzy and Walter Johnson. Murray touched on how Vance had his worst year in 1926 but seemed to have bounced back.

"When you remember that he struck out 17 batters in a 10-inning game, seven in succession in another and allowed only one hit in two successive games in 1925, it seems that he is earning his salary in spite of one bad year. More power to you, Dazzy!"[9]

Meanwhile, in Georgia, baseball fans were marveling at the pitching prowess of young Frank Chilton, a 19-year-old who was playing with a factory team until he was signed by the Atlanta Crackers. Pat Monohan, a scout for the Boston Red Sox, described Chilton this way: "What's he got? Say, lemme tell you, that kid's got the works. He's got the curves, good ones, he's got speed like one of these new little racers, a smart change of pace. He's got a good knuckler. Say, the kid's a wonder and if you think he ain't, you're crazy." All of which prompted the *Atlanta Constitution* to the ultimate praise on him: "This youngster [is] the reincarnation of Dazzy Vance."[10]

The real Dazzy Vance lost to the Phillies 7–6 on July 1 when Philadelphia scored two runs in the bottom of the ninth to beat him. Six days later, he tamed the Giants 3–2, though his teammates could get only four hits. James Harrison, writing for the *New York Times*, could not hold back his disgust for how some of the Giants performed, including future Hall of Famer Bill Terry.

"The reluctance of Mr. Will Terry to soil his spotlessly white uniform by sliding into home plate probably cost the Giants a ball game," he wrote. Terry was on third base, representing the tying run in the bottom of the ninth inning when a fly ball to left field created a situation for a play at the plate. The throw came in on a high hop and catcher DeBerry had to reach for. Terry could have scored easily by sliding in as

DeBerry while DeBerry's glove was extended to catch the ball. But Terry came in standing up. "Memphis Bill remained very erect and came into the plate in stately fashion, with head held high," according to Harrison. "He was rudely startled and shocked when DeBerry pinned the ball on his shoulder for the last out of the ballgame."

The writer saved some of his venom for New York third baseman Andy Reese, who kicked a ball for an error in the third inning. Harrison pointed out that Reese had been a star drop kicker for Vanderbilt University and that he had not lost his old skill. His error would have been a field goal on any gridiron, he wrote.[11]

On July 12, the Robins' lack of hitting was too much for Dazzy to overcome even in pitching his best game of the year. The Pirates scored one in the eighth and one in the ninth to beat the Robins 2–1. Vance struck out 11 and walked three. He lost his next three starts by scores of 5–3, 3–0 and 2–1. At the end of July, Vance had a four-game losing streak, his record was 10–10, the Robins were 41–52 and in their familiar position of sixth place, 15½ games behind the Pirates. Vance was leading the league in strikeouts again and was a .500 pitcher primarily because of the punchless lineup of the Robins. In nine of Dazzy's 20 starts, his teammates had supplied him with two runs or less.

The owls in the press box were hooting. This was a team that let go of Jack Fournier, Zack Wheat, Andy High, Burleigh Grimes and, two years earlier, Dutch Ruether. High was having a .300 season for the Braves and teammate Fournier was hitting .280. Wheat was hitting .323 for Connie Mack's Philadelphia A's. Grimes was on his way to a 19–8 season with the Giants and Ruether, whom the Robins dumped after his 8–13 season in 1924, was headed to the World Series with the New York Yankees.

For all of the player shuffling, the Robins were mired in sixth place and did not inspire optimism. "Look out below," is the universal cry, Kieran wrote in the *New York Times*. Uncle Robbie, who had been in baseball almost 40 years, was frustrated but he tried to take it all in stride. "I've booted my share of trades like the rest of 'em and the boys in the bleachers are entitled to howl a bit. You pay money for some bird who's supposed to be a wonder in the field and he can't catch the measles. You pay for a hitter and he couldn't hit the floor if he fell off a chair."

Robbie said he felt sorry for the pitchers. "We've kicked away enough games to win four straight pennants and a trip to Europe. Ain't it awful?" He would get no argument from most Brooklyn fans. To make matters worse, Babe Herman, the maverick on the base paths and the original "Dr. Strangeglove" in the field, was having a sophomore jinx year at the plate. Herman, who hit .319 in his rookie year with 11 home runs and 81 runs batted in, was hitting .270 and would finish the year with 46 fewer hits than he had in his rookie year.

There was a report that Larry Sutton and Nap Rucker, the Robins' chief scouts, reported to Robbie that there were no prospects worthy of bringing up to the big club. Go out again, Robbie told them, and find him some ballplayers. Find four good ballplayers. He then told them that at the end of the season, they would hold a meeting at Dover Hall, Robbie's retreat where he liked to hunt and fish. Rucker told him, "No deal. Not at Dover Hall." When Robbie asked why, Rucker said, "Every time I saw you at Dover Hall, you had a gun in your hand."[12]

Vance's last two losses in July were tough ones. On July 22, the Robins once again failed to score for him and this time got only one hit off Red Lucas as the Reds beat Brooklyn 3–0 — and two of the runs were unearned. The Robins' only hit was delivered by DeBerry in the sixth inning — "nothing more than a sickly dribbler that bounded lazily past Lucas," in the words of John Drebinger, then got past second baseman Hughie Critz and into center field. In Dazzy's next start on July 27, he lost a 2–1 decision to Vic Aldridge, the winning run scoring on a Paul Waner double in the bottom of the eighth.

The Robins' hitting woes continued at the start of August but they managed to have just enough offense to beat the Reds 2–1 for Dazzy's 11th win, but two straight setbacks by scores of 6–2 and 3–2 put him behind .500 for the year with an 11–12 record. He won two more games in August and went into September with a 13–12 record. It was not going to be a 20-win season for the Dazzler but he still had a shot at being the league's strikeout champion. Going into September, the Robins were 53–70 and in sixth place but lost 13 of their next 16 to plummet into seventh place. They finished the season winning 12 of their last 20. That boosted their record to 65–88 and yet another sixth place finish.

Vance was 16–15 for the year but that was a deceiving record considering how well he pitched. He led the league in strikeouts for the sixth straight year with 184; was first in fewest hits allowed per nine innings, 7.97; first in complete games with 25; first in strikeouts per nine innings, 6.06; and first in strikeout to walk ratio, 2.67. His 2.70 earned run average was third best in the National League.

Playing on a team like the Pirates or Yankees, the two pennant winners, Vance could have easily won 20 games. Here is a breakdown of the run support he got from the Robins: they scored three runs or less for him in 21 of his 32 starts. They were shut out four times, scored one run three times, two runs nine times and three runs five times. That means that in those 21 games, Dazzy would have had to hold his opponent to two runs or less to have a chance to win. He lost once 1–0, twice 2–1 and three times 3–2. The Robins were shut out four times in games Dazzy started (including the Red Lucas one-hitter). He salvaged a winning season for himself by winning four games in which the final score was 2–1, tossing two shutouts, each 3–0 victories and winning two other games in which the scores were 3–2 and 4–3. He only started one game in which he did not get the decision and the Robins won that one 6–5. In games Dazzy lost, the Robins averaged 1.6 runs in support of him.

Bill Doak, who was about a month older than Vance but who had been in the big leagues 10 years longer, marveled at Dazzy's skill on the mound. "When the ball isn't shooting up there so it can't be seen, it's curling up there so it can't be hit," said Doak. He said Dazzy got by with two pitches because he was so good with both of them. No slow balls or changeups. Just fastballs and curves.

"When Daz wants to fool a batter, he just whistles one past his chin," said Doak. Then he'll curve him on the outside corner. When the batter is expecting another fastball, he'll curve him again. When he's got him set up for a curve low and away, he'll bust a fastball right by him," said his teammate. Vance always said the best pitch is the unexpected one. Doak said, "It's a system that can't be beat."[13]

Dazzy's popularity throughout the country continued to grow as did his penchant for making good business deals. The Ken-Wel Sporting Goods Company in New York began manufacturing baseball gloves in 1919 and by 1924 had developed a pretty good business. It patented a glove that featured lace between the fingers. What the company needed now was a baseball star to endorse the product. It signed Dazzy Vance, for an undisclosed price, of course. Modifications were made for a "Dazzy Vance model" and it was patented and sold in 1927. By early 1928, it was being sold by Walford's Sporting Goods Store, 909 Pennsylvania Avenue Northwest, in New York City for $5, a little more than the average glove, which sold for $3.45. The Dazzy Vance glove was one of the most popular gloves of its era and is still a prized possession of collectors.[14]

IX

"I, for one, can't slow-ball 'em"

The Yankees and Pirates squared off in a World Series that didn't last long. The Bronx Bombers made short order of the Pirates with their Murderers' Row lineup that had Babe Ruth, Lou Gehrig, Bob Muesel, Earl Combes and Tony Lazzeri and pitching staff that included Waite Hoyt, Herb Pennock and, yes, Dutch Ruether, the old Robin. The Pirates countered with the Waner brothers, Paul and Lloyd, as well as a third future Hall of Famer, Pie Traynor. Vic Aldridge and Lee Meadows were mainstays on the pitching staff. The Yankees swept the series but, oddly enough, with that power-packed lineup, they scored the winning run of the series in the bottom of the ninth inning of the fourth game on a wild pitch by Pirates reliever Johnny Miljus.

The Pirates' season and World Series appearance had a spillover effect that involved the Robins. Pittsburgh had a great outfielder by the name of Hazen "KiKi" Cuyler who came up with the Pirates briefly in 1921, 1922 and 1923 and then hit .354, .357 and .321 in his first three full seasons with the Bucs. In 1927, Donie Bush took over as manager of the Pirates and guided them to the National League championship. But Cuyler, who was generally known as an easy-going individual and not a troublemaker, did not get along with his new manager. For one thing, Bush put Cuyler second in the batting order when he had become accustomed to batting third. The two men had words but Cuyler had no choice but to accept his new place in the lineup. Then, later in the season, Bush reportedly became upset when Cuyler did not slide in an attempt to break up a double play. Bush benched him and did not start him for the rest of the season and kept him on the bench for the entire World Series. It was no secret that Cuyler, who would hit over .300 10 times in his career and retire with a .321 lifetime batting average, was on the trading block. One of the teams interested in him was the light-hitting Robins. One of the players the Pirates were interested in was Dazzy Vance.[1]

Just two days after the World Series ended, the New York Times reported that the Pirates would be willing to send Cuyler to the Robins but would want Dazzy Vance from Brooklyn as part of the trade. Uncle Robbie was hungry for hitters but he would starve before he gave up the best pitcher he had. On Oct. 21, 11 days after the New York Times story, the Washington Post reported that the Cubs, Reds, Giants and Robins were all interested in obtaining Cuyler. Uncle Robbie and Brooklyn officials stayed in the hunt because the Robins needed hitting so badly, but Bucs' owner Barney Dreyfuss was now saying he wanted both Dazzy Vance and Jess Petty in return. Robbie was willing to consider a trade involving Petty but not Vance and certainly not both of them. "If Robby allows both men to depart, he might as well toss the rest of his club in the river and go fishing next season," the Post concluded.

The sweepstakes ended on Nov. 28 when Pittsburgh traded Cuyler to Chicago for Pete Scott, an outfielder who played in just 71 games for the Cubs in 1927, and Sparky Adams, a veteran infielder who led the National League in at-bats for the third straight year, scored 100 runs and batted .292. Scott played sparingly for the Pirates in 1928 and then retired. Adams played just two years for Pittsburgh and finished his career with St. Louis and Cincinnati. Cuyler had eight productive years with the Cubs and finished off his career with stints in Cincinnati and Brooklyn.[2]

Dazzy wintered in Florida as he had for the past few years. In his leisure time, when he wasn't fishing, he was playing golf. In November, he shot a 79 to win the qualifying round of the Clearwater Country Club's first tournament of the winter season. In December, he won a similar tournament in Dunedin. In January, he made headlines in Florida papers when he got an eagle two on the par-four 13th hole at Clearwater, a hole in which many of the best players had to settle for a score of six or seven because of all the ditches, brush and water that surrounded the hole. Dazzy told writers afterwards that he was proud of his game but that Jigger Statz, his Robins teammate, was the best golfer among major league players. Not long after that, Statz shot a 66 to win a tournament in San Gabriel, California — and beating some professional golfers in the process. Vance had an advantage over many other ballplayers because he was allowed to play golf during baseball season. Hitters on most teams were prohibited by their managers from hitting a golf ball because of all the bad habits it could cause in hitting a baseball — the theory first expressed by John McGraw.

Uncle Robbie couldn't snare any sluggers during the winter trading season but he did make a move to try to provide some stability to the gang that was well known now as the Daffiness Boys. He picked up Dave Bancroft from Boston who, at 36, was beyond his prime as a shortstop but had leadership qualities that were sadly lacking in most of the Brooklyn bunch. Bancroft had been around for a long time. Pat Moran had told Robbie that the acquisition of Bancroft was a big reason why the Phillies won the 1915 National League pennant. Now 13 years later, Robinson was hoping Banny could do the same for his ball club. Most recently, he had been team captain of the New York Giants pennant winners of 1921, 1922 and 1923 and had been player-manager of the Boston Braves for the past four years. For Bancroft, the chance to get out of Beantown must have seemed like clemency; the Braves finished eighth, fifth and seventh (twice) under his direction.

Robbie wanted Bancroft to be like an assistant manager on the field, directing the players and trying to keep them fired up. The problem was that they were veterans, they were used to Robbie pretty much letting them do their own thing and they weren't fond of following the instructions of a newcomer. Added to all of this was that Uncle Robbie agreed to assume the last year of Bancroft's contract with Boston, meaning he was easily the highest paid Robin with a salary of $40,000.

The Robins made other off-season moves— so many in fact that their lineup of regulars in 1928 included only three familiar faces: Herman moved from first base to the outfield; Carey remained in the outfield; and DeBerry stayed behind the plate. Newcomers included Del Bissonnette at first base, a rookie touted to be a long ball hitter; Jake Flowers, traded from St. Louis to Brooklyn for Bob McGraw, at second, replacing Chick Fewster, who retired; Harvey Hendrick at third in place of Bobby Barrett, who was released, stayed out of baseball for a year and then resurfaced to play one year with the Boston Braves; Bancroft at short, replacing Johnny Butler, who was traded to the Cubs for Howard Freigau, a utility infielder; and outfielder Rube Bressler, finishing up a 19-year career, who was picked up on waivers from Cincinnati. Herman and Bressler replaced Gus Felix and Jigger Statz in the outfield. Felix was released and Statz became a reserve player.

While the shakeup was taking place on the field, things were starting to boil over off the field. McKeever and Robbie continued their feud. During a party given in conjunction with the winter baseball meetings in New York, one of the party-goers tried get the two Brooklyn executives to smooth things over and actually got them to shake hands and agree to be friends. The next day, when Robbie arrived for work at the president's office at Ebbets Field, he offered a cheerful "hello" to McKeever as he passed by his office. "Rat, don't you talk to me," said McKeever. Uncle Robbie responded with his own verbal abuse and it was business as usual in the Brooklyn front office.[3]

Meanwhile, Vance was once again dickering with Robins' officials about his salary. It was different than it used to be. Charles Ebbets was no longer around to listen to the Dazzler's mathematical analysis of the importance of pitching to a ball club. Uncle Robbie was still club president as well as manager. But as spring training began, he said he wanted no part of further negotiations. "The matter of signing Vance is out of my hands completely," he said. "Dazzy is doing his negotiating with Mr. Frank B. York, who is acting for the directors of the ballclub."

It was obvious, though, that Dazzy and Robbie were on friendly terms. As spring training began for those who had signed, they were seen often playing checkers together in the hotel lobby while Max Carey looked around for someone to take him on in a game of chess. Robbie scoffed at chess, saying it had funny-looking little men and appeared to him to be "checkers gone bad." Writers noticed Robbie and Vance huddling privately several times away from the checker board. Both denied any negotiations were taking place. They said they were talking about the possibility of tapping some pine trees for turpentine on property they owned jointly in nearby Homosassa, a story most writers didn't believe.

On March 6, after a meeting between Vance, Robinson, York and John Scholl, another Robins director, Dazzy signed a contract for $20,000, making him the highest paid pitcher in the National League, meaning he was earning more money than Grover Cleveland Alexander of the Cardinals. Robbie was ecstatic and a little boastful. "I know how to handle Vance," he told the press, "and we both agree that my system has done much to make him a great pitcher."

He said he had always let Dazzy play golf between starts if he wanted to, so that was not a condition in his contract as had been speculated. Robbie said Dazzy was in excellent condition to start spring training and that he expected great things out of his star pitcher in 1928.[4]

The Robins were also counting on James "Jumbo" Elliott to have a good year in his second season in the starting rotation. "Jumbo" got his nickname because of his size — 6 foot 3 and 235 pounds. In 1927, he was 6–13 as a spot starter. If he could increase his wins into double figures, it would help take some of the load off of Vance and Petty.

While the Robins approached spring training with high hopes, as they always did, there were early indications that the personality of the ball club was not going to change much — that the daffiness of the Daffiness Boys still lived. That was apparent with the noisy arrival of Babe Herman on Feb. 26, a week ahead of schedule. Robbie said he was surprised to see him. Herman replied he arrived a lot sooner than he thought he would. He put his wife and child in his car nine days ago in Los Angeles, he said, and began his cross-country trip. It turned out that Babe couldn't drive any better than he could field. By the time he arrived in Clearwater, the auto had taken a beating, mostly because of all the objects it had run into along the way.

"Fenders, accessories, spokes and what-not shed themselves like leaves in autumn at every turn and bump in the trail and when he pulled up in front of the hotel, he seemed to have little more left than a steering wheel and a couple of license plates," reported the *New York Times*. Babe put it all in perspective when he said, "If I field as well as this car traveled, I ought to hold my job. I missed nothing."[5]

It was soon apparent why Herman showed up early. The rookie Del Bissonnette hit .375 with 30 home runs at Buffalo in 1927 and was a nifty first baseman. If Herman could play in the outfield, Robbie would have two big bats in his lineup, something the Robins desperately needed. So Herman came early and worked with Otto Miller, who hit fungo fly balls to him in the outfield. The press reported that he circled around and caught a surprising number of them. Drebinger told his readers it was even possible that Babe might learn to catch most of them.

One writer said Uncle Robbie's hitters were pacifists— they didn't believe in doing harm to anybody, and that Robbie had two things going for him — a good pitching staff and the presidential year. The Robins won the pennant in 1916, 1920 and nearly won it in 1924 — all presidential years— as was 1928.

The Robins opened the season on April 11 with Jess Petty on the mound, who pitched well enough to win but lost a 4–3 decision to the Philadelphia Phillies. The next day, Dazzy got some hitting support and breezed to a 6–1 victory with rookie Del Bissonette hitting his first major league home run and Harvey Hendrick, now the Robins' third baseman, hitting his second home run in as many games. He won again on April 18 when Brooklyn beat Boston 10–5. Dazzy was in control all the way, weakening in the eighth inning and allowing three runs, but by that time the game was well in hand. On April 26, Braves got to him for four runs early and the Robins fell back into one of their old habits— they didn't score. They only scored two runs for him in each of his next two outings, losing to both the Giants and Cardinals by scores of 4–2. On May 12, he pitched well again, but once again his teammates' bats were silent as the Cubs beat the Robins 3–0, saddling Vance with a record of 2–4. Since his first two starts when the Robins scored 6–1 and 10–5 victories, Brooklyn was shut out twice and scored two runs in each of his other two starts. He could easily have been 6–0.

On May 14, the Robins had a wild one with the Pirates at Forbes Field. After Brooklyn took the lead 7–6 with two runs in the eighth inning, Uncle Robbie went to his bullpen — and brought in Dazzy to try to hold the Pirates in check. As John Drebinger reported in the *New York Times*, "It is to be seriously doubted whether Horatius standing at the bridge had a more trying time of it than did Vance." He got the first two batters in the eighth but then gave up a single and two walks to load the bases. The inning ended when Lloyd Waner popped out. In the ninth, the Dazzler walked the first two men he faced, then retired the next three batters with no damage being done. Bill Doak got the win.[6]

After losing to the Giants 9–5 on May 22, Dazzy got his fourth win of the year and his first shutout on May 26 when DeBerry drove in the only run in a 1–0 victory over the Braves. Going into June, the Robins were 22–19 and in fifth place — but only five games behind the Cardinals. It was an unusual situation in that the team was staying afloat even though Vance was 4–5. Typically, for the past seven years, it had been Dazzy leading the way and the rest of the team struggling to stay above .500. This gave Robins fans hope that when Dazzy hit his stride, which he usually did in mid-season, Brooklyn would be in the thick of things to make another presidential year run at the championship.

Vance was still getting batters out with his bread-and-butter pitches, the fastball and the curve — more often than not, a fast curve so the batter didn't have time to figure out what was coming. "I, for one, can't slow-ball 'em," he told an interviewer. He said when he first started out in baseball, he tried to mix up his pitches. "I noticed the slow ones got pickled a lot," he said. Also, said Vance, fooling around with so many different pitches led to his sore-arm problems in his early years.

He didn't become a good pitcher until he mastered the curveball—and he had a lot of opportunities to practice it. "Take a look at that list of clubs that have had Arthur C. Vance as one of their pitchers," he said. And he rattled them off: the Yankees, then Pittsburgh, St. Joseph, Toledo, Memphis, Rochester, Sacramento, New Orleans and finally Brooklyn. "I was learning to master the curve ball and when I finally got back to Memphis in 1920, I had the thing all fixed," he said. The next year he was back in New Orleans. "When I joined the Pelicans and got some of the salubrious air of the Crescent City into my system, I was fixed and I have been doing fair to middlin' ever since," said the Dazzler.[7]

Vance won four of six decisions in June, including his second shutout of the year, a 4–0 blanking of the Cubs on June 17 and his first-ever win in relief, when Uncle Robbie called on him in a June 26 contest against the Braves. In that one, the second game of a double header, Boston jumped to a 5–3 lead against starter Bill Doak and relievers Jeff Petty and Rube Ehrhardt when Dazzy came on with two men on and nobody out in the eighth inning. He retired the side in order without any further damage being done. The Robins scored three in the ninth to take the lead. Ray Moss, the fifth Robins pitcher of the afternoon, blanked the Braves in the bottom of the ninth, giving Vance his eighth win of the season against six losses. It was the Robins' sixth straight win and, coupled with their win in the first game of the twin bill, put them in third place, six games behind the first-place Cardinals.

They didn't play for four games, then ended June with a double header split with the Phillies. The winning streak ended in the first game when Dazzy lost a grueling 13-inning matchup with Herb Pruett in which both pitchers went the distance. Drebinger in the *New York Times* said Vance lost because he got "a little too scientific" at the end. In the 13th, the Phillies had a runner on third. Dazzy worked carefully on the next two batters, not wanting to give either of them anything good to swing at, and wound up walking both of them, setting up force plays at any base. But Pinky Whitney singled up the middle to score two runs. The Robins got one of them back in the bottom of the 13th but it wasn't enough and Brooklyn lost 4–3. Drebinger told his readers the Robins "renounced strategy in the second game and won 13–5 on brute strength."[8]

Between July 22 and Aug. 15, Dazzy reeled off six straight victories, including his third shutout of the year, a 5–0 whitewashing of the Pirates on July 22. In five of the six wins, Vance allowed no more than two runs. But unfortunately, all six wins either came after a loss or snapped a losing streak. Dazzy's streak came to an end on Aug. 20 when he lost to the Cardinals 2–1. Then he came back with two more victories, including his fourth shutout. When he beat the Giants 4–2 on Aug. 31, he was 18–9 but the Robins were 61–64 and were now 15½ games behind the league-leading Cardinals.

It was at about this time that George Moriarty, manager of the Detroit Tigers, penned an article in which he bemoaned the fact that major league baseball had become a hitters' game and that pitchers had to find their own devices to counteract the lively ball. He mentioned three examples. Howard Ehmke of the Philadelphia Athletics had developed a hesitation pitch in which he went into his windup and then hesitated with his hands over his head before delivering the ball to the plate. The idea was to throw the batter's timing off. Moriarty said, "It has not greatly perturbed the sluggers." Another pitcher who changed his delivery style was Ted Lyons of the Chicago White Sox, who developed a method of rocking back and forth as he went into this windup in an effort to distract the batter.

"Although most pitchers find that subduing the maulers is difficult, now and then a pitcher bobs up with an effective new wrinkle. You know the slit-sleeve stunt used by Dazzy Vance to confuse the batsmen during the windup. The idea has not been widely copied," he wrote. Moriarty surmised that the star pitchers could get away with gimmicks better than mediocre pitchers because in lesser pitchers, the deviation might be seen as a lack of confidence. Not so with pitchers like Dazzy Vance.[9]

The Dazzler won four out of his last five decisions to finish the season with a 22–10 record, his best since his MVP year of 1924. But none of the other starters won more than they lost. Petty had another .500 season at 15–15. McWeeny, whom Uncle Robbie had picked to be a star a few years earlier, checked in at 14–14. Jumbo Elliott was 9–14. Del Bissonette would have been Rookie of the Year had they had one in those days. He hit .320 with 25 home runs and 106 runs batted in. Babe Herman did more damage to opponents with his bat than to his own team with his glove. He hit .340 with 12 homers and 91 runs batted in.

Frank Graham summed up the Robins' year succinctly. "What if Vance did win 22 games, lead the league in earned run average with 2.09

and in strikeouts with 200? The Robins finished sixth." Again. Where they had finished five out of the last six years.

Vance broke a pledge he had made five years ago and decided to take in a World Series game in New York. "After the Giants nosed us out back in 1924, I vowed I'd never attend a World Series game until I could pitch in one. But curiosity seems to have got the better of me," he said.

Robinson and Roscoe McGowen of the *Brooklyn Standard-Union* (later with the *New York Times*) went to St. Louis together to watch the series. In his hotel room, Robbie gave an interview to a young sports-writer from a suburban St. Louis newspaper.

"How would you pitch to Ruth," Robinson was asked.

"Walk him."

How about Gehrig?

"Walk him."

And Combes?

"Walk him."

How about Meusel?

"Put him on, too."

Robbie had the same answer for the first eight batters.

How about the pitcher, the young reporter asked.

"Pitch to him," said Robbie. "Let him win his own ballgame."

Robinson told another reporter, Dan Daniels of the *New York World-Telegram*, that the current Yankees team would have clobbered his old Orioles team of the 1890s. When that was published, many of the surviving Orioles, including Giants manager John McGraw, publicly disagreed with their old teammate. In fact, the feud between Robinson and McGraw, seemingly dormant for years, was reignited. Robbie's reaction: "I don't give a X$#@ what McGraw says."[10]

Though the results were no better than they had been for the past four years, the Robins felt they had an improved club in 1928. They had added more punch by inserting Bissonette at first base and moving Herman to the outfield and Harvey Hendrick provided some punch at third base with his .318 batting average and 11 home runs. Bancroft was in the waning days of his career but was a steadying force at shortstop. Carey also added leadership but was also at the end of his career. Johnny Frederick, a promising rookie, was brought up to replace Carey in 1929 and joined Herman and Bressler in the outfield. Other new faces included veteran catcher Vic Picinich, who came over from Cincinnati for Johnny

Gooch and Rube Ehrhardt; Eddie Moore, a second baseman picked up on waivers from Boston; and Wally Gilbert, who came up in 1928 but became the regular third baseman in 1929. Robbie hoped that Watty Clark, 12–9 in 1928 while splitting time as a starter and reliever, would step up and fill the void left by the trade of Jess Petty.

The *Washington Post* did a feature story on Vance, not only recapping his statistics from the previous season, but pointing out how the Dazzler was succeeding while playing for the lightest hitting team in the National League. The story also extolled Dazzy's sense of humor and illustrated with an anecdote that reflected the insensitivity of the times regarding the status of African Americans. According to the story, Dazzy was with a sportswriter in Clearwater when they came upon Jim, a "negro man" who worked for Vance. The man was wearing a suit and Dazzy kidded him, asking him where he got it. When the man replied that Vance had given it to him, Dazzy laughed and said he didn't remember that. Then, according to the story, the black man started telling the writer about Dazzy's pitching prowess. "When Mistah Dazzy fanned all them Jints [Giants] at the Polo Grounds in Noo York last summer and never let 'em get a run, the news was all over town. I was so excited, I quit work fo' de day." To which Dazzy replied, "Don't see how you could do that. I always thought a fellow had to start work before he could quit work." They all had a good laugh over it.[11]

Dazzy was good column fodder in other newspapers, too, during the winter. Grantland Rice wrote that just on the basis of winning the strike-out championship seven years in a row put Vance in a class with the greatest pitchers of all time. He also pointed out that Dazzy had worked most of his career with little run support from his teammates. Ballplayers who hit against both Walter Johnson and Dazzy had trouble determining who was faster, said Rice. "Sizing up the speed of a rifle bullet at close range is a half-step beyond the limit of the human eye. When you can't see 'em, they must look pretty much like the same thing."[12]

James S. Collins in the *New York World News* wrote that Dazzy was in a great bargaining position, not only because of his 1928 performance but also because of the loss of Jess Petty during the off-season. "Dazzy is said to have put a $22,500 price tag on his services. That's pretty high, but dirt cheap if, as reported, the club found it good business to pay Dave Bancroft something like $40,000 for performing at short last season," wrote Collins. He said at the bargaining table, Vance was like a bridge player with a handful of spades.[13]

Uncle Robbie had other problems with potential holdouts. Babe Herman, his best hitter — and his worst fielder — was reportedly out in California trying to catch fly balls hit with a fungo bat. The Robins were concerned that the Babe might seriously hurt himself as he trained to once again play in the outfield for Brooklyn. In ballgames, fly balls are hit occasionally to an outfielder. If Herman was trying to catch 100 balls a day hit to him out on the West Coast, the odds increased dramatically that he would get "skulled" by one of them.

Vance arrived at training camp in Clearwater on March 1, played golf for a few days and then went back to his home in Homasassa. The Robins had offered him $22,500 but it turned out Dazzy wanted $25,000 and not a penny less. The Robins' board of directors rejected his demand, and Robbie, as both club president and manager, was helpless. By March 11, the managerial side of him dominated his thinking. "We've got to have Daz. That's all there is to it," he told the press. Any chance the Robins had to be contenders in 1929 depended on Vance. He seemed to be telling the other directors, "Vance at any price." On the night of March 14, director John Gorman, also club secretary, announced that Dazzy would get the $25,000 he sought. With the signing of Vance — and with Herman already in camp safe and sound — Robbie was a happy man as he hit infield grounders, wearing his baseball uniform shirt and knickers. Spring training had become fun once again.

Glenn Wright, who came over from Pittsburgh in the Petty deal, was a good hitter and was expected to anchor the infield at shortstop, replacing the aging Dave Bancroft. Robbie thought Wright would provide some hitting punch to go along with Herman and Bissonette — and that would produce some runs for a pretty good pitching staff led by Vance.

Reality set in quickly in 1929. The Robins opened the season by losing their first five games. They never achieved a record of better than two games below .500 (6–8 on May 6). But they lost nine in a row after that. The ball club simply could not get any traction. In addition to the five-game losing streak at the start and the nine-game losing streak two weeks later, the Robins had four four-game losing streaks and another five-game string of losses.

Dazzy made his 1929 debut in the second game of a double header at Boston on April 19 and was hardly in mid-season form. He left in the seventh inning, down by three runs, in a game the Robins eventually lost 5–1. He struck out no one, walked three and hit two batters. Roscoe McGowen in the *New York Times* saw fit to refer to him as "the expensive Mr. Vance." Dazzy then reeled off three straight victories, including his first shutout of the year, a 2–0 victory over the Giants.

When the Robins began showing signs that this would be no different than the futility they showed every year since 1924, Westbrook Pegler, the czar of sarcasm among America's sportswriters, took them to task.

Pegler noted that the Robins seemed more confused than usual this spring "which probably constitutes a new record in the matter of free-style chaos." He pointed out that the athletes were not performing well, the front office was divided into two camps (the McKeever crowd who hated Robbie and the Robbie crowd who loved him), and that fans and sportswriters couldn't even agree on what to call the team — the Dodgers or the Robins.

Pegler accused the front office of not wanting to spend the money for good ballplayers. He recounted an incident several years earlier when Charles Ebbets was accused of hoarding his money rather than spending it on his team. Ebbets replied that he once offered the Cardinals $250,000 for Rogers Hornsby. After that comment was published, someone — probably a sportswriter — called Ebbets, identified himself as Sam Breadon, owner of the Cardinals, and said he would take Ebbets up on his offer. The Dodgers owner was so shocked, not realizing it was a prank, that he was "indisposed for a week," according to Pegler. The current management, he said, filled vacancies on the roster by trying to find players who wore the same size uniform shirts and pants as the players they were replacing so as not to have the added expense of new uniforms. As for this year's ball club, "strictly speaking, the Brooklyn club consists of Dazzy Vance inclusive," wrote Pegler.[14]

The borough of Brooklyn was cold, wet and windy in the spring of 1929. Robinson managed from the bench with a blanket covering his legs and he missed several games with bouts of tonsillitis. Carey ran the ball club in his absence. Bissonette was being treated for a sinus infection. Vance had been fighting a cold off and on and developed fever and chills along with it. He lost to the Phillies 7–4 on May 16, giving up two home runs to Lefty O'Doul in the cozy confines of the Baker Bowl in Philadelphia. Three days later, the Robins announced that the old Dazzler was too weak to make his next start. He went to a doctor who told him he was suffering from complications of influenza. The only thing that could help him was medications and bedrest. He was ordered to go home for several weeks.

The loss to the Phillies was the ninth in the nine-game losing streak that sunk the Robins. They were in eighth place with a record of 6–17. Vance had three of the six wins. He did not appear in another game until June 8. Robbie brought him into the game in a relief appearance against the Pirates. It was not a glorious re-entry. Pittsburgh scored five unearned runs and Dazzy gave up three hits without a strikeout or a walk in the one inning he pitched. He did not get the decision as Watty Clark had given up

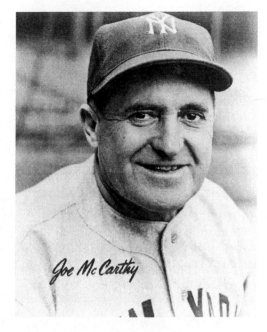

Joe McCarthy made the biggest name for himself as manager of the New York Yankees. His first big league managing job was with the Chicago Cubs where he complained to National League officials about Dazzy Vance's tattered shirt sleeve. (Courtesy Hall of Fame.)

the game winning runs long before Dazzy took the mound. On June 13, he made his first start in nearly a month and mowed down the Reds at Crosley Field, allowing just five hits in a 2–1 victory. He didn't get a decision in either of his next two starts, then lost a 3–2 decision to the Giants and Carl Mays on June 26. On June 30, in besting the Braves 5–3, Vance had a won–loss record of 5–4, the Robins had won four straight, their longest winning streak of the year, and found themselves in the unfamiliar territory of fifth place in the National League standings.

But the Robins faltered again in July, winning but 12 of 31 games, and Dazzy lost three out of his five starts during the month. Brooklyn went into Chicago in early August and lost three out of four to the Cubs. Vance did not pitch in the series but nonetheless was a hot topic for Cubs manager Joe McCarthy. McCarthy, like McGraw of the Giants, never passed up an opportunity to get an edge on an opponent, including playing mind games whenever an appropriate situation came up.

McCarthy complained publicly about one of Dazzy's trademarks—the tattered sleeve of his undershirt. McCarthy told the press that if Vance didn't buy a new undershirt, he would either buy one for him or complain to National League president John Heydler. McCarthy said when Vance wound up, the long slits in his shirt fluttered in the breeze, distracting Cubs hitters. That was the reason so many of them struck out, said McCarthy. It was a particular nuisance to Hack Wilson, who fanned four times the last time Vance faced him, said the Cubs manager.[15]

Dazzy spun many stories about the tattered sleeve. Early in his career, he denied cutting slits in it so that on a breezy day, it looked like a windmill when he was winding up. Ol' Daz said it was a lucky undershirt that he had worn for years and that it was beginning to wear out. Another time, when he had been retired for many years, he told the press that the sleeve never flapped in the batter's eye. He said when opposing batters and managers heard about the sleeve, they started imagining things.

It all started during a game with the Reds when Dolph Luque was still pitching for them. With Vance at bat and squared away to bunt, Luque threw a pitch high and inside—exactly what a pitcher should do when a hitter is obviously trying to bunt. Dazzy said the ball clipped him on the sleeve and tore it. Some fans started shouting to him about his cheap uniform.

Dazzy figured if the torn sleeve was noticeable, maybe he could play it to his advantage. "I told DeBerry when they came to the plate to act like, 'I can't see the ball with that thing flapping.' Sure enough, they all began to believe that the sleeve bothered them, though in truth, you couldn't see the sleeve when I wound up and threw."[16]

Word soon got around the league about Vance's sleeve, he said, and batters like Hack Wilson and managers like Joe McCarthy complained about it when, in fact, there was nothing to complain about, he said.

There were other myths that caused distractions in batters. Rube Bressler, before he joined the Robins, said Vance was impossible to hit on Mondays because that was the day that women in apartment buildings beyond the outfield wall did their wash and hung up their undies on clothes lines to dry—creating a white background behind Dazzy. Jimmy Johnston complained about an open window in an apartment building distracting him. Vance said a screen was put on the window to alleviate Johnston's concerns. "Ebbets Field was built in 1912 and that window never bothered anybody before. It was just his imagination," said Dazzy.[17]

The frustration of another losing season caused Uncle Robbie to publicly vent, even to the point of threatening to trade Vance — the man he said he could not live without when he was trying to sign him in spring training. What a difference, a few months later. What a difference, many losses later. In August, Robinson said, "I'll trade Vance this winter without a doubt. If I can make the right sort of deals, I'll trade most of the others of the Brooklyn club." The *Chicago Daily Tribune* reported "there is a strong suspicion in National League circles that the 38-year-old Vance is slipping as well as not trying."[18]

Dazzy contributed to his growing reputation of indifference with some bewildering acts. On July 16, in a game against the Reds, Vance inexplicably went into a windup three times with a runner on first. Each time, the runner stole second and each time the runner eventually scored in a game the Robins lost 5–3. The *Brooklyn Eagle* offered no explanation for the Dazzler's forgetfulness but did offer a solution.

"Some type of signal should be arranged to let Vance know when he is ready to deliver the ball with men on base," the newspaper suggested. "A shot might be fired across his bow as he steps on the slab. If that does not bring him out of his trance, a bat might be hurled at him from the bench."[19]

The trading of Dazzy Vance was good fodder for newspaper columnists for the next several weeks. The *Washington Post* postulated that it wouldn't happen because the trading of Vance violated one of the basic tenets of good business: buy low and sell high. "One needn't be a financial wizard to see it's a poor time to sell," the newspaper reported.[20]

Dazzy would never say so publicly but he had to feel some pressure. His manager had a love-hate relationship with him, he had missed a month because of the flu, his fastball had apparently lost some of its zip and it seemed like his team still struggled to get runs for him. Babe Herman was still hitting the cover off of the ball but his adventures in the outfield sometimes offset what he did at the plate. On Sept. 12, Dazzy was cruising along with a 2–1 lead over the Reds at Crosley Field. Horace Ford hit a fly ball to deep right field with Herman in pursuit of it. Babe misjudged the ball. Here's how McGowen described what happened next. "As the ball fell safe and rolled into rightfield, Herman's midsection struck the fence, his heels left the turf and his lanky form shot high into the air. For a moment, he poised like an acrobat on top of a giant swing.

Then he catapulted over into the stands." Herman was not hurt. Ford circled the bases. The Reds won 3–2, and Vance, accused in the press of "slipping" and "not trying," was saddled with his 12th loss of the year, matching his win total.[21]

The Robins never really recovered from their slow start. They finished at 70–83 and once again renewed their lease on sixth place in the standings. Glenn Wright, the shortstop picked up from Pittsburgh in the trading of Jess Petty, hurt his hand while playing handball and appeared in only 24 games for the Robins. He had but one home run and six runs batted in as Bancroft returned to the role of starting shortstop. Bissonette's home run total dropped from 25 in 1928 to 12 in 1929. Johnny Frederick picked up some of the slack with his 24 homers, 75 runs batted in and batting average of .328. And Babe Herman, the outfield acrobat, continued to sting the ball at the plate. He hit .381 with 21 home runs and 113 runs batted in. Ray Moss was a surprise on the pitching staff with his 11–6 record. After him, Dazzy, with a 14–13 record was the only other pitcher to win more than he lost. Watty Clark won 16 to lead the staff but he lost 19.

As for Dazzy, for the first time in his career, he failed to lead the National League in strikeouts, finishing with 126–74 fewer than his 1928 total. In addition to the flu bug that knocked him down early in the season, doctors also diagnosed him with rheumatism, for which he was going to undergo three months of extensive treatments in the off-season. No matter how the treatments would go, one thing was for certain. For the first time in his career, he was a question mark as the Robins looked to 1930.

X

No More Daffiness
(Well, Almost)

Wilbert Robinson was one of the most popular figures in baseball. Brooklyn fans knew him as the man who took no guff from John McGraw of the arch-rival Giants, and the man who brought pennants to Flatbush in 1916, 1920 and made a great run at it in 1924. The portly man with the big hat and the big smile was a drawing card throughout the National League as well. Fans came to the ballpark to see Uncle Robbie. All of these were reasons why Robinson was able to keep his job even though the Robins finished in sixth place every year since 1922 (when Vance joined the club), except for the 1924 season when they finished second. The best modern comparisons are perhaps Tommy Lasorda with the Los Angeles Dodgers and Sparky Anderson, particularly when he managed the Detroit Tigers. In each case, the managers were popular at home and on the road and there was never any question as to who was going to manage the ball club the following year. Another comparison might be Connie Mack, who managed the A's for 50 years because he owned the team. Robbie, too, was in the front office, but was not nearly as secure in his position as Mack was in his.

There is another comparison worth noting. Brooklyn fans were as loyal to the Robins in that era as Chicago Cub fans have been to their favorite team in recent years despite the futility of the team in trying to climb in the standings. As the 1930 baseball season approached, writer Frank Graham described the Brooklyn faithful this way: "Even they had abandoned all hope of ever seeing anything more exciting at Ebbets Field than an infielder booting the ball, an outfielder losing it in the sun or a runner losing himself on the bases. Yet, by the thousands and hundreds of thousands, they continued to attend the games."[1]

Things were heating up in the front office. McKeever wanted Robin-

121

son out, not just as the president of the ball club, but as manager too. Out altogether. Robbie had a faction of Ebbets heirs on his side, creating a standoff. McKeever even went so far as to contact the baseball commissioner, Judge Kenesaw Mountain Landis, for help in ousting Robbie. Not surprisingly, the judge said it was a club matter and a league matter and that the commissioner's office was not going to get involved. It became more of a league matter when word spread to other National League club owners that Robbie was in trouble. They not only had loyalty to him but realized what he meant to their ticket sales. The owners prevailed upon National League president John Heydler to intercede as an arbiter and bring peace to the Robins' front office.

Heydler came up with a plan to add a fifth person to the Robins board of directors, someone who, in effect, would be the tie-breaker, because McKeever and Robinson each had two strong backers on the board. The man chosen to be the fifth spoke on the wheel was Walter F. Carter, known as "Dutch," a Brooklyn lawyer, brother-in-law of Supreme Court justice Charles Evans Hughes, and an avid Robins fan. Carter would own no stock in the company. His only role was as adviser but, more importantly, as a board member, he had a vote on how the ball club would be run. With Carter's help, the directors reached a compromise: Robbie was out as club president. Frank York, the club's attorney got that job. Robinson got a two-year contract as manager. He headed for spring training in Clearwater with a renewed spirit and a determination to turn the ball club into a pennant contender once again. For all practical purposes, the daffiness days were over.

The status of Dazzy Vance was curious. Robbie seemed to have lost faith in him and, indeed, he wasn't much better than a .500 pitcher in three out of the last four years. He was a pain in the backside every year at contract time and in recent years had fallen victim to bouts of illnesses during the season. His lack of concentration in games, such as the times he would wind up with men on base, were also perplexing to Robins' management. Other club owners were aware of how Vance had fallen out of favor with his bosses. William Wrigley of the Cubs, whose team had just lost in the World Series to the Philadelphia A's, made it known he was interested in acquiring Vance. But for all the talk the previous season of unloading Dazzy Vance and all the interest shown in him by other clubs, Robinson knew he was still the heart and soul of the pitching staff. Dazzy wasn't a young man any more, but at his best he was still the best. So Dazzy stayed but Doug McWeeny departed. He was traded to Cincinnati for Dolph Luque, a native of Cuba and a 15-year veteran who won 27 games for the Reds in 1923 but had slipped to 5–16 for a poor Cincinnati team in 1929. In acquiring Luque, Robbie was reverting to a practice that had served him well over the years— squeezing one or two more good years out of old-timers.

"We got some good prospects in these kid pitchers but you can't tell when they'll blow," said Robbie. "When it looks like they're gonna win a game, they get all excited and go up in a balloon. That's where we could get a lot out of Luque."[2]

Vance showed up at spring training a few days late — exactly the kind of behavior Robins management disliked — but on March 8 he threw 27 consecutive strikes in batting practice, exactly the kind of behavior the Robins rejoiced in.

As the season got under way, the Robins were hoping for a resurgence from Bissonette at first base, Flowers was a mainstay at second, Wright was fully recovered from his hand injury and big things were expected from him as shortstop and dependable Wally Gilbert was at third. The outfield was solid with Herman, coming off a .381 season, and the veterans Bressler and Johnny Frederick. DeBerry was still behind the plate, sharing duties with Al Lopez. Vance, Watty Clark, Jumbo Jim Elliott, Ray Moss and the newly acquired Luque were the main forces on a strong pitching staff.

Clark got the opening day assignment and lost a 1–0 heartbreaker to Leo Sweetland and the Phillies on April 15. Dazzy got hit hard in his season premiere as the Braves beat the Robins 10–8. Clark was called on to pitch the third game of the season and lost a 7–2 decision to the Braves. On April 21, Luque made his debut with the Robins and got some run support as Brooklyn won its first game of the year in a 15–8 win over Boston. But two more losses put the Robins in eighth place, winning only one of their first six games. They ended the month on a high note, sending the Giants to their third straight loss after McGraw's troops had won seven in a row to start the season. Dazzy picked up his second win and Babe Herman hit his fourth home run in the 9–4 victory. It was the third straight win for Brooklyn, now 5–7 for the year after the dismal start.

The Robins put together four more victories, increasing their winning streak to seven before losing to the Cubs 3–1 at Wrigley Field. Dazzy took the loss and it occurred primarily because of one pitch — a ball Hack Wilson hit out of the ballpark with two men on. It was a tough loss, and yet, Brooklyn had been within one pitch of having an eight-game winning streak, something that hadn't happened in many years. Luque was proving to be a valuable addition to the pitching staff, Vance seemed to be back to his old form, Herman was hitting over .400 and Glenn Wright was playing well at shortstop and hammering the ball at the plate. On May 11, the Robins beat the Pirates 10–2 for Vance's third victory of the year, They got 18 hits with everyone in the lineup contributing — three from Bissonette and Herman, two from Vance, Flowers, Frederick, Wright and Bressler and one each from Gilbert and DeBerry. Dazzy held the Pirates to four hits. Vance won again on May 16, this time a 10–3 rout of the Reds in a 16-hit attack. After a loss to the Phillies, Brooklyn reeled off a four-game winning streak in which they beat the Phillies by scores of 3–0 and 7–5, crushed them 16–9 behing Luque and then beat the Braves 12–1 with Vance picking up his fifth win. With this sudden surge of success, the Robins found themselves in the unfamiliar territory of first place in the National League standings. Since their 1–5 start, they had won 17 and lost only 7 and were beginning to believe in themselves. There was nothing daffy about the way they were playing.

The Robins closed out the month with winning streaks of three games and four games, with a loss sandwiched in between. Dazzy shut out the Giants 7–0 on May 26 — the first time New York had been shut out this season — and then lost a 3–1 decision to the Phillies to close out the month. When Brooklyn fans awoke on the morning of June 1 and looked at the standings in their morning paper, here is what they found:

Team	W–L	Pct.	GB
Brooklyn	25–15	.625	__
St. Louis	23–17	.575	2
Chicago	23–19	.548	3
Pittsburgh	20–18	.526	4
Boston	18–18	.500	5
New York	17–22	.436	7.5
Cincinnati	16–23	.410	8.5
Philadelphia	12–22	.353	10

It was the latest in the season that the Robins had found themselves in first place since their pennant run of 1924. But in 1924, the Robins had been contending much of the year and made a final, futile charge at the end of the season. This year, they were in charge, at least so far.

After a forgettable 13–0 drubbing at the hands of the Cubs on June 6, Dazzy returned to his old form, holding the Reds to four hits in a 2–1 victory on June 11. When Moss beat the Reds the next day, the Robins had a four-game winning streak and had been in first place for two weeks straight. Nobody was taking them lightly and nobody thought of them as daffy any more. Uncle Robbie had waited a long time, and his days were probably numbered as their manager, but he had put together the winning combination this year.

Westbrook Pegler, ever the cynic, saw the Robins' success in a unique perspective. He mentioned the dislike that Steve McKeever and Robinson had for one another and yet Robbie's ball club was making tremendous profits for McKeever and making him look good and, at the same time, McKeever was stuck with Uncle Robbie as his manager and the Robins were making their manager look good. "Their interests are alike and yet contrary," wrote Pegler, "and neither one can enjoy this season's success because success for the one also means success for the other."[3]

Pegler noted a couple of other oddities about this year's ball club. Robbie didn't like to have foreign-born players on the team unless there was a teammate of the same nationality. They could room together and bond with other ballplayers better than they could if they were alone, he reasoned. One of the reasons he decided to pick up the veteran Cuban pitcher Luque from the Reds is that catcher Al Lopez, also a Cuban, was on the roster. And with that bit of logic, Robbie had a tough southpaw who had six wins under his belt by the middle of June. The other oddity: Babe Herman, the outfielder whose defense was "self-defense," was the only starter in the Robins' lineup without an error.

Brooklyn beat St. Louis in two out of three games at Ebbets Field, with Dazzy picking up the lone loss. The Robins then split a four-game series with the Reds with Vance losing a 2–1 classic with Larry Benton of Cincinnati picking up the win. They took the train to Chicago for a four-game series with the second-place Cubs, who were just one game behind the Robins. Robbie held a rare team meeting at noon on June 26, telling them their pennant chances depended on their ability to beat the Cubs, particularly on the road. "Go out and get the jump," he told them. "That's the way to beat them. The Athletics proved that."[4]

The Robins knocked out Charlie Root in the second inning when they got five runs out of an error, a hit batsmen, a double and four singles. Meanwhile, Dazzy mowed down the Cubs, one after the other, giving up a run on a ground ball out with a man on third in the sixth inning. Vance struck out six and walked one in the 7–1 victory that gave the Robins a two-game cushion in the standings.

Luque matched up with Guy Bush the next day in a game the Cubs won 7–5 to even the series but, more important, move them to within one game of Brooklyn with two more to play in the series. When Chicago won the next one 4–2, the two teams were in a virtual tie for first place with Brooklyn having the edge by just seven percentage points. Chicago came back the next day with its ace, Charlie Root, who had gone less than two innings in the opener. He was equal to challenge on this day, beating the Robins 5–1 and pushing them out of first place for the first time since May 29.

The crystal balls were a little hazy on July 4, the traditional day in baseball in which prognosticators often pick the pennant winners based on who was on top on that day. The Robins split a double header with the Giants and remained .002 of a percent ahead of the Cubs in the National League standings. They actually fell out of first place after the first game when New York beat Dazzy in 11 innings, 5–4. Watty Clark pitched well enough in the nightcap to gain the split. Brooklyn won 5–2 to edge back on top of the league.

Dazzy was at it his best on July 9 when the Robins beat the Braves in a double header. That, coupled with a Cubs loss, gave Brooklyn a two-game lead. Vance struck out nine, including Wally Berger three times on just 11 pitches. Babe Herman, still hitting just under .400 for the season, hit his 21st home run to aid the cause. Five days later, the Robins and Vance beat Pittsburgh 12–8 but Dazzy, for the first time all year, displayed the lack of concentration that had put him deep inside Robbie's doghouse in years past.

With Brooklyn ahead 7–1 after five innings, Pittsburgh got two in the sixth, two in the seventh, one in the eighth and two in the ninth. The Robins got four of their own in the sixth and owned a 12–3 lead with three innings to go. The late-inning assault of Vance's pitching allowed them to close the gap to 12–8. Glenn Wright was the hitting star with two doubles and two homers in four at-bats but writers gave equal space to Dazzy's squandering a big lead. "Vance saw an opportunity to do a bit of coasting and took advantage of it," wrote McGowen in the *New York Times*. "The result of Vance's rather lackadaisical lobbing was that the visiting batsmen got 12 of their 14 hits in the final four frames and scored seven runs."

The Robins opened a five-game series with the Cubs on July 16 followed immediately by a five-game series with the Cardinals. Chicago had stumbled a little and was now three games behind Brooklyn. Pittsburgh was in third place, six games out and the Cardinals were fourth, seven behind the leaders. The series opened with the two teams splitting a double header, the Cardinals winning the first game with Pat Malone besting Ray Moss 6–4, but Luque getting the best of Charlie Root in the nightcap with a 5–3 final. From Uncle Robbie's standpoint, it was two games out of the way with the Redbirds gaining no ground and Dazzy Vance waiting in the wings. He would pitch game five and be the safety valve, the stopper, in case the roof caved in before then. The third game was a battle that went 13 innings and forced Robbie to make a strategic change of plans. He brought Vance in from the bullpen in the ninth inning with the score tied 3–3. Dazzy held the Cardinals in check in the ninth, 10th, 11th and 12th innings but weakened in the 13th. The Cardinals scored three and won the game 6–3. Vance took the loss and worked four innings two days before he was scheduled to start.

When Sheriff Blake won a decision over Jumbo Elliott in game four, the Cardinals found themselves one game out with one more to play in the series. On July 19, Dazzy took the mound against Bob Osborn. Babe Herman hit his 22nd home run in the first inning to give the Robins a lead they held until the sixth inning. Hack Wilson hit his 26th home run with a man on in the sixth and a double and single accounted for another run as the Cubs took a 3–1 lead. Then in the eighth, Woody English led off with a single and KiKi Cuyler walked for Chicago. Uncle Robbie pulled Vance in favor of Babe Phelps. He walked Wilson and then got Riggs Stephenson to hit into a force-out at the plate. Charlie Grimm hit a ground ball right back to Phelps, who threw to the plate for the start of an apparent inning-ending double play. But DeBerry threw the ball way over Bissonette's head at first base—the *New York Times* said it was 20 feet over his head—and two more runs scored. The gravity of the error was magnified when the Robins scored three in the bottom of the eighth to cut the lead to 5–4. That turned out to be the final score. The Cubs left town in a virtual tie for first place, four percentage points behind the reeling Robins, losers of four in a row including two in which Dazzy Vance was the losing pitcher.

It was a disheartening series for the Robins—with the last game being the most disappointing. DeBerry's wild throw meant the difference between being tied with the Cubs and being two games up on them. But there was no time to look back. The Cardinals were coming in for five games. As the series with St. Louis opened, the standings showed the Robins barely ahead of the Cubs, followed by the Giants in third place five games out and the Cardinals fourth, six games out. In the opener, the Robins seemed shell-shocked from their series with the Cubs and lost 15–6. But the Giants beat the Cubs so Brooklyn maintained its fractional lead over Chicago. The next day, the two teams split a double header but the Cubs beat the Giants, inching into first place by a half-game. Twenty-four hours later, Hollis "Sloppy" Thurston took the mound for the Robins and pitched the game of his life as Brooklyn won 1–0. Thurston had been an off-season pickup for Robbie and a spot starter. This was the most important game of the year for him and he came through. The Robins closed out the series with a 4–1 victory with Luque getting the win.[5]

On July 24, the Reds got to Dazzy early in the first game of a double header. He was removed after $1\frac{2}{3}$ innings—his earliest exit of the year—after allowing three runs on four hits. Elliott and Moss went the rest of the way and pitched well but Cincinnati escaped with a 4–3 victory. Vance's record fell to 10–10. In the second game, Brooklyn won 9–0 in a game called after five innings because of both rain and darkness. The game took on comic overtones as Brooklyn took the lead 2–0 with two first inning runs. As the weather got worse, the Robins wanted to try to salvage a victory by playing at least 4½ innings. In their half of the fourth inning, with rain coming down and darkness setting in, Bissonette swung at the first pitch and tapped the ball weakly back to the pitcher. He then trotted leisurely down to first base to make sure he was an easy out. The next batter, Wright, swung wildly at three pitches, the final one being well wide of the strike zone. The next batter, second baseman Eddie Moore, laid down a bunt on the first pitch and fell flat on his face as he ran to first base. By this time, of course, the Reds knew what the Robins were trying to do—so they did what they could to prolong the inning. Cincinnati pitcher Benny Frey took his time fielding the bunt and when he threw to first, Joe Stripp, the first baseman intentionally dropped the throw. Moore was safe at first but, in the spirit of moving the game along, got himself picked off. The Reds went down in order in the top of the fifth, making it an official ballgame but the umpires signaled for play to continue. Brooklyn hammered out six hits in the bottom of the fifth and scored seven runs, all this after they had done their best to shorten the game just an inning earlier. The contest was called at the end of five innings with the Robins winning 9–0. Brooklyn's split, coupled with a Chicago win, cut the Robins' league lead to a half-game.

Two days later, Uncle Robbie called for Dazzy to come out of the bullpen to save an 8–5 victory for Babe Phelps over the Reds. He entered the game in the eighth inning at Ebbets Field to a chorus of both jeers and cheers from the fans who were not happy with him for losing his last three outings in the thick of a pennant race. He allowed a hit and then uncorked a wild pitch but got out of the inning. In the ninth, he disposed of the Reds quickly and quietly to preserve Phelps' ninth win of the year and the Robins' half-game lead over the Cubs.

On July 29, the Robins and Dazzy were sailing along with a 3–0 lead over the Braves when they nicked the old Dazzler for a run in the seventh and two in the eighth to tie the game. Watty Clark and Phelps kept the game tied until Boston scored a run in the 10th to win the game 4–3, hanging Babe with his third loss of the year against nine wins. But the Cubs also lost so the Robins maintained their game-and-a-half lead and picked up another game on them by the end of the month. But Vance had failed to win in his last four appearances— two as a starter and two in relief. It was his longest dry spell of the season and, of course, was coming at a critical time for Brooklyn. With two months left in the season, the standings were:

	W–L	Pct.	GB
Brooklyn	60–39	.606	—
Chicago	58–41	.586	2.5
New York	55–44	.556	5
St. Louis	48–49	.495	11
Pittsburgh	48–49	.495	11
Boston	45–53	.454	14.5
Cincinnati	44–52	.458	14.5
Philadelphia	32–63	.337	26

Nobody knew it then — there was no reason to even suspect it — but the Cardinals were about to go on a two-month tear in which they would win 44 of their remaining 57 games. The Robins, meanwhile, dropped 19 of 31 games in August, erasing the 11 game lead they had on the Cardinals and setting up a great stretch drive in September for both teams.

Dazzy got back on the beam on Aug. 3 when he a won a 1–0 thriller over Carl Hubbell and the Giants. The only run of the game scored when Hubbell walked Jake Flowers with the bases loaded in the bottom of the ninth inning. He won again on Aug. 7 when Uncle Robbie once again used him in relief against the Pirates. Jumbo Elliott started for the Robins but weakened early and Robbie summoned Vance in the second inning after pinch-hitting for Jumbo in the top half of the inning. Dazzy pitched seven strong innings and Watty Clark finished it up by pitching the ninth as the Robins won 6–4. They left Pittsburgh and boarded a train for St. Louis for their last western trip of the year. They were a confident bunch, holding what was now a 3½ game lead over the Cubs. That confidence was not diminished when they opened the series with an 11–5 victory with Ray Phelps besting Jesse Haines. That kept them 3½ ahead of the Cubs and the Cardinals were floundering in fourth place with a record of 52–53, 12 games behind the Robins.

But the Cardinals started to light the fire that would blaze for two months. They won the next day, 4–3, in a game highlighted by a Robins triple play that started when Herman made a spectacular catch at the right field wall. Cardinals base runners Chick Hafey and Jim Bottomley were not able to get back in time. But that was all for naught as the Cardinals pushed over a run in the bottom of the ninth off of Freddie Heimlach and Vance, in relief of Clark. Heimlach took the loss but Vance gave up the winning hit. The Cardinals also won the next three, giving them four in a row over the Robins. The fourth win, by a score of 7–6, knocked the Robins into second place because the Cubs had won four in a row while Brooklyn was losing four. All of this occurred on the brink of a four-game series with Chicago at Wrigley Field.

The Cubs and Robins were in a virtual tie for first place when 45,000 fans packed Wrigley Field to watch Sheriff Blake go up against Dazzy Vance. They were not disappointed. Both pitchers went the distance in an 11-inning thriller won by the Cubs. It was the sixth straight win for the Cubs, the fifth straight loss for the Robins. Both streaks ended the next day when the Robins exploded for a 15–5 victory. But they lost the next two games and left town two games behind Chicago. The race was tightening up. New York was in third, 3½ games out and the Cardinals were fourth, eight behind the leaders.

Dazzy won his next start, tossing a shutout at the Pirates on Sunday, Aug. 17. But the Robins fell into a pattern that had plagued them in previous years—a 10-day period where they just didn't hit. Brooklyn lost seven in a row including one shutout, four games where they were held to just one run and two games where they managed to score three. Vance suffered one of the losses, a 4–1 decision to the Reds on Aug. 22. The Robins were now in third place, 4½ behind the Cubs. The Giants had slipped into second, three games out. The Cardinals remained in fourth and were eight behind the Cubs.

By the end of the month, Chicago had opened up a five-game lead on the second place Giants and looked poised to win their second straight championship. Brooklyn was third, six games back and the Cardinals were fourth, 6½ back. But baseball is full of surprises and an amazing thing happened in September. When the Robins lost to the Braves 6–0 on Sept. 2, Dazzy suffered the loss, the Robins fell to fourth place, still six back of the Cubs. But then, just when they appeared to be down and out, Uncle Robbie's troops won 11 consecutive games to reclaim first place on Sept. 14. The amazing turnaround happened like this:

Sept. 6 — Robins 22, Philadelphia 8. Winning pitcher Luque; Sept. 7 — Robins 5, New York 2. Winning pitcher Vance; Sept. 8 — Robins 8, Philadelphia 2. Winning pitcher Moss (first game); Sept. 8 — Robins 11, Philadelphia 4. Winning pitcher Elliott; Sept. 9 — Robins 3, Chicago 0. Winning pitcher Phelps; Sept. 10 — Robins 6, Chicago 0. Winning pitcher Luque; Sept. 11 — Robins 2, Chicago 1. Winning pitcher Vance; Sept. 12 — Robins 7, Cincinnati 3. Winning pitcher Moss; Sept. 13 — Robins 4, Cincinnati 3. Winning pitcher Phelps; Sept. 14 — Robins 8, Cincinnati 3. Winning pitcher Thurston; Sept. 15 — Robins 13, Cincinnati 5. Winning pitcher Moss.

Obviously, the three-game sweep of the Cubs was crucial. Vance was the winner in one of them, striking out 13 and giving up just five hits in a 2–1 victory. One of the hits was Hack Wilson's 48th home run.

While the Robins were winning 11 straight between Sept. 6 and Sept. 15, the Cubs were 3–6, the Giants were 4–6 and the Cardinals were 8–2. That created a turnaround in the standings so that the Robins were once again on top — by 6 percentage points over the Cardinals and 10 percentage points over the Cubs. The top three teams were separated by a game and a half in the standings with two weeks to play.

	W–L	Pct.	GB
Brooklyn	84–60	.583	—
St. Louis	82–60	.577	1
Chicago	82–61	.573	1.5
New York	78–65	.545	5.5
Pittsburgh	74–68	.521	9
Boston	67–78	.462	17.5
Cincinnati	55–85	.393	27
Philadelphia	49–94	.343	34.5

The schedule makers couldn't have envisioned this kind of pennant race when they set up a three-game series between the Robins and the Redbirds beginning Tuesday, Sept. 16, at Ebbets Field while the Cubs took on the Giants at the Polo Grounds at the same time. And nobody could have predicted what happened to the Cardinals on the eve of the series. The Cardinals had a righthanded pitcher named Flint Rhem, who won 20 games for their 1926 pennant winners and had consistently won in double figures for them. But Rhem was as good with highballs off the field as he was with fastballs on the field. He rivaled Grover Cleveland Alexander, his teammate for three years, as the biggest drinker in the National League. And on the night of Sept. 15, the night before the Cardinals' biggest series of the year against the first-place Robins, Rhem disappeared. He was not in the hotel all night and nobody saw him until he showed up at the ballpark moments before game time on Sept. 16 looking bleary-eyed, disheveled and hungover. He said he had been standing in front of the hotel the night before when a taxicab pulled up. Two men got out of the cab and motioned for him to come over to them. Then they pushed him into the cab at gunpoint. Rhem said he was driven to some place in New Jersey where he was forced to guzzle several cups of whiskey. New York newspapers played up the story as possibly an attempt by gamblers to favor the Robins. The Cardinals had the police investigate but Rhem could not identify where he was taken in New Jersey. As for the St. Louis writers—columnist J. Roy Stockton, in recalling the incident years later, said, "Flint says he was kidnapped. Who am I to spoil his good story?"[6]

For Brooklyn, the man Uncle Robbie wanted on the mound for the opening game of the series was the pitcher he still considered his ace — Dazzy Vance. Dazzy had come on strong of late, beating the Giants and the Cubs in his last two starts. He was 16–13 on the year. Cardinals manager Gabby Street went with Wild Bill Hallahan, who had been with St. Louis for five years and was having his finest season. Wild Bill was not a misnomer as a nickname. In 1930, he led the National League in both strikeouts and walks. In his 12-year major league career, he walked more batters than he struck out in six of those seasons. The night before the big game, Hallahan slammed a car door on his pitching hand. He didn't break any bones but had a blister on one of his fingers. With Rhem nowhere to be seen and Hallahan with a sore pitching hand, the Robins' chances for victory increased before either team had even taken the field.

When Vance took the mound, it was evident, as usual, that he was not concerned with his physical appearance. Indeed, he may well have intended for his looks to be a distraction. His uniform shirt was loose and drooped below the belt of his pants. The seat of his pants was black as if he had been sitting in a mud puddle. The sleeve on the undershirt of his pitching arm was tattered with long slits that fluttered when he went into his windup and fired the ball toward the plate. It was classic Dazzy.

Westbrook Pegler wrote that Vance appeared to be the essence of "shiftlessness" and someone to be thought of as a "no-good and a loafer." He described Dazzy's uniform as a "mildewed and tattered get-up" that was all an affectation to hide the fact that "a wise old noodle may ratiocinate beneath a soiled and sweaty cap and that rags are royal raiment when worn by certain parties."[7]

In the sixth inning, Old Daz pulled off a play that gave credence to Pegler's reference to the "wise old noodle" and showed beyond doubt that he was in full concentration mode on this afternoon. Sparky Adams led off with a base hit and got around to third on an infield out and a long outfield fly. Vance worked the count to 0–and–2 on Chick Hafey. The next pitch, by conventional thinking, would be a "waste pitch" out of the strike zone. As Dazzy went into his windup, Adams took off for the plate and had a terrific jump on the play. Vance saw him out of the corner of his eye but could not do anything to stop him without balking. So he fired the pitch at Hafey who could not get out of the way in time. The ball hit him. The result was he went to first base as a hit batsman and Adams had to go back to third. George Watkins then popped out to end the inning.

Vance said later that incident with Hafey was one of only three times in his entire career that he purposely hit a batter — and he wasn't angry at any of them. He said he hit KiKi Cuyler of the Pirates because the Pittsburgh bench had been needling him all day and that Cuyler just happened to be in the batter's box when Ol'Daz had had enough. The other time he hit someone intentionally was in a game against the Giants. He plunked George Kelly right after Irish Meusel had hit a home run off of him.[8]

For the first six innings of the fateful game against the Cardinals, Hallahan was even more effective than his more famous counterpart. In fact, he retired the first 18 Robins in order and had a perfect game going into the seventh. Dazzy had scattered a hit here and there but the game remained scoreless with three innings to play. Hallahan made it 20 in a row by retiring the first two batters in the seventh. Then Babe Herman slapped a ball back to the pitcher, and Wild Bill, who hadn't walked a batter all game, picked that moment to throw wildly. First baseman Jim Bottomley couldn't handle the toss and the Robins had their first base runner on Hallahan's error. He settled down quick and got Glenn Wright to hit an easy fly ball to center to end the inning.

Harvey "Gink" Hendrick broke up the no-hitter with a single in the eighth inning of what was still a scoreless tie. Hallahan picked him off, a miscue that was magnified when Mickey Finn followed with a single. But Finn tried to stretch it into a double and barreled into shortstop Charlie Gelbert as the throw came in. There was a powerful collision between the two men. Gelbert fell to the ground and dropped the ball. Finn walked around in a daze. But nobody had called time out. Frankie Frisch picked up the ball and tagged Finn for the third out of the inning. The oddity was that Hallahan faced only three men in the inning though two of them had singled. It was a 0–0 game going into the ninth inning and when both teams went scoreless, the battle moved on to extra innings.

In the tenth, Andy High, once a teammate of Dazzy's, pinch-hit for Gelbert and led off with a double. Hallahan sacrificed him to third. Taylor Douthit then singled home what proved to be the winning run. But the Robins went down fighting. Glenn Wright opened the bottom of the tenth with a double. Hallahan pitched carefully to Bissonette and walked him. Hendrick sacrificed them to second and third. Flowers batted for Finn and drew an intentional walk.

Al Lopez came up to the plate with all sorts of possibilities facing him. A base hit could win the game for the Robins. A sacrifice fly would tie it. An out would keep the hope alive for the next hitter — Vance — or most likely a pinch hitter. Lopez hit a sharp ground ball to Adams at deep short. He knocked the ball down, then retrieved it and flipped to Frisch for the force-out at second. Frisch's throw to Bottomley at first was in time to nail Lopez. Double play. Game over. In retirement many years later, Vance said the 1–0 loss to the Cardinals was the toughest of his career. Uncle Robbie said after the game, "It took Al exactly 15 minutes to get down to first base."

The loss snapped the Robins' 11-game winning streak and put them in a virtual tie with the Cardinals with St. Louis ahead by 1 percentage point. But the loss seemed to take the heart out of the Robins and at the same time invigorated the Cardinals. St. Louis won the next two games 5–3 with Sylvester Johnson beating Dolph Luque and 4–3 with Burleigh

Grimes the winner over Ray Phelps. Brooklyn's tailspin continued with two losses to Pittsburgh and one to the Giants and one to the Phillies. The loss to Philadelphia, their seventh in a row following the 11-game winning streak, plunged them into fourth place where they would remain the rest of the season. It was a heart-breaking end to a heart-throbbing season for the Robins and their fans.

But much credit was due the Cardinals who were 48–49 going into August, 11 games out of first place. They compiled a 44–13 record from that point on, including a 21–4 mark in September. And they had accomplished it with a couple of Robins cast-offs, High and Grimes.[9]

The Robins finished at 86–68, winning 16 more games than they had in 1929 and they moved up two places in the standings, from sixth to fourth. Still, the feeling of being in first place with two weeks to go and then seeing it slip away left them with a double-edged set of emotions— huge disappointment and yet a determination to come back next year and finish the job. The 1–0 loss to the Cardinals was the breaking point of 1930. Had Al Lopez' ground ball been a foot or two to the left of Adams, who knows what would have happened the rest of the season.

Vance finished at 17–15, but once again his record was deceiving. In 11 of his 32 decisions, the Robins scored two runs or less. His 2.61 earned run average led the National League and he was tied with Charlie Root of the Cubs for most shutouts with four. He was first in the league in fewest hits allowed per nine innings, first in fewest walks per nine innings and second only to Hallahan in strikeouts. His 17 wins were fourth best in the National League.

Joseph Cardello, a member of the Society for American Baseball Research, calls Vance's 1930 season one of the 10 best in baseball history despite the 17–15 record. Cardello points out that in the two-month period between April 25 and June 26, Dazzy had an earned run average of 1.68 with nine complete games—and it would have been 1.16 except for one game in which he gave up seven runs in six innings.

In a year for the hitters, when Hack Wilson hit 56 home runs and drove in 191 runs, and when the National League as a whole hit .303, Vance's league-leading earned run average of 2.61 was well ahead of the second-place finisher, Carl Hubbell of the Giants at 3.87. That remains the largest difference between the top leaders in earned run average in major league history.

"At first glance it's hard to understand how anyone with a 17–15 record could be compared with Ron Guidry in 1978, Walter Johnson in

1912, Grover Cleveland Alexander in 1915, Lefty Grove in 1931, Dazzy Vance himself in 1924, Bob Gibson in 1968 or any other legendary season you'd care to mention. But the statistics are revealing."[10]

The Robins had a good year because they finally achieved a balance of good hitting and good pitching. The acquisition of Dolph Luque prior to the start of the season paid off as the Cuban won 14 and lost only 8. Ray Phelps was 14–7, Jumbo Elliott was 10–7 and Watty Clark compiled a 13–13 mark and would have been credited with six saves if that statistic had been kept in those days.

Babe Herman had a fabulous year, hitting .393 with 35 home runs and 135 RBIs. He didn't lead the league in any of those departments because Bill Terry hit .401 and Hack Wilson hit 56 home runs and drove in 191.

Glenn Wright had the kind of year everyone expected of him, hitting .321 with 22 homers and 126 RBIs. Bisonnette hit .336 with 16 home runs and 113 runs batted in. The lowest batting average among the starters was Finn's at .278. Wally Gilbert hit .294, Rube Bressler hit .299, Lopez hit .309 and Frederick hit .334.

The 75 days that the Robins spent in first place gave everyone, including the front office, a taste of what being on top was like — and they all wanted more of it. More than 1 million fans had jammed into Ebbets Field during the season and there was every reason to believe that more would come next year — if there was room for them. McKeever and York had begun a plan to expand the bleachers. Now they wanted the work to speed up. The new seats would not be ready before the season started — but they'd in place for the World Series, if there was one.

As winter settled in, so did Dazzy Vance, ready to partake in one of his favorite pastimes next to golf and fishing. He was going to do what he always did — hold out for more money — for as the Dazzler approached his 40th birthday, for all his aches and pains, his hobo appearance on the mound and slightly less zip on his fastball, he was still the best pitcher on the Robins' staff. He was still the man Robbie wanted on the mound when the money was on the line. As spring training of 1931 approached, the money was on the line again — and Ole Daz wanted his share again.

XI

"He was what you call superstitious"

When Dazzy Vance struck out seven Chicago Cubs in a row on Aug. 1, 1924 ... and when he fanned 17 Cubs on July 20, 1925 ... and when he threw a one-hitter against the Phillies and followed that up with a no-hitter against them on Sept. 8 and Sept. 13, 1925 ... and when he got caught in the base-running gaffe where three men wound up on third on Aug. 15, 1926 ... and when Dazzy lost the 1–0 heart-breaker to Wild Bill Hallahan on Sept. 16, 1930, that was the turning point in the pennant race ... all of these games had a common thread. Dazzy's family was not there. He didn't want them there any time he pitched.

Dorothy Vance Williams, Dazzy's daughter, said, "He was what you call superstitious. He really didn't think it was appropriate for us to be in the stands while he pitched. So, on days when he started, we couldn't go to the games."

The same family rule held true when Dazzy was summoned from the bullpen, said Mrs. Williams, who was born in Memphis the year before her father made it to the big leagues. "During the times he would come in during the middle of a game, we were told ahead of time that he was going to come in and pitch soon," she said. When they got the signal, that meant it was time to leave. "We just got up and left the stadium. It became quite natural after a while," she said.[1]

Edythe Vance had three seats reserved for every Robins home game and used them as often as she could, except of course when Dazzy was pitching. She and Dorothy would sit behind the visitors' dugout so they had a clear view of the Robins in their dugout. "I'll never forget the Brooklyn fans," she said many years after her husband retired. "I loved them. They were enthusiastic. They'd cheer loudly and they'd razz the home team and players when they played poorly. The players enjoyed it all, even the razzing"—this from a woman who didn't follow baseball or particularly like it when she and Dazzy were courting in 1916.[2]

Many baseball personalities made their way to the Vance home in Florida during the winter months. Babe Ruth was a frequent visitor and Dizzy Dean and little Dorothy Vance enjoyed each other's company. "To me, these guys were just people my mother and father knew. I really didn't know any better," said Dorothy. "I grew up with the attitude that these players were just acquaintances of my parents and this was the way they made their living—by playing baseball."[3]

Bernie Neis, a reserve outfielder with the Robins from 1920 through 1924, was a good friend of the Vances and helped Dazzy manage some of the property he bought in Homosassa and worked as an unofficial hunting and fishing guide for guests, including the visiting ballplayers such as Ruth and Dean.

While much of Dazzy's professional life was quite public, he kept his family life separate from his baseball life. There is little record of his home life except for an occasional photograph published in a newspaper—such as one of him helping his wife in the kitchen of their home in Omaha in 1924 and another, also in Omaha, of him shoveling snow outside a cigar store he owned.

Edythe Carmony Vance was an intelligent, stately, well-read woman described as "very ladylike" and who didn't know a whit about baseball and couldn't have cared less when she met Charles Arthur Vance when he was playing ball in Nebraska. The two courted for about a year and then were married on March 7, 1917. A son, Donald Brewster Vance, was born later that year. Dorothy, the second child, was born in 1921. Tragedy struck the Vance home in 1920 when Donald, not yet three years old, stumbled and fell into a cauldron of hot soap his mother was making. He died from his injuries.[4]

The family traveled and moved often as Dazzy's early career took him from one city to another. Donald was born in Omaha. Dorothy was born in Memphis. In 1925, the Vances started living part of the year in Homosassa, Florida, not far from the Robins' spring training camp in Clearwater. Eventually, Dazzy purchased a 120-acre estate in Homosassa and, if that wasn't enough proof that he wanted to make that a permanent home, he called the place 'Dun Rovin.'"[5]

There is ample evidence that Dazzy loved children and loved being around them. Frequently, he took part in Robins promotions in which he and other players appeared at department stores for autograph-signing sessions back in the days when autographs were free and ballplayers welcomed the attention they got. Also, in the off-season, Dazzy helped with boys' baseball programs in the Homosassa–Clearwater area well into his retirement. At Ebbets Field, it was a familiar sight after a game to see Dazzy emerge from the clubhouse in street clothes, with a cigar lodged in the corner of his mouth, and throngs of kids waiting to get his autograph. Sometimes, Edythe and Dorothy smiled and waited patiently as their husband and father tried to accommodate all the little folks who had waited for him to come out.

Perhaps Dazzy was motivated by the memory of the son he lost at such a young age and poured affection out to little boys like he would have to his own son. Or maybe it was just his good-hearted, fun-loving spirit — the sort of thing teammates experienced with his kangaroo courts and opponents endured with his fabled tattered sleeve — that Dazzy was able to apply to the younger generation. Whatever, that spirit was evident.

Dorothy said her father loved interacting with kids. "Dad always liked being around children," she said. "He always gave away a lot of autographs and he would sit down and talk with any of the kids who were interested in baseball."

She said one time he even arranged for a young boy to move in with the Vance family for a while because Dazzy thought the boy had potential as a ballplayer and wanted to work with him. The youngster's family consented and the boy stayed at the Vance home. "That's just the way he was," said Dorothy. "If someone had an interest in the game, Dad would go out of his way to help out."[6]

One of the boys he helped was a lad by the name of Gene Allen who recalled this experience with Vance. He said he had a blister on a finger when he was pitching a game for Crystal River High School that Vance attended. "When the game was over, he walked over to me and said, 'Young man, I'd like to ask you a question. Why did you throw all your pitches with this finger up in the air?'" Allen said he was stunned by the attention he was getting from one of the all-time great pitchers. "I just looked down and saw this World Series ring — 1934 St. Louis Cardinals — and said (to myself) 'This man is the most.'" The two developed such a relationship that Allen later pitched for Vance's West Citrus (Fla.) semipro team and, with Dazzy's help, he got a tryout with the Detroit Tigers.

"Dazzy was always helping guys get tryouts. I don't know anyone else who could have trained me where I could have gotten as much out of the game as I did with Dazzy," said Allen. "When Dazzy Vance spoke, people in the baseball world stopped and listened."[7]

Edythe Vance said Dazzy had compassion for youngsters and it made for difficult times when kids had the dream but not the skills to be good ballplayers. "We had boys come here from all over," she said, referring to the couple's home in Homosassa Springs. "It was a sad thing to see boys who wanted desperately to succeed but didn't have the talent. They were broken-hearted when they couldn't make the grade. On the other hand, there were boys who had the talent but just drifted along, not using it," said Mrs. Vance.[8]

As the 1931 baseball season approached, a story was reported throughout the country about a 17-year-old kid in Chattanooga, Tenn., who got some help from Dazzy Vance. The youngster's name was Jackie Mitchell and the story was about Mitchell signing with the Chattanooga Lookout minor league baseball team. The unusual aspect of the situation was that Jackie was a girl. She would be given every opportunity to make the team, said club owner Joe Engel. The only special provision is that her mother would travel with her and act as chaperone.

Jackie credited her early interest in baseball to a fellow who used to be her next door neighbor in Memphis ten years earlier — Dazzy Vance. "Dazzy Vance taught me how to throw the ball," she said. Her father agreed. Joe S. Mitchell said, "Vance took quite a liking to my daughter. He used to show her some of the tricks of the trade."

Dazzy's friendship with the little girl was reported throughout the country when the youngster signed with Memphis. Team owner Engel was experienced enough to know when there were big bucks to be made. He arranged for Mitchell's debut to be in an exhibition game on April 1, 1931, when the Lookouts played the New York Yankees.

When Babe Ruth learned a girl would be pitching to him, he was dismayed. "I don't know what's going to happen if they begin to let women into baseball," he said. "Of course they will never make good because they are too delicate. It would kill them to play every day." He paused and then said, "By the way, how big is she?" He was told she was five foot, seven inches. He yawned and said, "Well, I don't know what things are coming to."[9]

On the big night of April 2, 1931, before a sell-out crowd, Mitchell faced the Yankees and struck out both Babe Ruth and Lou Gehrig. (Ruth gallantly took three strikes and Gehrig swung wildly at three pitches.) Mitchell's career as a baseball player did not reach great heights but she did play for the House of David team two years later. Once again, the family credited Vance for his early encouragement. Mitchell said Dazzy was impressed at how straight she could throw a ball for someone as young as she was. That, and the fact that she was a lefthander, made him think she had a future if she worked at it, she said.

When the news was reported that Mitchell had signed with the House of David, many of the stories recounted her appearance against the Yankees two years earlier. For her family, reality may have set in with the passage of time. When her father was asked if he thought Babe Ruth struck out on purpose against her, he replied, "I don't know." But they thanked Dazzy Vance every chance they got for the encouraging words and direction he had given to Mitchell.[10]

Not every child was thrilled with Dazzy. He liked to tell the story about the day in Brooklyn when he was walking near the grandstand during batting practice. A boy of about 10 years old shouted at him, "Hey, Dazzy, throw me a ball." Dazzy said he didn't have a ball with him so he just kept walking, pretending that he didn't hear the youngster. "Hey, Dazzy. Please throw me a ball," the lad pleaded. Dazzy said he looked around and there were no balls on the ground near him. So again he kept on walking. Before he got out of earshot, he heard the young man shout at him again. "Hey, Dazzy," the kid yelled, "I hope the Giants beat your brains out."

XII

"They do the unexpected and the unexplainable"

Just about the time Jackie Mitchell was pitching for the Chattanooga Lookouts and crediting Dazzy Vance with teaching her some tricks of the trade, Dazzy was holding forth on some of his other tricks of the trade — holding forth and holding out — for a bigger salary in 1931.

Dazzy had proven to be a lot of things over the years — he could talk with the best of them, drink with the best of them, pull pranks with the best of them and certainly pitch with the best of them. He was an expert marksman, an excellent pool player and was probably good enough to be a professional golfer. But the Ol' Dazzler was also a shrewd business-man and he proved it just about every spring by calling the Robins' bluff.

Thus, on Feb. 24, 1931, Vance made the short trip over to Clearwater from Homosassa Springs to join the other players in spring training. He had not signed a contract yet and therefore could not work out with his teammaters. But the *Washington Post* reported, "Mr. Vance is not a malignant holdout. His is a very mild case," and that he was expected to sign soon.[1]

He would be joining a club with a little different cast of characters as the Robins' brain trust worked during the winter to bring Brooklyn a championship in 1931. The biggest acquisition was Francis Joseph "Lefty" O'Doul, a hard-hitting outfielder with the Phillies who hit .398 and .383 the past two seasons. Infielder Fresco Thompson came along in the deal. O'Doul did not come cheap. The Robins parted with Clise Dudley, Hal Lee, Jumbo Elliott and cash. Robbie wanted O'Doul and Herman to bat back to back in the lineup.

Another key acquisition was pitcher Joe Ben Shaute, a left-hander who had been released after eight years with the Cleveland Indians where he had been a 20-game winner in 1924. Shaute fit in nicely with Robbie's preference for working with veteran pitchers to try to squeeze one or two more good years out of them. Westbrook Pegler called Shaute another one of Robbie's "salvage jobs" and said Shaute was released by the Indians after coming down with a "headache in his throwing arm."[2]

Two other hurlers would get the chance to make the major league club. One was Clyde "Pea Ridge" Day, a champion hog caller from Pea Ridge, Ark., whose minor league resume looked a lot like Dazzy's, skipping from one town to another trying to make the grade. He would have fit in well a few years earlier with the Daffiness Boys because Pea Ridge was loud, eccentric and no one had to ask him twice to demonstrate his hog calling ability.[3]

The other pitcher with great potential was Van Lingle Mungo, a 19-year-old who could throw as hard as any Brooklyn pitcher, past or present, including Dazzy Vance, but had trouble getting the ball over the plate. Robins scouts thought that if he could ever find his control, he could be one of the all-time greats. With Uncle Robbie, the ex-catcher, as his mentor, Mungo looked like he was a project worth taking a chance on.

Meanwhile, on April 1, Vance ended his holdout by signing for $23,000, thus ending about a two-week period in which the veteran hurler played golf while his teammates worked out. Vance posed for pictures with an obviously delighted Wilbert Robinson and assured the press that "everything is OK." The annual ritual was over — Dazzy's name was on the dotted line.

As the 1931 baseball season approached, Brooklyn fans were excited, and so were the writers who covered them. John Kieran, a columnist for the *New York Times*, wrote that the Robins had the most colorful team in either league. He described the cast of characters:

Babe Herman — "a one-man show all by himself ... who got his batting style from slapping paint on battleships."

Dazzy Vance — "the Homo of Homosassa, an itinerant golfer and rare raconteur. He pitches too."[4]

Alfonzo Lopez — "the catcher who rolls his own cigars and can, upon request, sing to a Spanish guitar."

Pea Ridge Day — "the hog caller from the Ozarks." A story that made the rounds about Pea Ridge was the time when he was a young ballplayer for Cincinnati and staying at a fancy hotel for the first time. He got into bed but was bothered by a light coming from a clothes closet. The door to the closet was slightly ajar. Ridge did not know it but the light came on automatically when the door was open and went off automatically when it closed. He got out of bed and searched the closet in vain for the light switch. Finally, he told his amused roommate Art Nehf, "Well drat it, let it burn. I ain't paying for it." He then slammed the closet door and, of course, the light went off.[5]

Uncle Wilbert Robinson —"one of the biggest figures in baseball, measured in any direction."

Despite all the pre-season ballyhoo, the Robins stumbled out of the gate, opening the season with a four game series at Boston and losing all four games—convincingly. After losing 7–4 and 9–3, Dazzy made his 1931 debut and pitched reasonably well until Charley Wilson touched him for a three-run homer in the seventh inning. The Braves won 7–4. It wouldn't have been that close except that Babe Herman also had a three-run homer. The Robins opened their home season against the Phillies and dropped a 6–4 decision in 10 innings. They finally got a win behind Joe Shaute, the veteran they picked up from Cleveland as the Robins won 10–5.

On April 20, Dazzy received word that his mother, Sarah Elizabeth Ritchey Vance, had died in Omaha, at the age of 79. He left the team to be with his family and did not pitch again until May 3. By that time the Robins had lost 10 out of 14 games and were in seventh place, six games behind the league-leading Cardinals. A record crowd of 35,316 packed Ebbets Field to watch Dazzy match up with Carl Hubbell, the great Giants pitcher. The Robins won 4–3, getting one of their runs without a hit or an error. In the sixth inning, Fresco Thompson walked, stole second and dashed all the way home on an infield ground out. Dazzy picked up his first win of the year and the Robins had a modest three-game winning streak. In Vance's next time out, the Pirates beat him 4–3 in a game at Ebbets Field in which Dazzy was booed by the crowd — not for his pitching but for coming up to bat when the crowd thought a pinch hitter was in order. When Dazzy popped out, the boos got louder. The only consolation was that only about 5,000 people were at the game, compared to the 35,000 in his last start.

On May 22, Dazzy picked up his second win but it was costly. In the ninth inning of a game at Philadelphia, Pinky Whitney, the Phillies' third baseman, whistled a line drive right back up the middle that caught Vance defenseless. The ball hit him flush in the face, creating an ugly bruise and about a two-inch cut on his cheek. He was forced to leave the game. Jack Quinn came in from the bullpen to preserve Dazzy's second victory.

It was not known immediately if he would miss a start because of his facial injuries but they didn't turn out to be any more than a cut and a bruise. So he was back out on the mound in his regular turn on May 29 and mowed down the Giants 3–2. It was a significant win for Uncle Robbie's boys. It not only showed that Vance was fully recovered from his injury, a key development if the Robins were going to be a contender. The win was the first of what would be a five-game winning streak for Brooklyn that would bring them to the .500 mark for the first time all season at 20–20. Since their 2–10 start, the Robins were 18–10 and showing signs of being the feisty crew that nearly won the pennant the year before.

But the Robins lost their next two games to the Cubs, including a 9–8 decision in which Dazzy took the loss, evening his record at 3–3. At Cincinnati four days later, Vance pitched well but was not around at the end when the Reds beat the Robins 2–1 in 11 innings. The Robins continued to draw big crowds at home. More than 30,000 were on hand on June 18 when Brooklyn split a double header with the Cubs. Dazzy won the first game, won by the Robins 7–5, in which Vance gave up 11 hits but stayed out of big trouble by also fanning 11. Luque was the loser in the second game as the Cubs won 8–0. Vance picked up a win in relief on June 21 when he came in for Ray Phelps in the ninth inning with the Robins ahead by a run. He gave up two singles, the second of which scored the tying run. He got the win when the Robins pushed across a run in the bottom of the ninth.

Four days later, he lost a heart-breaker, 1–0, to the Cardinals. The winning run scored on a steal of home by George Watkins in what Roscoe McGowen described as "one of the most extraordinary double steals in major league history." Dazzy had a perfect game going after six innings but the Robins had not scored off Paul Derringer either. Vance retired the first two batters in the seventh inning, making it 20 in a row for the game. Then Watkins, with two strikes on him, surprised everyone by laying down a bunt. Third baseman Charlie Gilbert raced in, fielded the ball cleanly, but slipped as he started to make his throw. The no-hitter was gone. Jim Bottomley then hit a clean single to center and Watkins went all the way around to third. Dazzy had a habit, when there was a runner on first, of lobbing the ball over a couple of times and then firing it over a third time to try to throw off the runner's timing. He did the same thing on this day. On his second lob over to first, Watkins broke for the plate. By the time Bissonette could get the ball to catcher

Lopez, Watkins had slid in with the first, and as it turned out, the only run of the game.

But all in all, the Robins had a good month. They had put together 3 five-game winning streaks in June and early July and were eight games over .500 at 40–32 after winning a double header from the Giants on the Fourth of July. Vance was 7–4 and was consistently being matched against the best pitchers in the league. In three of his starts, his mound opponent was a future Hall of Famer — Carl Hubbell (twice) and Eppa Rixey. The National League standings at the end of play on July 4 looked like this:

Team	W–L	Pct.	GB
St. Louis	45–27	.625	___
New York	40–29	.580	3.5
Brooklyn	40–32	.556	5
Chicago	38–31	.551	5.5
Boston	36–36	.500	9
Philadelphia	31–40	.437	13.5
Pittsburgh	28–41	.406	15.5
Cincinnati	26–48	.351	20

Toward the end of June, Kieran in the *New York Times*, took a look at the races in both leagues and surmised the Athletics were continuing to win, and the only sign of cracking was the wisecracking of their players, particularly Jimmy Dykes and Mickey Cochrane. In the National League, the Cardinals were the best, he said, with the Giants and Cubs chasing them. He expected the Robins to move up and be contenders, and, by the Fourth of July, they had moved up, in third place and a half-game ahead of the Cubs. But the Robins, who had played well the past couple of seasons, still had not shaken the image of being free spirits. "They always add plenty of fun to the race," wrote Kieran. "They do the unexpected and unexplainable…. More power to the jolly Robins. They liven up the game."[6]

Dazzy lost his next two starts 4–3 to Boston and 3–2 to St. Louis. On July 18, he was the winning pitcher in an 8–6 win over the Cubs — but he wasn't the big story of the day. That honor went to Jack Quinn, the 46-year-old relief pitcher who came in for Dazzy in the ninth, had bases-loaded jams in the ninth, tenth and 11th innings and still won the game. In the ninth, all three Cubs outs were on plays at the plate. Five days later, Vance took his worst pounding of the year, giving up eight runs before he was mercifully removed in the fourth inning of what turned out to be a 17–6 pasting at the hands of the Pirates at Forbes Field. Dazzy was now 0–3 in his last four starts and was 7–7 for the year with a team that was 10 games above .500. It was an unusual position for the Ole Dazzler whose winning percentage had surpassed his team's winning percentage every year he had been in the major leagues. He got back on the winning track with a 5–0 shutout of the Reds and then got a no-decision in a game at Philadelphia where he hurt his hand in a freak accident. He swung and hit a pitch from Clise Dudley in the third inning but broke his bat in the process. He also hurt his hand, either by the bat splintering or scratching him with the jagged part of it. In any case, he pitched another inning before removing himself from the game. The Robins ended July in fourth place, with Chicago sneaking ahead of them into third.

In seven starts, Vance was 2–3 for the month and 8–7 for the year — not bad for a 40-year-old but way below par for him. Dazzy thought he should be a 20-game winner every year and wanted to be paid that way. The Robins paid him that way every year with the expectation that he would achieve that goal. Going into August of 1931, the Robins were still in the race but it was obvious that Ole Daz would be lucky to win 15 games.

Sportswriters were paying more attention to Paul Derringer, a pitcher for the Cardinals, who was being compared to Vance because of his overhand delivery, hopping fastball and sharp breaking curve. Derringer, a 25-year-old rookie, was on his way to winning 18 games for the Redbirds in the start of a career that would see him win 223 games for the Cardinals, Reds and Cubs. In 1931, he credited much of his success to Burleigh Grimes, the former Robin who was now with the Cardinals and who Derringer said worked with him by the hour in spring training to teach him the tricks of the trade.

Meanwhile, in the American League, writers were kidding that Connie Mack, the A's manager, was the best outfielder in the American League. Mack, of course, was long past the days of putting a glove on and going out in the field. Instead, he stayed in the dugout, wearing a business suit and hat like he always did, and would position his outfield by motioning with a rolled up scorecard. He was regarded as the best in the business at having his outfielders properly placed, making their defensive tasks easier.

The Robins lost eight out of 10 games in mid–August to drop to just one game above .500. They remained in fourth place but were now

15 games out of first and the pennant race was quickly getting away from them. Dazzy lost to the Giants 3–2, then beat the Braves 4–2. An 8–5 loss to the Cardinals was the Robins' fourth defeat in a row. When he beat the Cubs in a 5–3 decision on Aug. 19, he brought his season record up to 11–8 and now, despite his age, was the winningest pitcher on the Robins' staff.

The Robins played well the rest of the way but had dug too deep a hole for themselves in August. They finished at 79–73, good for fourth place in the National League but not good considering the high hopes of management and players at the start of the year. Watty Clark finished strong and had a 14–10 record. Shaute, who had come over from Cleveland, was 11–8. Vance took some hard-luck losses and was 11–13. Lefty O'Doul led the hitters with a .336 average. Herman had an off-year for him. His .313 average was 80 points lower than his 1930 average. Bissonette hit only 12 home runs.

Once again, Vance's record was deceiving. Of his 13 losses, three were by scores of 3–2, two were by scores of 2–1, two were by scores of 4–3 and one was by a score of 4–2. With another clutch hit here and there by the Robins, that 11–13 record could have been 19–5. But it wouldn't have mattered much in the standings. Brooklyn finished 21 games behind the first place Cardinals.

The big question now was whether Uncle Robbie was finished. In the compromise worked out during the front office turmoil, he had been relieved of his front office duties but was allowed to stay on as manager for two years—and that time was now up.

At the end of August, when the Robins' fate seemed sealed, Westbrook Pegler speculated on Robinson's fate in his syndicated column. Noting the manager's popularity with the press and the fans despite presiding over mediocre ball clubs for many years, Pegler wrote: "If he should happen to lose his job, in spite of the most insistent newspaper claque that ever befriended a man with small troubles, he will have to admit that press and public gave him a long hearing and a square deal."

Pegler said Robinson's tenure with the Robins, almost 18 years, was remarkable considering the club hadn't won a pennant in a decade and the manager had been fussing with the front office, and vice versa, for almost that long. "Uncle Wilbert isn't really a quick manager, and on his record and ability alone, without his personal character to warm the cold facts, might have been unjobbed a long time ago," wrote Pegler. The thing that saved him, said the writer, was how Uncle Robbie had endeared himself to the fans of Brooklyn — and they to him.[7]

The ax fell on Oct. 23 when the Brooklyn board of directors voted unanimously not to renew Uncle Robbie's contract and instead, offer the managerial job to Brooklyn coach Max Carey, the former great outfielder of the Pittsburgh Pirates. Robinson received the news in a telegram sent to his winter home in Dover Hall, Ga.

Kieran in the *New York Times* bade farewell to Uncle Robbie. "Like Falstaff, he was not only witty himself but the cause of wit in others," he wrote. "He was not an intellectual. He knew baseball as the spotted setter knows the secrets of quail hunting, by instinct and experience."

Kieran said Robinson had been involved in baseball for 50 years and the separation would not be easy. He concluded, "No man can walk out on a lifetime of associations without a wrenching of something in the region of the heart."[8]

As for Carey and the Dodgers management, one of the first questions they had to answer among themselves was what to do with Dazzy Vance.

XIII

Days of Diminishing Dazzle

Maximillian Carnarius grew up in Terre Haute, Ind., and was preparing to be a Lutheran minister when he decided that baseball was his calling. He shortened his name to Max Carey and was one of the premier outfielders in the National League from 1911 to 1929. Most of those years were with Pittsburgh but when the Pirates unloaded some players in 1926 when they challenged the authority of Fred Clarke over manager Bill McKechnie, Carey came over to the Robins. He was a Pirates coach in 1930 but then stayed out of baseball for a year, tending to business interests in St. Louis. When he accepted the job as Brooklyn's manager, he faced two immediate challenges: he was following in the footsteps of a legend, Wilbert Robinson, and was working for an organization that wanted a winner and wanted it soon. The ball club was once again the Dodgers—a name they never officially dropped when they were known unofficially and affectionately as the Robins.

In the winter of 1931, the trade winds were blowing fiercely in the National League. Newspapers were reporting the impending trade of Dazzy Vance to the Cubs straight up for Pat Malone. The Cubs were also dangling the name of Hack Wilson, the slugger who hit 56 home runs in 1930 and hit only 13 in 1931. Wilson eventually went to St. Louis along with pitcher Bud Teachout in exchange for the well-traveled veteran Burleigh Grimes, whose greatest years were when he teamed with Vance as the one-two punch on the Brooklyn pitching staff. A month later, Wilson was traded to Brooklyn for Bob Parham, a minor league pitcher, and $45,000. It wasn't so much the decrease in his power numbers that bothered club owners about Wilson as it was his bawdy lifestyle. He was among the league leaders in alcohol consumption. When he came to New York to meet with his new manager, he brought his six-year-old son, Bobby, with him and told Carey he had turned over a new leaf.

150

Carey was diplomatic. "Don't go out nights, Hack," he said. "You might catch cold."[1]

Meanwhile, Dazzy was in his top off-season form, engaging in three favorite winter sports—fishing, golfing and holding out for more money to play baseball. He said he was expecting a salary cut after his 11–13 season but the contract offered by Brooklyn surprised him. "It looks like the depression is still on," he said. "There will have to be some dickering about the terms before I sign." Contract terms were not disclosed by Vance, who said he did not want to be treated like Bill Terry was with the Giants. Terry had been asked to take a 40 percent cut. If the same was true with Vance, it would mean the Dodgers wanted to slash his pay from $22,500—the highest of any pitcher in the league—down to $13,500. "I had expected a reduction, but nothing like this," said Dazzy. Then, applying some of that mathematical logic that used to confound Charlie Ebbets a decade earlier, Dazzy told the press, "The club management can go up a lot easier than players can come down on contract terms."[2]

On Feb. 25, the Dodgers announced that Vance had signed after conferring with Carey in Clearwater. Terms were not disclosed but the *New York Times* reported the salary was believed to be $15,000. The club also announced the signing of Waite Hoyt, the great Yankees pitcher, whose name was often hidden in the shadows behind those of Ruth, Gehrig, Lazzeri and the rest of the Murderer's Row crew but who was a mainstay on that pitching staff.

As the Dodgers began spring training, they realized immediately that the change in regime from Uncle Robbie to Max Carey also meant a change in routine. Carey insisted that his ball club be in top physical condition and instituted a daily program of what Vance called "Carey Calisthentics." The new manager said, "I consider conditioning paramount. These players can play ball. What we're chiefly trying to do here is to get them in the top shape physically. We expect to keep them that way throughout the season." It was quite a departure from the past for players like 41-year-old Vance, who used to tell Robbie that he trained like he pitched: one day of work, four days of rest.

Carey was all business but he did add a bit of color to the atmosphere when he hired Casey Stengel as one of his coaches. Casey, a popular player who had spent part of his career with the Dodgers, had been managing at Toledo. Now he would bring his baseball experience and his jovial attitude back to Brooklyn. The fans especially greeted the news warmly.

One player conspicuous by his absence was Babe Herman, who, like Wilson, had seen his numbers slide in 1931, particularly his batting average, from .393. to .313. He too was asked to take a salary cut and refused it. So while his teammates were doing push-ups and jumping jacks in Clearwater, Babe was working out at his home in California, not far from the Giants' training camp. One afternoon while he watching the Giants work out, Willie Hennigan of the *New York American* came down from the press box and approached him.

"Have you heard the news, Babe?" he asked.

"No," said the Babe.

"You've been traded to Cincinnati."[3]

There was no question about it. The old days were over. In a matter of a few months, Uncle Robbie was gone, Babe Herman was gone, Dazzy Vance was hanging on, and the changing of the guard included Max Carey, Hack Wilson and Casey Stengel. Not long after the season started, it also included the veteran first baseman George Kelly, picked up from the Giants when Bissonette got hurt. O'Doul was counted on to have another great year and the Dodgers expected big things from Clark, Vance, Hollis Thurston and Van Lingle Mungo on the pitching staff.

Max Carey had a Hall of Fame career as an outfielder for the Pittsburgh Pirates and, late in his career, with the Robins. When Wilbert Robinson ended his long tenure as Brooklyn manager, Carey was picked to take over. (Courtesy Baseball Hall of Fame.)

The departure of Herman prompted baseball pundits to recall some of his great antics in a Brooklyn uniform —"tripling" into a double play; heading for second and criss crossing with a base runner headed back for first; taking a lit cigar out of his pocket and smoking it; playing the outfield as if he was wearing a tennis racket instead of a mitt.

Eddie Collins, the great A's second baseman, was taking in the sights at spring training as a spectator. When the topic of conversation became Herman's adventures on the field, Collins said he couldn't top the three men on third story — but he could come close. He told of a time the A's were playing Detroit and had a man on first. The runner took off for second in an attempt to steal. The shortstop and second basemen got confused as to who was to cover the bag. So they both went for it. The shortstop, looking at the second baseman, ran into the umpire and they both tumbled to the ground. The second baseman, looking over toward the shortstop, ran into the base runner and they both toppled over. "Four men down and nobody out," said Collins.[4]

The Dodgers opened the season by splitting two games with the Braves. Waite Hoyt, ever popular in New York, got the opening day assignment but was not equal to the task as Boston roughed him up in an 8–3 loss. Watty Clark evened things up the next day with an 8–2 win. Next up was Dazzy Vance. Which Dazzy would appear? Brooklyn fans wondered, as did Max Carey and, for that matter, much of the baseball world. Did the Ole Daz still have it?

The answer seemed apparent after only a few innings. Vance set down the visiting Phillies, one after another, and had a no-hitter going after six innings. Coupled with his last four innings of work in spring training, Dazzy had 10 consecutive no-hit innings until Don Hurst singled cleanly to right in the seventh. Vance gave up just one other hit in registering a 5–0 shutout. But Dazzy's early season problems, which had plagued him the past few seasons, reappeared when Vance complained of a sore arm after absorbing a 4–1 loss to the Braves in his second start in a game in which he was removed in the sixth inning. His bad fortune continued in Philadelphia, where, unable to pitch because of his arm trouble, he was hit on the left thumb with a ball during batting practice. The Dodgers reported that it was his arm and not his thumb that kept him out of the rotation. He returned to the mound on May 2 and just missed getting his second shutout. He outpitched Carl Hubbell as Brooklyn beat New York 3–1. The only run the Giants got was unearned, scoring on a throwing error by Tony Cuccinello, who had taken over the second base duties for the Dodgers. But in his next start, the Cubs clobbered him and he didn't make it out of the third inning in a 12–5 loss in which Burleigh Grimes won his first start for Chicago. It was not only Cubs bats that did in Ole Daz. As Irving Vaughan reported in the *Chicago Daily Tribune*, "Vance started dispensing charity in the noisy third. Herman walked. English walked. Moore walked. So did Vance, but to the shelter of the dugout."

His roller coaster season continued with a good outing on Friday the 13th of May as Brooklyn disposed of the Cincinnati Reds 5–3, but he followed that with a less than stellar performance in a 9–4 loss to the Giants. On May 26, he pitched well enough to win against Boston but three unearned runs killed him and the Braves won 4–2. Dazzy closed out the month by winning a 3–2 decision over the Braves, evening his record at 4–4 for the year. Going into June, Carey and his Dodgers were on a bit of a run, having won three in a row, and were now in fourth place but just 5½ games behind the first place Cubs. They won their fourth straight on June 2 when on-again–off-again Vance was on again in the first game of a double header against the Braves but another streak of wildness forced him from the game. Winning 6–1 in the ninth inning, Dazzy walked three straight pinch hitters and had a 2–0 count on the next batter when Carey yanked him. Jack Quinn got the last two outs without a run scoring. The Braves won the second game 5–1 to stop Brooklyn's winning streak at four. Dazzy won the next three of his next four starts, with a no-decision in between, then lost in 11 innings to the Phillies. When all games were completed on July 4, Vance had an 8–5 record and the Dodgers were in a good-news–bad-news situation. The bad news— they were in seventh place. The good news— they were just 5½ games out of first place in the crazy National League race.

Team	W–L	Pct.	GB
Pittsburgh	37–29	.561	___
Boston	39–34	.534	1.5
Chicago	37–34	.521	2.5
Philadelphia	39–38	.506	3.5
St. Louis	35–35	.500	4
New York	32–34	.485	5
Brooklyn	35–38	.479	5.5
Cincinnati	34–46	.425	10

Dazzy won his ninth game of the year on July 9 when the Dodgers scored seven in the ninth to beat Pittsburgh 9–3. He then dropped a 4–1 decision to Guy Bush and the Cubs and a 5–3 decision to Wild Bill Hallahan and the Cardinals. He pitched one of his best games all year on July 24, striking out 10 Phillies in a 5–4 Dodgers victory that snapped a five-game losing streak for his 10th win and beat Dizzy Dean and the Cardinals on July 29 for win number 11. He had to wait 12 days to get his next win and that was in relief when Brooklyn beat Cincinnati 10–9 in 13 innings. Ole Daz hurled the last five innings and allowed just one hit. In his next outing, he came out on the short end of a 7–4 decision to the Giants.

The Dodgers had a terrific August, due in large part to the hitting of O'Doul and Wilson and the mound mastery of Watty Clark, who was having his best year in the big leagues. Brooklyn had two six-game winning streaks in the month as well one of four games and went into Chicago for a crucial series with the Cubs in second place, just 3½ games behind Chicago, who had taken over the league leadership. While his teammates went to Chicago, Dazzy went to New York for treatment of a sore arm. Chicago banged the Dodgers' pitching around for 26 runs in a three sweep in which Brooklyn lost by scores of 7–4, 9–3 and 10–4. Dazzy got back in time to be one of three Dodgers relief pitchers to come on in relief of Sloppy Thurston. The ball club headed out of town still in second place but now 6½ behind the leaders.

Vance struggled in September and didn't pitch after Sept. 15. The Dodgers played well but were never really in the race after the three-game sweep by the Cubs in August. Chicago went on to win the championship. They eventually lost the World Series to the New York Yankees, a series made famous by Babe Ruth's called shot — or was it? — off of Charlie Root, who swore to his dying day that Ruth never called anything.

For the Dodgers, Hack Wilson had a great comeback year, hitting 23 homers and driving in 123 runs. O'Doul hit a league-leading .368 with 21 homers and 90 RBIs. Watty Clark won 20 and lost only 12, but no other starter could muster more than 13 wins. Beyond Clark, it was a .500 pitching staff with Mungo at 13–11, Vance at 12–11, Thurston at 12–8, Quinn at 3–7, Shaute at 7–7 and Phelps at 4–5. Waite Hoyt, picked up from the Yankees, was released in mid-season with a 1–3 record.

Sportswriter Frank Graham summed up the season by saying the Dodgers had done well in finishing in third place. But the front office was frustrated once again. They had put in new bleachers because the ballpark couldn't hold all the people who had wanted to see the Robins play, even in their most eccentric Daffiness Boys era. Maybe it was the daffiness that was missing, said Graham. "Whether or not it was because Robbie and the other old heroes, save Vance, had gone, the crowd never really warmed up to this team and reacted only tepidly to the fact that O'Doul won the batting championship with a mark of .368," wrote Graham.[5]

With Cincinnati, Babe Herman played in all but six games. He hit .326 with 16 homers and 83 runs batted in. He also led the league with 19 triples. He made 13 errors in the outfield, the same number he had with Brooklyn the year before. Cincinnati finished in last place, 30 games behind the champion Cubs.

Not long after the World Series was over, rumors were rampant about possible trades. The Associated Press reported that a deal involving four ball clubs was imminent. If it came about it would be the biggest transaction in baseball history. Supposedly, Boston's slugging outfielder Wally Berger and Herman of the Reds would wind up with the Giants where they would join Mel Ott in the outfield. Kiki Cuyler and Gabby Hartnett would move from the Cubs to the Braves, Freddy Lindstrom would go from the Giants to the Cubs and veteran pitcher Pat Malone was to end up in Cincinnati. "Before long, the fruit may fairly rain down," the wire service reported.

Dodgers owner Steve McKeever said he had set aside $220,000 for player transactions and manager Max Carey made no secret of the fact the Dodgers were interested in getting Jim Bottomley from the Cardinals. McKeever said the ball club was interested in getting two quality pitchers. It had already signed Walter Beck, who won 27 games for Memphis in 1932.

Amid all the talk and speculation, the Associated Press reported flatly, "The only man definitely considered on the [trading] block in Brooklyn is Dazzy Vance, the veteran who used to burn up the league."[6]

Talk persisted all winter about the Dodgers dumping Dazzy. Carey paid a visit to Vance at the pitcher's Homosassa home but insisted the conversation had to do with salary and nothing else. On Feb. 5, 1933, Carey told the *New York Times* Dazzy was not for sale but Brooklyn would listen to anyone willing to part with a quality player. "All this talk about selling Vance is rubbish," said Carey. "If a club were to approach us on a deal offering us a player that would help us, we would naturally be interested."

But when Carey was asked to name his starting pitchers for the coming season, he mentioned Watson Clark, the lefthander who won 20 games in 1932; Van Mungo, the young fireballer; Ray Benge, who had come over from Philadelphia; and Beck, who the Dodgers hoped might be the next Dazzy Vance.[7]

Three days later, the Dodgers traded Vance to the Cardinals. Brooklyn included utility infielder Gordon Slade as part of the deal. In return, the Dodgers got Owen Carroll, a righthanded pitcher and Jake Flowers, a second baseman, who had been a teammate of Vance's with Brooklyn earlier in his career. It was Slade, and not Dazzy, who was the key player in the deal for the Cardinals. Their regular shortstop, Charlie Gelbert, was badly injured in a hunting accident in which he tripped and his gun went off, shattering several nerves in his legs and mutilating his instep. Surgeons saved the leg and eventually Gelbert returned to the big leagues. But not in 1933. So the Cardinals needed a shortstop, and they got one in Gordon Slade. Vance, one of the greatest pitchers in his era, was a throw-in in the deal. The deal turned out to be forgettable for both teams. Slade hit .113 in 39 games for the Redbirds and was out of the starting job by May 7 when St. Louis acquired Leo Durocher to play short. Meanwhile, Carroll lost 20 games, the most in the league, for Brooklyn in 1933.

The trading of Dazzy Vance truly marked the end of the Wilbert Robinson era in Brooklyn, one in which Vance was the leader on and off the field of ballplayers who knew how to play and knew how to have a good time. Gone were Jack Fournier, the first baseman and bookie; Burleigh Grimes, the spitballer who was far from through when the Robins gave up on him; Babe Herman, the great hitter but adventuresome fielder and base runner; the hotel rooms that served as both kangaroo courts and speakeasies; and now Dazzy Vance, the winningest pitcher in Brooklyn history at the time he was traded.

John Drebinger, who covered Vance from the time he came up to the major leagues, wrote a piece for the *New York Times* in which he traced Dazzy's legacy, starting with that remarkable 1924 season. Uncle Robbie put up with a lot because he needed the Dazzler to dazzle, but in the end, as it turned out, Dazzy needed Robbie too.

"With Vance's ascendancy also came a new era of prima-donna showmanship which not even the higher-salaried Babe Ruth deigned to employ," wrote Drebinger. "In contrast to the easy-going Babe, the Dazzler proved himself a hard and shrewd businessman and repeatedly became one of baseball's most stubborn hold-outs."

Beyond that, said Drebinger, Vance demanded special privileges that he thought were befitting the National League's top-paid pitcher — things like insisting on four or five days between starts, avoiding relief pitching, and being permitted to play golf whenever he wanted to during the baseball season even though golf was prohibited for his teammates.

"To all of these whims, Robbie obliged without a murmur on the theory that so long as the Dazzler performed with brilliancy, nothing was too good for him," according to Drebinger.[8]

Sometimes Dazzy stretched Robinson's patience to the limit such as the times he seemed to lose concentration on the mound, complained about ailments that Robby considered pretty minor — and then there were the holdouts for money, no matter what kind of year he had the year before. Daz was a handful, no doubt about it, but Robinson knew he couldn't win a pennant without him.

The Dodgers front office, reacting to public criticism of the trade, was blunt in explaining why Vance was expendable. Management cited these reasons:

- In return for a total salary of $63,000 over the past three years, Dazzy won a total of 40 games.
- He did not win a game after mid–August and complained of a lame arm that took him out of the starting rotation for a crucial series with the Cubs in which the Dodgers lost all three games.
- He violated team rules of discipline, which might have been acceptable to Wilbert Robinson but were not to Max Carey.
- Progressive laziness.[9]

It was not the kind of ending that the Dodgers or Vance could have envisioned or would have wanted. Uncle Wilbert Robinson, about to manage the Atlanta Crackers in the Southern League after a year out of baseball, might have shaken his head in disbelief at the news — or he might have seen it coming.

XIV

The Quest for 200

Sportswriter and historian Fred Lieb described the St. Louis Cardinals of the early 1930s as "frolicsome, exuberant spirits with boundless energy." They came to be known as the Gas House Gang — Jay Hannah "Dizzy" Dean and his brother Paul "Daffy" Dean, Pepper Martin, Joe Medwick, Frankie Frisch, and Leo Durocher — the shortstop whom New York writers had dubbed "the all–American out." They knew how to have a good time but their first priority was winning. "We haven't any room for softies," said Frisch, who would rise to be the manager of this ball club. Lieb was unabashed in his praise. "With due respect to the powerful Yankees of the Babe Ruth era, the most colorful picturesque club of modern baseball was ... the famous Gas House Gang of St. Louis." And now, in addition to Dizzy and Daffy, they had Dazzy. They also had an old teammate of Dazzy's at Brooklyn, Burleigh Grimes, still grinding it out just as Vance was trying to do.

Dazzy was 42 and his role was to be a spot starter who would also make occasional relief appearances. The adjustment was tough. He was no longer the king who could come and go as he pleased, train when he wanted to, play golf when he wanted to and turn up his nose at the front office. He was a hanger-on.

Manager Gabby Street gave him his first start in the first game of a double header with Pittsburgh on April 23 and Ole Daz got clobbered. He allowed three runs in the first inning and was removed with nobody out in the second, having given up six hits and absorbing the loss. His next start had some of the old-time hype to it that Dazzy loved during his prime. The Cardinals went to Brooklyn and 35,000 fans showed up to see Vance make his first appearance at Ebbets Field since the trade. He fared better than he did in his first start, allowing two runs on five hits in six innings. He did not get the decision in a 4–2 Cardinals loss. On May 18, Cardinals starter Jim Mooney could not get out of the first

159

inning against the Dodgers in St. Louis and Dazzy was brought in from the bullpen. Once again, he had trouble getting anybody out. He pitched three innings and gave up seven runs on seven hits. Mooney took the loss in a game won by the Dodgers 14–5.

A game on June 6 was best remembered for what happened before it started. Reds pitcher Paul Derringer and Dizzy Dean of the Cardinals, crossed paths with one another as each walked across the field before the game. Derringer said Dean had been "riding him hard" all year and he asked Dizzy if he meant what he said. "Every word," said Dizz, upon which Derringer punched him in the face. (Afterward, Dean claimed he blocked the punch and invited photographers to take pictures of his face.) When Dizzy grabbed Derringer, both fell to the ground in a heap. The fight was broken up when 42-year-old Dazzy Vance sat on both of them until other players came to break up the fight.[1]

Vance had his best relief stint on June 21 when pitched the last two innings of a 7–5 Cardinals win against Brooklyn. He allowed one scratch hit and struck out three. A week later, he got a start and gave up two runs on five hits in four innings before being lifted for a pinch hitter. He took the loss in a game won by the Braves 3–0. The Cardinals started the second half of the season by getting clobbered by Brooklyn 10–4 but Dazzy turned in another good relief appearance. He pitched three innings and allowed one run on one hit and did not get the decision.

By this time, the Cardinals had decided that Dazzy could fill an important role in long relief, even if it just meant eating up some innings in games that were decided early. Such was the case when the Pirates jumped on Bill Walker for five runs in the first inning of a game on Aug. 1. Dazzy came in after Walker had retired only one batter. He pitched the next 5⅔ innings and surrendered four runs on nine hits. Dazzy got a rare start on Aug. 21 against Brooklyn because St. Louis had a stretch of double headers and few off days. The regular starters needed a break and Dazzy could help provide it. He did about as well as he was doing in middle relief — and lasted about as long. He pitched four innings and gave up two runs on seven hits. The Cardinals won 6–2 so Vance had done his job — he kept them in the game — but Walker got the win in relief. Dazzy left after giving up successive singles in the fifth inning. Walker came in and got Joe Hutcheson to hit into a triple play to end the inning.

Dazzy picked up a win in a relief assignment on Aug. 28. He came into the game against the Giants in which the Cardinals were losing 6–5.

He gave up a couple of hits but the Redbirds scored seven in the ninth to take a 12–6 lead. Dizzy Dean mopped up in the ninth inning and allowed two more runs—but Vance got the win. He was rewarded for his effort by getting a rare start against the Cubs at Wrigley Field on Sept. 3. Irving Vaughan of the *Chicago Daily Tribune* described what happened:

"The Cubs don't seem to know that the one time terrible Dazzy Vance is just an old fellow coasting downhill. They let him shine yesterday." Dazzy struck out nine in a 3–1 Cardinals victory. Babe Herman, his old teammate from the daffiness days fanned three times. "Vance was in such a frisky mood that he refused to stop short of anything less than a performance as he habitually showered on the Cubs in other days."[2]

By season's end, Dazzy had compiled a 6–2 record in 28 appearances, 11 as a starter and 17 in relief. His season in a nutshell:

G	IP	H	BB	SO	ERA
28	99	105	28	67	3.55

Those weren't the quality numbers of the Dazzy Vance of old, but the old Dazzy Vance figured they were good enough to keep him in the big leagues a little longer. At least he hoped so. In early January 1934, reports began to surface that the Reds were interested in Dazzy and that the Cardinals no longer were. St. Louis general manager Branch Rickey declined to comment one way or another. It became official on Feb. 6, when the Reds' new owner, Powell Crosley Jr., announced that the ball club had purchased Vance in a straight cash deal. Terms were not announced but it was believed Cincinnati got Dazzy for the $7,500 waiver price.

After the deal was made, Bob O'Farrell, the Reds' manager, called Dazzy at his home in Homosassa Springs and asked him if he was in shape for the coming season. Dazzy talked about the call as he entertained writers one day at spring training. The way Dazzy told the story: "'Shape?' says I. 'You get a gun and follow me through these jungles all day and you'll see who needs to be in shape.'"

With that, Ole Daz was off and running with one story after another. He told of how a few weeks earlier, he was driving on a highway when he came across a bear in his patch. He said he got out of his car and drew his .22 caliber pistol. "Say, a good big sparrow could laugh at a gun like that." He said the bear came within 20 yards of him when another man appeared and shot the bear with his .12 gauge shotgun. "So I didn't have to pester the bear with my cap pistol," said Dazzy.

Then the conversation turned to dogs and someone wondered how many Uncle Wilbert Robinson had at his home in Dover Hall, Ga. Dazzy said he didn't know how many his former manager had, but Ole Daz had 12 of his own. Then he told of the time that Paul Waner showed up at Homosassa to do some hunting. Dazzy said he gave Waner and his hunting partner his best dogs and sent them on their way. "They put up about a million birds and Paul and the feller with him fired 85 times and how many birds do you think they got? Ten," said Dazzy. "I said to him it's that same kind of hittin' that won the pennant for the Giants last year. You better do better than that this year." Waner just grinned, he said.

Next topic — his arm. "Listen, grandson," Dazzy told one of the writers, "In 1916 a scout looked me over and said the way I threw the ball, my arm wouldn't last three years. Well I'm here and my arm's here. Where's he? And who cares?" He adjusted the cigar in the corner of his mouth.

He picked the Cubs to win the pennant. Someone said the Giants, who were defending champs had the chance for improvement. "Yes, and with chances of de-provement, too," said Dazzy. He pointed out that last year the Giants' entire pitching rotation stayed healthy the entire year. That wouldn't happen again. "De-provement" would set in. "Accidents and wear and tear and roughage, as you might say."[3]

O'Farrell, Dazzy's new manager, was optimistic that his new acquisition would help lead the Reds out of the cellar, where they finished in 1933. "Dazzy has shown me so far that he is not only determined but ready to pitch another season of good ball," said O'Farrell. But, it didn't happen. O'Farrell gave him a start in the second game of the season against the Cubs, a day after Lon Warneke held the Reds to one hit on opening day. The Cubs got eight runs on 10 hits off Dazzy in eight innings of work as Chicago won 8–4.

Irving Vaughan of the *Chicago Daily Tribune*, who had seen Vance pitch many times in the past decade, wrote, "The Cubs today made Dazzy Vance feel every one of his 41 [sic] years. They hit the old fellow without respect for age or previous service.... There were 10 hits off the pitcher who in previous years figured he was having an off day if a dozen Cubs didn't fold up on strikes."[4]

A week later, Dazzy faced the Cubs again in Chicago's home opener

Dazzy's tenure with the Cincinnati Reds was short and uneventful, but he still had the big wind-up with the high leg kick that made him the most successful pitcher in the National League for several years. (Courtesy Hall of Fame.)

at Wrigley Field and couldn't get out of the first inning. He gave up three runs on five hits while retiring only two batters. That was all the Cubs needed in a 3–2 victory. On May 5, he made a relief appearance against the Dodgers and uncharacteristically walked three batters in succession after giving a hit. His totals for the day were two innings pitched, one run allowed, two hits and the three walks. On June 13, he was brought in to stop the bleeding in a game won by the Giants 12–1. Dazzy pitched three innings and gave up two runs on seven hits.

Lee Allen, in his history of the Cincinnati Reds, gives short notice to Vance's time with the ball club. "Dazzy Vance's comeback attempt was an utter failure," he wrote. "He appeared in only two games, lost them both, and moved on." Actually, he started two games but appeared in six. Nonetheless, his conclusion regarding Dazzy's efforts would be hard to dispute. On June 25, Vance was sold to the Cardinals for the waiver price of $7,500.[5]

What St. Louis needed from Dazzy was more realistic than what Cincinnati anticipated from him. The Reds were hoping the old warhorse would take his place in the starting rotation, rally the troops and march them out of last place and into the land of respectability in the National League standings. The Cardinals, on the other hand, were in a pennant race — and pennant contenders are always looking for more pitching. If Dazzy could come in and pitch an inning or two here or there, if for no other reason than to give the front-liners a breather, he would contribute mightily to the cause.

Dazzy had lost some speed off his fastball and his curve didn't act like it fell off a table top anymore. But what got him in the most trouble at this stage in his career was control problems. He was walking more batters than he used to, putting himself in a position where he had to get the ball over the plate. And when he did, that's where the lack of speed or sharp curve hurt him. A case in point was a July 14 game at Ebbets Field. Bill Walker started for the Cardinals, his first game back since fracturing a forearm two months before. The Dodgers nailed him for two runs on five hits in 2⅔ innings. Vance came in and got the third out of the inning. But in the fourth, he gave up a base hit, hit a batter, got a strikeout and then walked the next two batters, forcing in a run. Then, just trying to find the strike zone again, he tossed one down the middle that Tony Cuccinello rapped for a single, driving in two more runs and Dazzy was through for the day. The Dodgers won 10–2.

Five days later, he relieved Walker again in a game against the Dodgers but in different circumstances and with a much different result. Dazzy came on in the eighth inning with St. Louis holding a 5–3 lead. There were two out and Brooklyn had runners on first and third. Ole Daz struck out Al Lopez to end the eighth and then pitched a 1–2–3 ninth inning.

On July 22, manager Frisch needed a helping hand of a different kind from his veteran. The Cardinals were playing a stretch of games with double headers and few off days and Frisch needed someone to give him some good innings and hopefully give his starting rotation a break. So he sent the 43-year-old Vance out to hurl the second game of a double header against Boston. Dazzy responded by going the distance, allowing two runs on seven hits, striking out five and walking only 1. His strikeout of Wally Berger in the eighth inning was the 2,000th of his career. But more important, coupled with the Cardinals' 5–4 victory in the first game of the twin bill, St. Louis was now in third place, just four games behind the league-leading Giants and a game back of the second-place Cubs. It was Dazzy's second start for St. Louis—the other was a July 1 outing that ended in a 2–2 tie with Cincinnati—and his first complete game.

On Aug. 8, Vance and the rest of the baseball world received a shock with the news of the death of Wilbert Robinson in Atlanta. Uncle Robbie, who was 70 and who had taken over as owner and manager of the Atlanta Crackers in the Southern Association, collapsed in his hotel room and died of a brain hemorrhage. The Associated Press obituary made particular mention of his ability to develop good pitchers and to get the most out of his pitching staffs. "To the modern fan, Dazzy Vance, sensational strikeout king of 1924 and voted the National League's most valuable player that season, stands out as the most notable of Robinson's products," the wire service reported.[6]

On Aug. 14, Vance gave Frisch another outstanding performance, pitching seven innings against Philadelphia before retiring because of a blister on his finger. He gave up only one run on three hits and struck out six but left with the game tied 1–1. The Cardinals scored four in the eighth to make a winner out of reliever Jess Haines. The Cardinals remained in third place, now 6½ games behind the Giants.

This was the same week when Frisch ran into problems with two of his other pitchers, the Dean brothers, Dizzy and Paul. Both refused to go to Detroit to participate in an exhibition game. Frisch fined Dizzy $100 and Paul $50 and then suspended them indefinitely when, upon hearing of their fines, they refused to suit up for their next game. Dizzy went to Chicago to plead his case with Commissioner Kenesaw Mountain Landis. Paul went home but returned to the ball club after signing a statement acknowledging he was wrong in refusing to go to Detroit and wrong to have refused to put on his uniform in defiance of Frisch. By the end of the week, Dizzy was also back.

With all of that as a backdrop and the Cardinals still in the pennant race, Vance took the mound against the Phillies on Aug. 16 and gave up two runs in the first inning. Frisch didn't want the game to get out of hand so he inserted Paul Dean, just back from his suspension, in the second inning. The Cardinals scored 10 runs in the next four innings and tacked on two more in the eighth to provide Dean and St. Louis with a 12–2 victory.

On Aug. 26, Dazzy filled the other role that Frisch had in mind when the Cardinals signed him. Tex Carleton got hit hard in the first inning of the first game of a double header against the Dodgers. When the damage was done, Brooklyn had six runs before the Cardinals had even come to bat. Vance relieved Carlton in the first inning and pitched 3⅔ innings, giving up one run on four hits. St. Louis lost 11–5 but came back to win the second game 7–2 behind the pitching of Wild Bill Hallahan. Two days later, Vance was once again called on in a mop-up role and worked one inning of scoreless relief as the Dodgers beat the Cardinals 10–1.

As September began, St. Louis had moved into a second-place tie with the Cubs but both were 5½ games behind the Giants. But the Cardinals, not powerful but feisty with Pepper Martin, Leo Durocher, Joe Medwick and Frisch leading the way and Paul and Dizzy Dean behaving themselves, went on one of those late season tears that are frequent yet unexplainable in baseball. They had winning streaks of five in a row between Sept. 5 and Sept. 11, seven in a row between Sept. 16 and Sept. 23 and finished the season with a four-game winning streak between Sept. 27 and Sept. 30. Dizzy Dean threw shutouts in his last three starts on his way to winning 30 games for the season. The Cardinals were 21–7 for the month and cruised home with the National League championship, outperforming the Giants, who were 13–14, and the Cubs, who were 12–15 for the month.

The World Series matchup pitted the upstart Cardinals against the Detroit Tigers. Dazzy was ecstatic about getting into his first World Series and was at his storytelling best as the St. Louis players arrived at their hotel in the Motor City. "It took me 13 years to get in and now I'm just a relief pitcher," said Vance. "But I sneaked in just the same." He said 13 had always been a lucky number for him, pointing out he threw a one-hitter against Philadelphia on Sept. 13, 1925, and followed that up with a no-hitter. "And in my 13th year, I escaped from Cincinnati and into World Series dough."[7]

Dazzy was on a roll. Someone asked him about clashes between ballplayers and umpires that he had witnessed. He said he remembered a time a player was called out on a close play. He jumped up and stormed the umpire. The ump, fearing a physical confrontation, backed up and stretched his arms up in the air. Dazz said the player shouted at him, "Hey, put your hands down. You're the burglar, not me."[8]

The Cardinals won two out of the first three World Series games, with Dizzy picking up a win in Detroit in the opener and Paul winning the opener in St. Louis. In that one, Frisch had Dazzy Vance warming up in the fifth inning but Dean got out of a jam and Dazzy didn't get into his first World Series game. That occurred the next day, on Oct. 6, when Dazzy came on in the third inning in relief of Tex Carleton. The inning started innocently enough with a fly out to right field and a strike-out. Then Mickey Cochrane doubled down the right field line and Charlie Gehringer and Goose Goselin both walked to load the bases. Billy Rogell singled to center, scoring Cochrane and Gehringer and moving Goselin around to third. Frisch had seen enough of Carleton and summoned the old warrior, Vance, from the bullpen, to face Hank Greenberg. It was a scene reminiscent of the 1926 World Series when the aging veteran, Grover Cleveland Alexander, was summoned by the Cardinals to face Tony Lazzeri of the Yankees with the bases loaded. Alexander struck out Lazzeri to put out the fire. Dazzy fired a strike past Greenberg on the first pitch. On the next pitch, Greenberg rapped a single off of Durocher's glove at short. Had he fielded it cleanly, there would have been an easy force out at second or a play at first to end the inning. As it was, another run scored. Marv Owen then hit a ground ball that took a high hop on Pepper Martin. He leaped to get it but threw wide to first. The bases were loaded once again. Dazzy then struck out Pete Fox to end the inning.

In the fourth inning, he got a strikeout and then surrendered a walk. There was a bad throw on a steal attempt allowing the runner to go all the way to third. Then Dazzy uncorked a wild pitch, giving the Tigers a run. Vance struck out Cochrane and got Gehringer on a ground out to end the inning—and end Vance's World Series career. The Cardinals won the series in seven games. It is best remembered for the incident in which Detroit fans showered Cardinals outfielder Joe Medwick with bottles and other debris, prompting Commissioner Landis, who was in attendance, to order Medwick off the field and out of the game.

In the off-season, Vance headed home to Homosassa Springs to hunt and fish and entertain friends, including ballplayers, who headed his way for a little fun and relaxation. One thing different from past off-seasons was that Dazzy no longer staged his annual holdouts. Now, it was more a matter of holding on, hoping to live the dream for yet another season. But on March 29, 1935, he got the message he dreaded. The Cardinals gave him his unconditional release. Frank Frisch thanked him for his time and service and told him he was free to seek employment with another team. Two days later, the Dodgers, now managed by Casey Stengel, said they were willing to give him a tryout. No promises, no contract yet. Just a tryout. It was almost a demeaning offer for a man who had won 190 games in a Brooklyn uniform and had led the league in strikeouts seven years in a row. And yet, it was his old team willing to give him one more shot. Dazzy jumped at the chance.

On April 6, Casey gave him the ball to start an exhibition game against Brooklyn's Montreal farm club. Dazzy pitched five innings, allowing one run on three hits. The *New York Times* reported after the game "there would seem to be no doubt" that Vance had made the ball club because he had exceeded expectations. There was no immediate word from the Dodgers brass. But a week later, Stengel announced that Vance had signed a contract and would be part of the Dodgers pitching staff. No one revealed the terms of the contract but Casey let it be known that Vance would be paid more than the Cardinals paid him the previous year.

On April 14, in one of the last pre-season games, Dazzy started a game against the New York Yankees at Ebbets Field. It was a tremendous homecoming for the Dazzler. "The old master received one of the greatest tributes of his long career when he emerged from the dugout to start his warm-ups," wrote Roscoe McGowen in the *New York Times*. "Practically every spectator rose to his feet and cheered Vance for a full minute."[9]

He gave up three runs on three hits in three innings, but the Dodgers scored three in the first and four in the second and had the game so well in hand that most of the fans' attention was on Dazzy, despite some high-powered folks on the other side such as Ruth and Gehrig.

On April 25, the Dodgers beat the Phillies 12–5 in the home opener at Ebbets Field. Vance was called on to come in the eighth inning to try to preserve the victory. He gave up a run on three singles in the eighth and pitched a perfect ninth. But what was notable about his appearance was the reception he received in walking in from the bullpen for his first appearance as a Dodger in a regular season game since 1932. Again, McGowen, who witnessed the crowd reaction in the exhibition game against the Yankees: "The ovation accorded Vance when he appeared in the exhibition game against the Yankees was multiplied a thousand-fold yesterday. When he ambled to the mound to start the seventh, the entire crowd rose and stood cheering him until the umpire signaled the start of the inning."[10]

Dazzy's last year in baseball was 1935 with the Dodgers. He ended his career with 197 wins — and thought he could have achieved his goal of 200 had Casey Stengel, his last manager, used him more effectively. (Courtesy Hall of Fame.)

Dazzy was lucky to have a job in the big leagues at his age but he was nonetheless frustrated because his only goal now was to win his 200th game. He was six shy of it and it would be difficult to accomplish coming out of the bullpen. He worked an inning and a third on May 5 and did not get a decision in a 9–2 loss to the Pirates. On May 15, he turned in a great performance but took the loss. He relieved Johnny Babich with nobody out in the first inning and held the Cubs to one run for the next eight innings. He tired in the ninth and surrendered four runs as Chicago won 8–4 in what would be Dazzy's longest outing all year. Ten days later, he was once again in a mop-up role, pitching two innings of a 10–3 loss to the Cubs. He got his first win of the year — and the 195th of his career — when the Dodgers rallied to beat the Phillies 11–9 on June 7. Dazzy became the pitcher of record when Brooklyn scored four runs in the eighth inning to take the lead for good in the game. He won again eight days later when he was hurriedly brought in to pitch after Van Lingle Mungo injured his thumb fielding a ground ball. Vance came on in the fifth and worked five scoreless innings to get his second win of the season.

He improved his record to 3–1 on June 23, 5⅓ innings and allowing one run on five hits as the Dodgers beat St. Louis 10–6 in the second game of a double header after getting pounded 16–2 in the first game. On July 12, Dazzy entered the game in the seventh inning at Crosley Field in Cincinnati with the Reds and Dodgers tied at 3–3. He might have stayed out of trouble but an error in the eighth inning by shortstop Lonny Frey kept the inning alive. The Reds scored two and beat Dazzy and the Dodgers 5–4. Vance made several other relief appearances but didn't get a decision in any of them. On Aug. 9, he was the winning pitcher when the Dodgers beat their Allentown, Pa., farm team 3–1 in an exhibition game.

On Aug. 23, the Cardinals swept a double header from the Dodgers at Ebbets Field. At the end of the *New York Times* story on the games, there was this item, published almost as an afterthought to the game coverage: "The unconditional release of Dazzy Vance was announced before the game. This may wind up the once-famous hurler's baseball career. The three games he had won for Brooklyn had left him just three short of the 200 mark he was aiming for."[11]

Dazzy was perhaps surprised and surely disappointed that the Dodgers released him. He had looked forward to getting his 200th career win and his pride may have prevented him from the realization that, at age, 44, he was more of a liability than an asset, that a team could get the same kind of performance out of someone half his age but with a chance to develop whereas Dazzy's skills were diminishing. Blinded by the notion that he was denied the chance to reach his 200th win — when in fact he was actually given the chance just by the fact the Dodgers signed him — Dazzy never quite forgave Casey Stengel for using him exclusively in relief.

"In August, I had been in about 20 games and not doing too badly but I made one bad pitch to Gus Mancuso and Casey never used me again. That Stengel didn't give me a chance to win 200 games when I needed only three is my only regret," said Vance in an interview with the *New York Journal-American* 20 years after he retired.

He remembered the incident well. He said the Dodgers were beating the Giants by one run, there were two outs and nobody on and he had two strikes on Mancuso. Dazzy threw him a curve ball and he hooked it foul. Al Lopez, the catcher came out and suggested that Dazzy throw a fastball under his chin and then come back with another breaking ball away. Dazzy told his catcher he'd rather waste a curveball outside and then come back with the high, hard one. "How he reached that curve, I don't know, but Gus hit a double," said Vance. The next batter walked and then Joe Moore singled to center, scoring Mancuso with the tying run. "And there went my last chance to win No. 198," said Vance.[12]

In an interview with David Condon of the *Chicago Daily Tribune*, also 20 years after he retired, Dazzy pointed to another game that cost him dearly—the May 15 contest against the Cubs in which Stengel brought Dazzy on in relief in the first inning and he pitched effectively until the ninth inning when he wilted and gave up the winning runs.

"[On] this afternoon, a coach wore me out chasing fungoes for two hours before the game," said Dazzy. Dodgers starter Johnny Babich couldn't get anybody out in the first inning and Stengel called on Vance to relieve. Dazzy pitched eight innings. Before the start of the ninth inning, Dazzy said he told Stengel, "I'm all in. Get someone ready." He said Stengel replied, "That's the trouble. You pitchers never are in shape. Well, go one more inning." He did, and the Cubs scored four runs. "That game did me in," said Vance.[13]

It was a difficult end to his major league baseball career, but for the man who was often accused of being lazy though highly successful on the ball field, a life of leisure awaited him because he had planned it so well while he was playing.

The land baron of Homosassa Springs, Fla., was coming home.

XV

"I never liked spring training anyway"

Within a month of being released by the Dodgers, Dazzy was pitching for the Brooklyn Bushwicks, one of the nation's top semi-pro teams, and he seemed comfortable with his situation.

"Why should I feel badly about hurling for the Bushwicks?" he said. "We got a good club, probably the best in the semi-professional ranks. Age catches up with all of us. I'm still good for three to six innings. I'm having my first fling, too, at pitching against Negro teams."[1]

That was true. In Vance's era in the big leagues, blacks were not allowed. It prevented Dazzy and others in the major leagues from competing with and against the great stars of the Negro Leagues such as Josh Gibson and James "Cool Papa" Bell who was said to be so fast that he could turn off the lights and be in bed before the room got dark.

"I'll stand those Nashville Elite Giants—I guess that's what they call 'em — on their heads, probably work against the Elmhurst Grays and go as far as I can against the New York Black Yankees. Believe me, some of those black boys can hustle," said Dazzy.[2]

Vance said he wasn't sure whether he'd be back in 1936 to play for the Bushwicks. That would depend on how well things went with the baseball school he was planning to open with George Earnshaw at his home in Homosassa Springs, Florida. The school would feature many major league players and former players, all of whom had specialties. Vance and Earnshaw would work with pitchers. Al Lopez, who lived in Tampa, would work with catchers. Joe Stripp signed on to work with infielders and Bernie Neis, Vance's teammate in the old days at Brooklyn, would be the mentor for would-be outfielders.

A writer who interviewed Vance wrote, "So, at 42 [sic], you find the comely old Dazzler — a trifle thicker around the middle, a trifle thinner around the skull, a few more wrinkles in that kindly, grinning face, tanned by 20 or more years of major league sun — looking ahead."[3]

The Dazzy Vance School of Baseball opened in the spring of 1936. He limited enrollment to 25 and put the boys through a strict and inflexible regimen — orange juice at 8 a.m. followed by "road work" followed by breakfast followed by classroom lectures. Then it was time to go to the ball field where the boys did calisthenics and leg work. It was after all of this that the youngsters were allowed to pick up bats and balls and gloves and take part in general instruction on the field. Then teams were selected and the boys played against each other. Sometimes prizes, such as baseballs autographed by the 1935 Dodgers, were offered to the winning teams.

The school went well, so well in fact that Dazzy took some time away from it to go to Kentucky where he was paid very well by an advertising agency to talk a little baseball to well-heeled customers of the agency.

The baseball school, the speeches, the many guest appearances — all were sidelights to what he wanted most and what he had carefully planned — a quiet, comfortable life in Homosassa, the place that he compared on more than one occasion to heaven. If Dazzy had a talent that was even greater than pitching a baseball, it was being a wise businessman. His infamous holdouts with the Dodgers not only provided him with lucrative contracts for six months of work, but also gave him money to invest. And he decided early on to invest it in Homosassa and Homosassa Springs. He first came to the area on a fishing trip in 1923, or maybe it was 1924; that date got lost with the passage of time. Florida experienced a land boom in the Roaring '20s and Dazzy bought some land. When prices began to fall as the Great Depression began to settle in, Ole Daz not only held on to the land he had, he steadily purchased more at rock-bottom prices. By the time he retired from baseball, he had 3,300 acres of land, according to one newspaper account, and owned most of Homosassa Springs, according to many newspaper accounts.

By 1937, his holdings included the Homosassa Springs Hotel, a 50-room Spanish-style stucco structure sitting right on the edge of a fisherman's paradise — nine miles from the Gulf of Mexico and adjacent to beautiful springs, said to contain youth-restoring properties, also owned by Dazzy. He owned a fleet of fishing boats, the general store, the docks and the baseball field nearby. The post office was just down the way from the hotel and Dazzy's niece, the daughter of his brother, Boyd, was the postmistress. Boyd was the captain of the *Dazzmarine*, his cabin cruiser. The local gas station was operated by the husband of another of Boyd's daughters. The hotel had a gift shop run by Dazzy and Edythe and down the road a ways was a woodworking shop that produced everything from furniture to boats. That too was owned by the Vances.

Ballplayers came to Homosassa and Homosassa Springs, a few miles to the east, to relax, hunt and fish, and swap baseball stories with the king of storytellers. Often, after dinner, they would sit around a roaring fire in the big fireplace in the lobby of the hotel — Babe Ruth, Dizzy Dean, Paul and Lloyd Waner, Burleigh Grimes and many others. Bernie Neis, Dazzy's teammate in Brooklyn, was also his teammate in Homosassa. He was the fishing guide and was known as one of the expert fishermen in all of Florida.

Dazzy had planned his retirement and planned it well. He not only owned most of the town but when the Florida tourist boom returned and land values increased with the law of supply and demand, many people looked to settle on the Gulf Coast. He sold them land at prices extraordinarily higher than what he had paid.

Something had to give — and it turned out to be the baseball school he and Earnshaw and Neis operated in the spring of 1935. Dazzy got out of it after one year. He never quit helping kids play baseball but he didn't want the regimen of running the baseball school. "I never liked spring training anyway," he said.

It wasn't just ballplayers who dropped in on the Ole Dazzler. Many of his sportswriting friends made their way over to Homosassa Springs and were amazed at what they saw.

George Cassidy wrote, "Dazzy Vance has become the Baron of Homosassa Springs, the idol of the hunters and fishermen.... When he slipped out of baseball for good last year, he slipped into his new character as easily as a snake shedding an old skin for a new one." Cassidy tells of how fishermen from around the country gather around the great fireplace at night and tell nothing but the truth, of course, about their catches of the day. Sometimes, he said, Dazzy, coming in from the Gulf where he was aboard the *Dazzmarine*, would join the storytellers and match them "yarn for yarn, telling of the 40-pound grouper and razor-toothed barracuda. Or maybe of shooting duck that morning among the margrove swamps." Cassidy ended his piece by telling how Dazzy wanted to get a highway built in the area that would be right on the path to his hotel. If that came to be, said Cassidy (and eventually it did), the towns-people would just shake their heads and say, "He's done it. Ole Dazzy did."[4]

When sportswriter Sid Mercer caught up with him one day in 1937, he was giving a casting lesson to two old friends from Brooklyn. Mercer described the scene in much the same way he used to describe Dazzy on the mound at Ebbets Field. "Pitching with a sidearm motion and without a windup, Dazzy Vance drew back his trusty right — and launched a long trout cast that struck within a foot of the piling he had picked out as a target."

After the casting exhibition, which was done on a dock in front of his fishing lodge, he and Mercer got in a rowboat and Dazzy took the writer for a tour of the area as they headed for Homosassa, four miles away. Vance pointed to a building partially hidden by trees and said that was where President Grover Cleveland threw a party now and then. "I guess old Grover was the fishingest president we ever had," said Dazzy. "He knew where to git fish."

Mercer was mesmerized by what he saw. He called Homosassa Springs "one of the sights of Florida." He described how they fed the Homosassa River at the rate of 70,000 gallons an hour and hit a depth of 90 feet in one area. He said thousands of fish in more than 20 varieties inhabited the water and hundreds of them swam in schools near the surface — and some of them were "real big fellows."

"He may be all through with baseball but they are never going to hold any benefits for the old Dazzler," wrote Mercer.[5]

Bill McCullough paid a visit and noted that Vance, once the crown prince of storytelling in baseball, was on his way to capturing a similar reputation spinning tales about fishing. It seemed that everyone who visited Dazzy came away talking about the fireside chats after dark in the lobby of his hotel. "Vance seldom talks baseball but will spend half the night telling you how to hook a big grouper or a kingfish," wrote McCullough.[6]

Dazzy would often come in from a day of hunting or fishing, with boots, slacks, shirt with pockets on each side and open at the collar, floppy hat cocked back on the top of his head exposing most of his forehead, and a cigar — sometimes lit — in the corner of his mouth. And oh how the stories flowed. Sometimes he'd recount his baseball days — how he had Hack Wilson psyched out with the ragged sleeve and how his best pitch was "the unexpected one" and how the toughest out for him was a little-known outfielder named Curt Walker. "No matter where or how I threw the ball, he'd unload it," said the Daz.

Wilson, who hit 56 home runs in 1930, the same year Vance struck him out four times in one game, always said Dazzy was the toughest pitcher he ever faced. Wilson would go back to the bench and say, "I'll get him next time." A teammate once kidded him by saying, "The only hit you've ever gotten off of him is in conversation."

He said what made Babe Herman such a tough hitter was that Babe never thought about what he was going to do in the batter's box. "How can you outsmart someone who doesn't think?" said Daz. And Woody English was another tough out. "Woody was a sarcastic hitter. He'd look one way and hit another."

Dazzy said Van Lingle Mungo could have been another Dizzy Dean if he had possessed Dizzy's disposition — but he didn't. "Dizzy put pressure on the hitter by making the hitter think he, and not Dizzy, was the chump," said Dazzy. Vance said he struck Hank Greenberg out in the 1934 World Series by talking to him, kidding him, and getting him to relax at the plate. Then Dazzy bore down and got him on strikes. Often, when Vance told his stories, his sides would shake as he laughed.

Dazzy was a .150 lifetime hitter in the big leagues but he liked to tell of the time he got three hits off of Bill Sherdel of the Cardinals. "I kinda felt sorry for Willie that afternoon," said the Daz. "He had no idea I was a slow-ball hitter but I found out that years ago as a kid on our farm in Nebraska," he said.

Dazzy said the family was having problems with rats. Someone got a ferret and stuck it down a hole. Dazzy was told to go down a little ways to where there was another hole. When the ferret chased the rats out, Dazzy was supposed to club them with his baseball bat. Out scampered a rat, and Dazzy swung and missed it. And another and another with the same result. "Musta missed 50," said the Dazzler. "Then came one fellow nice and slow. I swung and flattened it. Unfortunately, that was the ferret. From that point on, I knew I was a natural slow-ball hitter."[7]

He said his toughest loss was the 1–0 ten-inning thriller against the Cardinals in 1930 that ended the Dodgers' 11-game winning streak and sent them on a tailspin and the Cardinals on the road to the World Series. He lamented that if Al Lopez, his buddy and frequent fishing companion, had run just a little faster on the last play, the game would have been tied and Brooklyn surely would have eventually won it.[8]

Dazzy had a good supply of hunting and fishing stories too. He loved to tell the one about the guide he hired to help guests make their way through the hunting and fishing preserve in Homosassa Springs. The guide went into the woods on what was supposed to be an expedition of a couple of hours, but he wasn't seen again for three days. When he returned, Dazzy said to him, "What happened? Did you get lost?" And the embarrassed guide said, "No, no. I wasn't lost. I was just bothered a little." Dazzy's sides would almost always shake when he told that one.[9]

Much has been said and written about Vance's hotel. His home was between Homosassa and Crystal River, constructed of palmetto logs that were stood on end rather than being horizontal to the ground. Originally, the house was one story with two bedrooms. Dazzy later added a large room as a second story that he used as a trophy room. Entry to the second-floor room could be gained from a large porch on the back of the house which was about 50 feet from the edge of the Hall River. He cut a small boat basin at the river's edge. The river at that point was full of jungle-like reeds and grasses that needed to be cut to create channels for the boats. Dazzy called the growth "hummock."[10]

In the late fall of 1938, Dazzy became ill with a cold that got progressively worse. On Nov. 6, he was admitted to Morton F. Plant Hospital in Clearwater where it was determined he had lobar pneumonia. Dazzy said later that he was transported to the hospital in a laundry truck, lying on a mattress in the back, because he was too sick to wait for an ambulance to arrive. His condition initially was described as "favorable" but got progressively worse and at one point he was listed as "critical." For two weeks he was fed intravenously and was on oxygen inhalation. On Nov. 23, his doctor and personal friend, Dr. Lucien Dickerson, reported that Dazzy had a good day but was still seriously ill. He gained strength and seemed to be on the road to recovery when he had a relapse in December. On Jan. 3, 1939, the hospital issued a statement which reported that Dazzy was progressing "satisfactorally." In February, he was well enough to receive visitors but his right lung was still being drained. Dazzy said the hole in his lung felt as big as the Bedford Avenue gate to Ebbets Field.

During his illness, he often became delirious and would drift off into unconsciousness that produced unusual dreams, he said later. In one of them, he hit a home run and wanted to get out of bed to run the bases. In another, he was going to join a baseball team managed by Jim Bottomley, the old Cardinals first baseman, but arrived too late and so they made it a football team. In late February, Dazzy was released from the hospital, 70 pounds lighter than when he was admitted.[11]

It was in April of that year that sportswriter Bill Corum ran into him in Clearwater as the Dodgers broke camp and started heading north for the start of the baseball season — the time of year when Vance said "the old jeepers creepers" started to set in. Corum said it was obvious that his recent illness had "cut deeply into what once seemed to be boundless health and strength," but Ole Daz still had his sense of humor.

"For six weeks," said Dazzy, "St. Peter had me in the bullpen and it took a long time for me to get up enough gimp to remind him I was still a starting pitcher." He said when he left the hospital he had to add 18 notches to his belt to keep his pants on. He would have been in the hospital sooner, he said, but it took four weeks to convince his wife he was sick. She just thought he was being lazy again, said Daz. He invited Corum to come over to Homosassa where the fishing was so good, he said, "you can catch your own trout right in the skillet in which you're going to cook it."[12]

Dazzy recovered completely from the pneumonia but was on doctor's orders to watch his diet and his alcohol intake — "darn the luck," he said — and enjoyed making periodic trips back to Brooklyn for old-timers games and fund-raisers. He was still idolized at Ebbets Field as he discovered on Sept. 22, 1940, when two teams of old-time Brooklyn players— the "Robins" and the "Dodgers"— played a three-inning exhibition game. Dazzy was reunited with his old battery mate, Hank DeBerry. Another old Brooklyn catcher, Otto Miller, was also there as was Del Bissonette, Bernie Neis, Rube Bressler, Andy High, Joe Stripp, Zack Wheat and Rube Marquard. Dazzy pitched the first inning for the "Dodgers" and, without the high leg kick or blazing fastball, managed to retire the opposition without allowing a run. In the pre-game introductions, the crowd showed enthusiasm for all but saved its most thunderous applause for Dazzy and Zack Wheat.

Dazzy gave up active participation in the Dazzy Vance School of Baseball about a year after he started it in 1936 to devote more time to his business dealings and to his well-planned life of leisure. But he never gave up his interest in helping youngsters. He started a youth baseball program in Citrus County in the early 1940s and coached the West Citrus team to a league championship in 1954. In 1946, he sold his hotel and, by that time, had sold much of the 3,300 acres of land he once owned, all of which added to his considerable wealth.

He returned to Brooklyn frequently for old-timers games and charity events. In 1947, he was named to manage the Brooklyn Eagle All-Stars in a three-game amateur tournament sponsored by the *Brooklyn Eagle* with proceeds going to the Brooklyn Amateur Baseball Foundation. He joked with writers about the old days and said he wished Brooklyn would have had a double play combination like the '47 Dodgers had with PeeWee Reese at shortstop and Eddie Stanky at second base.

"When I was in Brooklyn and had to pitch with runners on first and third, I could never count on the fellows behind me making a double play," said Dazzy. "The only way I could

Dazzy was a popular performer at Dodger old-timer games. He loved coming back to Ebbets Field — and the press loved to have him back because he always had great stories to tell. (Courtesy Hall of Fame.)

cut off that run was to strike out that second-out batter. That was the only thing on my mind."

Someone asked him if it was true that he had a season in which he completed every game he started. Had he said "yes," no one would have doubted him. But he didn't. Instead, he told reporters of a little known statistic about him — as if he had saved it for this occasion. "There were two years in a row (1924 and 1925) when I won 50 games and never had another pitcher help me win any of them," he said. "In other words, all the games I won I finished."[13]

On the morning of Jan. 19, 1955, Dazzy Vance was driving along Highway 19, the road he lobbied to have built, not far from his home in Homosassa, when a highway patrolman flagged him down. "I thought he was going to give me a ticket," said Dazzy. Instead, the officer told him he needed to go home, that a photographer was waiting for him at his house.

Dazzy said he suspected something good might be happening

because he had heard the Hall of Fame voting results were to be announced that day. Indeed, he had made it, becoming the first player in the history of the Brooklyn Dodgers to be voted in to the Hall of Fame.

The story of Dazzy being stopped by the traffic cop has been told and retold and like so many of Dazzy's stories, it makes a good yarn. And it may be the absolute truth. But Dazzy knew what day the Hall of Fame inductees would be announced. His name had been on the ballot every year since 1942 and he had been creeping up toward the 75 percent requirement for induction since 1947.

The Hall of Fame balloting results had gone like this:

1947: Carl Hubbell, Frankie Frisch, Mickey Cochrane and Lefty Grove elected; Vance 13th in votes with 31.6 percent.

1948: Herb Pennock and Pie Traynor elected; Vance 14th in votes with 19 percent.

1949: No one elected; Vance 13th in votes with 21.5 percent.

1950: No one elected; Vance 12th in votes with 30.9 percent

1951: Mel Ott and Jimmie Foxx elected; Vance 11th in votes with 30.9 percent

1952: Harry Heilmann and Paul Waner elected; Vance 8th in votes with 44 percent

1953: Dizzy Dean and Al Simmons elected; Vance 6th in votes with 56.8 percent

1954: Rabbit Maranville, Bill Dickey and Bill Terry elected; Vance 6th in votes with 62.7 percent.

Those elected in 1955 were: Joe DiMaggio, 88.8 percent; Ted Lyons, 86.4 percent; Dazzy Vance, 81.6 percent; Gabby Hartnett, 77.6 percent. Further down the list were two men who would eventually make it — Max Carey, Dazzy's former teammate who was also the manager who traded him; and Hack Wilson, the great slugger who had trouble hitting Dazzy throughout his career.

Vance became the first member of the Brooklyn Dodgers to be elected to the Hall of Fame. Induction ceremonies would be held in July in Cooperstown, New York, but Brooklyn was not about to wait that long to celebrate. Within a week, he was the guest of honor at the New York Baseball Writers Association dinner and was publicly recognized in Brooklyn on "Dazzy Vance Day." Brooklyn borough mayor John Cashmore read a proclamation adopted by the borough's governing council that cited how Dazzy "courageously refused to yield to discouragement

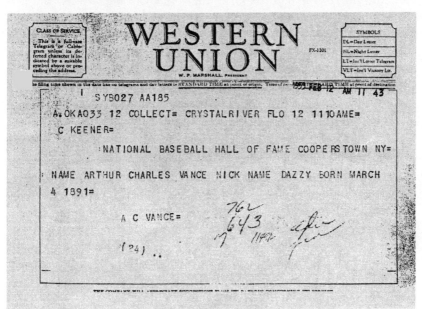

The filing time shown in the date line on telegrams and day letters is STANDARD TIME at point of origin. Time of receipt is STANDARD TIME at point of destination.

NUMBER   RECEIVED AT   CHECK

Dated   ARTHUR DAZZY VANCE   COOPERSTOWN, N.Y. 2/11/55

To   HOMOSASSA, FLORIDA   Telephoned 3:00 P.M.

WE NEED NAME YOU SELECT AS OFFICIAL AND YEAR OF BIRTH FOR DATA ON

YOUR HALL OF FAME PLAQUE. ROSCOE MCGOWEN'S STORY FEBRUARY 9TH

SPORTING NEWS CHANGES ARTHUR CHARLES TO CLARENCE ARTHUR. THERE IS

CONFLICT IN YEAR IN WHICH YOU WERE BORN. MCGOWEN'S STORY GIVES 1891

BY YOURSELF 1893 IN RECORD BOOKS WHILE A FRIEND SAYS 1896. WE WILL

APPRECIATE PROMPT TELEGRAM COLLECT, IF YOU WILL UNTANGLE THIS DAZZY

MYSTERY. SHOULD WE USE ARTHUR CHARLES OR DO YOU PREFER CLARENCE ARTHUR.

YOUR INFORMATION WILL BE AGREEABLE HERE. WARMEST WISHES.   SID C. KEENER

THE COMPANY WILL APPRECIATE SUGGESTIONS FROM ITS PATRONS CONCERNING ITS SERVICE

The filing time shown in the date line on telegrams and day letters is STANDARD TIME at point of origin. Time of receipt is STANDARD TIME at point of destination.

1955 FEB 12 AM 11 43

SYB027 AA185

A.OKA033 12 COLLECT= CRYSTALRIVER FLO 12 1110AME=

C KEENER=

    NATIONAL BASEBALL HALL OF FAME COOPERSTOWN NY=

NAME ARTHUR CHARLES VANCE NICK NAME DAZZY BORN MARCH

4 1891=

        A C VANCE=

        (24)..

Dazzy Vance was named "Charles Arthur Vance" but he preferred "Arthur Charles Vance" or "A.C. Vance" and was known for a while as "Clarence Arthur Vance." All of this confused officials of the Hall of Fame who telegrammed Dazzy on Feb. 11, 1955, wanting to know how he should be identified on his plaque. Also, there was confusion over his date of birth. Vance responded with a telegram the next day. Note that he signed it "A.C. Vance." (Courtesy Hall of Fame.)

and adversity during an earlier part of his career, and eventually became the greatest pitcher in the history of the Brooklyn Dodgers … and serves as an inspiration to young Americans and especially to millions of our youth who idolize great baseball players."

Vance told a cheering audience in the borough council chambers, "I feel the same way Columbus must have felt when he looked out from his ship and first saw land." He said there are four phases in a baseball player's life: first, learning how to play the game; next, breaking into organized ball; third, the thrill of being the most valuable player or pitching a no-hitter or getting into the World Series—"fortunately, I made all three," he said; and fourth, "if you're lucky enough to get into the Hall of Fame, you've had it all." He paused momentarily to compose himself, ran his hand through his now thinning white hair, and said, "Now there's nothing left for me but to let nature take its course."[14]

At a dinner the night before, Dazzy thanked the writers who had voted him into the Hall of Fame and then provided them with an All-American schmooze. "The boys in the press box were responsible for 75 percent of my success," he said. If someone wrote something nasty about him, said Dazzy, he'd say to himself, "I gotta show up this illiterate so-and-so. If someone wrote something nice about me, I'd say 'there's a right smart young feller and I can't let him down.' So I'd bear down even more," he said.

Dazzy said when he was a rookie with Brooklyn in 1922, the Dodgers were headed to the Polo Grounds for a series with the Giants. One of the writers covering the Giants wrote, "As if things aren't bad enough, the Giants still have to face Dazzy Vance and Burleigh Grimes." Vance said that one line thrilled him and he's never forgotten it.

Once again, Ole Daz was on a roll and he had an audience that didn't want him to quit. He talked about his mastery of Hack Wilson over the years and how Wilson once told him that his weakness was any pitch Vance threw to him. Dazzy also recalled the time Sammy Bohne of the Cincinnati Reds broke up his no-hitter with two outs in the ninth inning. That night, while he was having a beer, he ran into Sammy. He said he told him, "I'd be the last man in the world ever to ask another ballplayer to lie down and give me a gift of a no-hitter. But I'd advise you never to take a toe-hold on me at the plate again." And, would you believe it? said Daz. "He never got another hit off me in his life."

Dazzy also talked about present-day ballplayers. He said he marveled at the change-up of the Yankees' Whitey Ford, describing it in typical Vance fashion. "He throws it with his pulse," said Dazzy.

The evening after the "Dazzy Vance Day" ceremonies, Vance lit the "hot stove" at the Long Island Dodger Boosters' Club at the Garden City Hotel where he wowed the crowd with still more stories. The next day, he returned home to Homosassa where he could pick back up on the life that he had so carefully chosen — hunting, fishing, chatting and, as he told his friends in Brooklyn, letting nature take its course.[15]

The Hall of Fame induction ceremonies at Cooperstown in July were subdued compared to the Brooklyn celebrations but all of the events brought forth a new generation of fans. Dazzy got a taste of how his achievements withstood the test of time when he arrived in New York and was greeted at the train station by a group of cheering Cub Scouts, waving at him and seeking his autograph. In Brooklyn, he posed for pictures with fans, with ballplayers and with politicians who knew a good photo op when they saw one. In one of the more obvious staged photos, Dazzy, in coat and tie, demonstrated his famous wind-up, for Johnny Podres, a young Brooklyn left-handed pitcher, on the steps of the Brooklyn City Hall.[16]

In the next few years, Dazzy didn't venture far from Homosassa Springs except to attend baseball old-timer functions in New York. There was the day in Yankee Stadium, not long after the Hall of Fame inductions, when 20 Hall of Famers, including Ty Cobb, Bill Terry, Ray Schalk, Joe DiMaggio, Lefty Grove and Vance were recognized; and the "game" on Aug. 14, 1955, at Ebbets Field where the crowd roared when Vance took the mound and his old teammate Zack Wheat got into the batter's box. Nobody seemed to mind that 64-year-old Dazzy and 67-year-old Wheat had long ago lost their zip.

In 1957, Dazzy ventured over to St. Petersburg in January for an old-timers all-star game matching former stars of the American and National leagues. Ed Rousch, Heinie Manusch, Johnny Allen, Rip Sewell and Wes Ferrell were there, but the biggest applause was saved for Nick Altrock and Tommy Leach, both 80 and at one time roommates with the Louisville ballclub in 1898.

On Feb. 15, 1961, Dazzy got up in the morning and spent a typical day in Homosassa Springs. He cleared some underbrush — "hummock," as he called it — from around his house and hauled it away in his jeep. When he returned, he met with Ken Smith, a writer and Hall of Fame historian. They sat on his porch, beneath the big moss trees along the winding river, and he reminisced about the old days but also reflected on the importance of good pitching in the current era. "No manager will win if he doesn't have an instinct for pitchers," said Vance. "Many try to run a club without a knack. A pitcher detects the boss's ignorance quickly. Our manager, [Wilbert] Robinson, who used to catch, knew pitchers so completely, he could smell one."[17]

It was vintage Vance — insightful, colorful, learned. The comments were published posthumously. The next day, Dazzy dropped dead in his home, two weeks shy of his 70th birthday. The cause of death was a coronary thrombosis. His doctor, A.R. Miller, left no doubt that Dazzy died quickly at 5:50 a.m. On his death certificate, in the box labeled "interval between onset and death" Dr. Miller wrote a zero.

Tributes poured in from all over the country. Fred Lieb in *The Sporting News* called him "one of the game's outstanding pitchers and foremost personalities." Murray Robinson wrote in the *New York Journal-American*, "He was born to be a big-leaguer, and when he finally arrived, he carried himself with dignity, even in play."

Frank Graham, who knew him well and wrote about him often, said Vance wasn't the kind of guy who was ever going to build a bridge or design an airplane. His interests and skills were less sophisticated. "All he ever wanted to do was play baseball, go fishing or sit in the sun. Everywhere he went, and he went about everywhere in this country, he made friends and had laughs."

Famed syndicated columnist Red Smith recognized the same qualities in Dazzy that Graham did, and expressed them this way. "Surely nature intended him from the beginning to be just what he was—the gifted, gregarious, gaily unrepentent leader of the Merry-Andrews who played baseball — whenever the spirit moved them."

In 1951, Dazzy talked with Richard Fay Warner of the *New York Times*, who came to visit him in Homosassa Springs. He said that Vance chatted with him, shifting a chewed stump of a cigar in his mouth, while he was doing a little work on a boat. Dazzy told Warner, "The Suawanee River has its course here in Florida and ends here. I am going to do the same, huntin' and fishin'."[18]

His daughter, Dorothy Williams, talked in a 1994 interview about how her father wanted to live out his days. "He really believed deep down in his heart that Citrus County was the most wonderful place in the world," she said. "His one wish was to live the rest of his life there and die in his home on Halls River Road. And that's what he did."[19]

Death came on a day when many of his beloved Dodgers and hundreds of other ballplayers were preparing to head south to prepare for another baseball season. In his inimitable style, if he could have, Ole Daz would have laughed till his sides would shake once more, considering the timing of his demise.

After all, as he said, he never did like spring training.

Appendix

Dazzy Vance Statistics

Vance, Charles Arthur
Also known as
   Vance, Arthur Charles
Also known as
   Vance, Clarence Arthur
Nickname: Dazzy

Born March 4, 1891, Orient, Iowa. Died Feb. 16, 1961, Homosassa Springs, Florida. Height: 6 feet, 2 inches; weight: 200 pounds. Bats right, throws right. Elected to Hall of Fame: 1955.

Year	Team	W–L	Pct.	ERA	G	IP	H	BB	SO
1915	Pitt/NY (A)	0–4	.000	4.11	9	30.2	26	21	18
1918	NY (A)	0–0	.000	15.43	2	2.1	9	2	0
1922	Brklyn	18–12	.600	3.70	36	245.2	259	94	134
1923	Brklyn	18–15	.545	3.50	37	280.1	263	100	197
1924	Brklyn	28–6	.824	2.16	35	308.2	238	77	262
1925	Brklyn	22–9	.710	3.53	31	265.1	247	66	221
1926	Brklyn	9–10	.474	3.89	24	169	172	58	140
1927	Brklyn	16–15	.516	2.70	34	273.1	242	69	184
1928	Brklyn	22–10	.688	2.09	38	280.1	226	72	200
1929	Brklyn	14–13	.519	3.89	31	231.1	244	47	126
1930	Brklyn	17–15	.531	2.61	35	258.2	241	55	173
1931	Brklyn	11–13	.458	3.38	30	218.2	221	53	150
1932	Brklyn	12–11	.522	4.20	27	175.2	171	57	103
1933	StL. (N)	6–2	.750	3.55	28	99	105	28	67
1934	StL/Cin	1–3	.250	4.56	25	77	90	25	42
1935	Brklyn	3–2	.600	4.41	20	51	55	16	28
16 years		197–140	.585	3.24	442	2967	2809	840	2045

World's Series

Year	Team	W–L			G	IP	H	BB	SO
1934	StL (N)	0–0	0.00	.000	1	1.1	2	1	3

Chapter Notes

Chapter I

1. *Time* magazine, Oct. 7, 1946
2. Bill Corum, *Off and Running*, (New York: Henry Holt & Co., New York, 1959), p 98.
3. Corum, Bill, "Memories Walk on Lonesome Street," *New York Times*, April 6, 1939. Bill Corum was one of the nation's top sports writers when he ran into Dazzy Vance on that Clearwater street corner. His column appeared in newspapers throughout the country on April 6, 1939. Corum had many claims to fame as a writer. One of them was coining the phrase "a run for the roses"—a reference still used today to describe the Kentucky Derby horse race.
4. *Ibid.*
5. *Ibid.*
6. *Ibid.*
7. Frank Graham, "Graham's Corner," *New York Journal American*, Feb. 17, 1961.
8. Widely quoted, as are many stories about Wilbert Robinson, "Uncle Robbie," the legendary Dodgers manager.
9. Graham, *The Brooklyn Dodgers* (New York: G.P. Putnam's Sons, 1945), p 113.
10. Murray Robinson, "Murray Robinson Says," *New York Journal American*, Feb. 19, 1961.
11. Widely quoted.

Chapter II

1. The author is indebted to Marilyn Geidel of Orient, Iowa, for her insights and observations of Orient in the late 1800s.

2. Gary Vance, a retired sheriff's deputy in California and great-nephew of Dazzy Vance, provided details of the Vance family history as well as observations and remembrances of his relative.
3. F.C. Lane, "How Dazzy Got His Name," *Baseball Magazine*, October 1923.
4. The story of Vance's early experiences with baseball changed over the years. When Dazzy first related it to F.C. Lane in 1923, the playmate was a neighbor kid and not his brother Fred and a ball of yarn served as the baseball. The rest of the story, as told to Harry T. Brundidge of the *St. Louis Star-Chronicle* seven years later, is pretty much the same.
5. The account of Vance's wildness as a Hastings High School pitcher was reported in a sidebar story with Vance's obituary in the *Omaha World-Herald* on Feb. 17, 1961.
6. Harry T. Brundidge, "Vance Traces His Start to His Boyhood Days When a Barnyard Served as the Diamond," *St. Louis Star-Chronicle*.
7. *Ibid.*
8. *Ibid.*
9. Wagner, probably with the help of a ghostwriter, wrote a series of articles for the *Atlanta Constitution*. Under the headline, "Honus Wagner's Own Baseball Story," the strikeout of the rookie and the mention of Sam Crawford was published Feb. 13, 1916.
10. Honus Wagner, "Honus Wagner's Own Story," *Atlanta Constitution*, Feb. 27, 1916.
11. F.C. Lane recounted the tale of the beaning in the October 1923 issue of *Baseball Magazine*.

12. Dazzy recounted his injury for Furman Bisher in an article published in the Aug. 20, 1955, issue of the *Saturday Evening Post*. In the earlier interview with Brundidge, Vance said he was suspended without pay from the Columbus team and had to borrow money to get home. He said he borrowed money for the railroad ticket from a pitcher named Tom Blodgett and that Larry Pratt, a catcher, gave him $2 meal money. He paid back Blodgett but had trouble locating Pratt. Several years later, when Vance was a star pitcher with the Brooklyn Dodgers, he received a letter from Pratt, who by that time was a successful druggist in Illinois. The letter said, "Dear Dazzy, Please pay me that $2 you owe me. If you send me a check for it, I'll promise to frame it, not cash it."

13. Among those names in that third tier of players who had to make their own way to Macon was Urban Shocker, who had a 4–3 record for the Yankees that year and went on to win 187 games with them in a 12-year career. He won 20 games or more four years in a row for them (1920–1923) and was one of their starters in the 1926 World's Series against the St. Louis Cardinals.

14. "Dazzy Vance Has Long, Hard Claim to Fame," *New York Herald Tribune*, Nov. 18, 1922.

15. "Dazzy Vance Blanks Crackers in Fast Game," *Atlanta Constitution*, May 15, 1918.

16. "Dazzy Vance Daubs Crackers With White," *Atlanta Constitution*, June 4, 1918.

17. "Birmingham's Rise Features Southern," *Atlanta Constitution*, May 9, 1920.

18. "Daz Escapes From Farm," *New York Herald Tribune*, Feb. 7, 1955.

Chapter III

1. Charles C. Alexander, *John McGraw*, (New York: Viking, 1988) p 28.

2. There are several stories related to the creation of duckpin bowling — but all accounts say it originated at The Diamond, owned by McGraw and Robinson. One account has it that the manager of the

place, Frank Van Sant, asked workers to sand down some well-worn regulation-size bowling pins. By the time the overzealous workers had completed their job, the pins were too small to use. A new game was developed, using a smaller ball with the smaller pins. *The Book of Duckpin Bowling*, by Henry Fankhauser and Frank Micalizzi, says The Diamond already had the smaller balls, which were used in variations of traditional bowling, such as using five pins instead of ten. Battered old pins were intentionally whittled down to create the new ten-pin game. All accounts agree that the game got its name because McGraw and Robinson thought the pins looked like ducks flying around when struck by the balls.

3. Alexander, *John McGraw*, pp. 170–171

4. Graham, *The Brooklyn Dodgers*, p. 47.

5. *Ibid.*, p. 87.

6. *Ibid.*, p. 86.

7. *Ibid.*, p. 84.

Chapter IV

1. "Giants Pound Vance and Defeat Robins," *New York Times*, April 13, 1922.

2. "Pitching of Vance Helps Robins Win," *New York Times*, May 1, 1922.

3. Graham, *The Brooklyn Dodgers*, p. 86.

4. Widely quoted.

5. Smith was 3–6 for the Robins in 1923 and never appeared in the major leagues again. Mitchell has at least two claims to fame. He was the best man at the wedding of another Nebraska pitcher, Grover Cleveland Alexander. In 1920, he was the batter when Bill Wambsganss, Cleveland second baseman, executed an unassisted triple play in the World's Series.

6. "Giants Tie Robins in 9th, Win in 11th," *New York Times*, May 3, 1923. It is obvious from the prose that the newspaper's "home team" was the Giants and that the writer, in this un-bylined story, enjoyed needling Uncle Robbie, the former coach under John McGraw.

7. On Sept. 16, 1975, Rennie Stennett

of the Pittsburgh Pirates went 7-for-7 in a 22–0 drubbing of the Chicago Cubs, becoming the only player in the 20th century to accomplish that feat.

Chapter V

1. McGraw was quoted at length in the *New York Times* on March, 4, 1924. Managers throughout the years have been known to issue bans on certain practices. When Whitey Herzog took over as manager of the St. Louis Cardinals, he banned television watching in the clubhouse for a while. "Do you think it will affect the team's chemistry?" a reporter asked. "No, and I don't think it will hurt their history or geography either," said Whitey.

2. Dean was not related to Dizzy or Daffy and didn't pitch like either of them. He won five more games for the Giants in 1924 but lost 12. He had a respectable 10–7 record in 1925. He was shipped to Philadelphia, where few pitchers did well, and after an 8–16 season in 1926 he appeared in only four games in 1927, splitting his time between the Phillies and the Cubs. He was through in the major leagues at the age of 24 with a lifetime record of 24–36. The description of how he pitched in his major league debut is from the April 18 *New York Times*.

3. Graham, *The Brooklyn Dodgers*, p. 93.

4. Bressler described Vance's sleeve in Lawrence Ritter's baseball classic, *The Glory of Their Times*. Other players as well as Vance himself describe how he cut the sleeve of his undershirt in tatters to confound the hitter, a practice eventually banned in the major leagues.

5. "Dazzy Vance is Chosen Star of National League," *Chicago Tribune*, Dec. 2, 1924.

6. "Petulant Rhino Considered Less Dangerous Than Dazzy," *Atlanta Constitution*, March 24, 1925.

7. This appeared as part of a series of anecdotes about ballplayers in a feature distributed by Associated Editors Inc. and published in the *Los Angeles Times* Aug. 6, 1924. Accompanying it was a cartoon depicting Dazzy in a baseball uniform with a pistol in his hand.

8. The "second fiddle" reference is in a lengthy biographical piece on Burleigh Grimes published in the *Washington Post* on Jan. 12, 1925.

9. Graham, *The Brooklyn Dodgers*, pp. 94–95.

Chapter VI

1. A thorough account of the salary dispute was included in a special report to the *New York Times*, published March 7, 1925.

2. Yager's column appeared in the *Brooklyn Eagle* and was reprinted in the *Washington Post* on April 1, 1925. Doak stayed out of baseball for two years and then returned to pitch for Brooklyn in 1927 and 1928, ending his career with the St. Louis Cardinals in 1929. Ruether had a combined record of 45–22 in three years with Washington and the New York Yankees after the Robins gave up on him.

3. The picturesque account of the match-up of Dazzy Vance and Babe Ruth appeared in the *New York Times* on April 7, 1925. The story reported that about 12 boys were sitting in the tree watching the game but none were on the branch that Ruth broke off with his home run.

4. Graham, *The Brooklyn Dodgers*, pp. 96–98.

5. The *New York Times* reported on June 15 that the Brooklyn Robins defeated Cincinnati in Zack Wheat's first game as Robins manager. It reported on Aug. 5. that Wilbert Robinson was returning at Robins manager. Frank Graham, in his book, *The Brooklyn Dodgers*, does not make reference to specific dates, but provides anecdotal evidence that the switch took place and the problems that occurred with it. Yet, such references as the *Baseball Encyclopedia*, *Total Baseball* and the National Baseball Hall of Fame make no reference to Wheat's brief tenure as manager, nor do the Internet Web sites baseball-reference.com, baseballlibrary.com and Retrosheet.

6. There are many variations to the stories on how Dazzy got his nickname.

Dazzy told the original story many times about how a neighbor used the expression "dazzy" instead of "daisy" and the young Vance boy picked it up. It is not known whether he embellished the story to include the bases-loaded strikeout to give the press a good yarn or whether the Hastings incident actually happened. What is known is that Dazzy was known as Dazzy before he pitched for Hastings. The story of the strikeout appeared in the *New York Times* on June 28, 1925.

7. Dazzy's recounting of the Bottomley, O'Doul and Berger strikeouts appeared in Arthur Daley's "Sports of the Times" column on Oct. 11, 1953. There are some points of confusion in the anecdote about Bottomley. Dazzy said he got the sign from manager Wilbert Robinson but the game occurred when Zack Wheat was the acting manager with Robbie paying more attention to the front office.

8. Kennedy's list, published Aug. 1, 1925, in the *Atlanta Constitution*, is a little suspect because of inconsistent record keeping prior to the 20th century. One peculiar statistic from the list is that seven of the top strikeout performances occurred in the same year — 1884.

9. The opportunity never panned out. Wheat played one more year with Brooklyn and finished his career with the Philadelphia Athletics in 1927. As for the Cubs, Wheat was right about his assessment of their managerial merry-go-round. After starting the 1925 season with Bill Killefer, Rabbit Maranville took the reins in midseason and was replaced by George Gibson. The Cubs then gave Joe McCarthy his first big league managing job starting with the 1926 season.

10. A vivid account of the fight is included in Richard Vidmer's game story in the Aug. 8, 1925, edition of the *New York Times*.

11. *Los Angeles Times*, Aug. 11, 1925.

12. Corgan played in 14 games for the Robins in 1925 and in 19 games for them in 1927. That was the extent of his major league career — 33 games, 104 at-bats, 23 hits, no home runs and one run batted in.

13. Vidmer's account was published in the *New York Times* on Sept. 9, 1925.

14. Vance's consecutive pitching gems still rank among baseball's best. The best dual performances still belong to Johnny Vander Meer of Cincinnati, who pitched consecutive no hitters on June 11, 1938, against Boston and on June 15, 1938, against Brooklyn. Lon Warneke of the Chicago Cubs pitched consecutive one-hitters to start the 1934 season, beating Reds on April 17 and the St. Louis Cardinals on April 22. Perhaps the hard-luck pitcher of all time was Toronto's Dave Stieb, who threw consecutive one-hitters on Sept. 24 and Sept. 30, 1988, the first against Cleveland, the second against Baltimore, losing both no-hitters with two out in the ninth inning. He started the 1989 season with a one-hitter against the New York Yankees, giving him three consecutive one-hitters spread over the end of one season and the beginning of the next. No discussion of consecutive hitless innings can be without mention of Harvey Haddix's performance against the Milwaukee Braves on May 26, 1959, when he threw a perfect game for 12 innings, only to lose the no-hitter and the game in the 13th inning.

15. Arthur Daly wrote about the Vance-Fletcher banter in his "Sports of the Times" column in the *New York Times* on Aug. 19, 1954. The story has the Dazzler's flair for keeping an audience enthralled — but also shows how he ignored baseball tradition of not mentioning a no-hitter that was in progress.

16. *Washington Post*, Sept. 14, 1925.

17. On April 14, 2002, Ron Wright of the Seattle Mariners had a day at the plate that could easily be compared to Grimes' misfortunes. Wright struck out, hit into a double play and hit into a triple play. The reason Wright's day could be considered worse: It was his major league debut and he has never appeared in another big league game.

Chapter VII

1. Graham, *The Brooklyn Dodgers*, pp. 100–101.

2. Robbie was quoted in the *New York*

Times on March 13, 1926. McWeeny had a 4–10 record in limited action in three seasons with the White Sox (1921, 1922 and 1924) and did not pitch in the major leagues in 1925. He pitched four years for the Robins and never lived up to the potential Wilbert Robinson saw in him, compiling a 33–45 record. He appeared in eight games with Cincinnati in 1930 and then retired from baseball with 37 wins, 57 losses and an earned run average of 4.17.

3. Pegler sized up the Robins in a column published in many newspapers, including the *Atlanta Constitution*, on March 14, 1926.

4. *New York Times*, March 21, 1926.

5. Bob Feller of the Cleveland Indians recorded the only opening day no-hitter on April 16, 1940, against the Chicago White Sox. Lon Warneke of the Chicago Cubs threw a one-hitter to start the season against the St. Louis Cardinals on April 17, 1934, and Dave Stieb of the Toronto Blue Jays allowed just one hit in an opening day start against the New York Yankees in 1989.

6. *New York Times*, May 23, 1926.

7. Graham, *The Brooklyn Dodgers*, pp. 100–105. Tales involving the Daffiness Boys have been widely reported over the years. The ones recounted here were capsulized by Graham in his book.

8. The *Washington Post* reported the difference of opinion on Dazzy's ailments in a story published July 7, 1926.

9. *New York Times*, July 8, 1926.

Chapter VIII

1. *Los Angeles Times*, Nov. 6, 1926.

2. *New York Times*, March 1, 1927.

3. John Kieran, *New York Times*, March 26, 1927. In the same column, Kieran made reference to Dazzy Vance investing much of his baseball riches in Florida real estate. Kieran said Dazzy forgot to sell before the bottom fell out of the market but as time would tell, Vance steadily increased his holdings and had a retirement home, business and recreation waiting for him when his baseball days were over.

4. Graham, *The Brooklyn Dodgers*, p. 110.

5. *New York Times*, April 28, 1927. Richard Vidmer's story outlined the problems of all three New York managers—John McGraw of the Giants, Miller Huggins of the Yankees and Robbie. McGraw and Huggins had the challenge of how to keep their teams on top of the league. Robbie had to figure out how to get the Robins out of the National League cellar.

6. *New York Times*, May 15, 1927. Kieran's column that day made mention of oddities throughout baseball, including the career of Shucks Pruett, a lefthander with the Phillies, previously with the Browns. Pruett had an undistinguished career but faced Babe Ruth 11 times—and struck him out nine times. No one ever did better against the Babe. Kieran mentioned in the same column that "Dazzy Vance has returned to something like his real form," giving Brooklyn fans hope for a pleasant summer.

7. Frank Graham recounts these incidents and many more in his book, *The Brooklyn Dodgers*.

8. John Drebinger, "Robin's Onslaught Repulses Pirates," *New York Times*, June 12, 1927.

9. Feg Murray, "Again a Dazzler," *Los Angeles Times*, July 10, 1927. It is interesting to note that Murray identifies Vance as "Realtor, marksman, golfer and comedian," as if these were all marks of distinction. Gary Vance, Dazzy's great-nephew, said one of the things he remembered about Uncle Dazzy was that he was good at just about everything he tried. It is, of course, well documented that he was a great baseball pitcher and that he was an excellent golfer. He started investing in Florida real estate when he was making big money in baseball and it provided him with excellent retirement income. Gary Vance confirmed that Dazzy was an excellent marksman and, one thing Murray didn't mention, was Vance's pool playing. Gary Vance said if Dazzy missed a shot on the pool table, it was either because he was taking it easy on someone in a friendly game — or trying to lure someone into a game with higher stakes.

10. Tom Thompson, "Dazzy Vance The Second Joins Atlanta," *Atlanta Constitution*, July 9, 1927. Despite all the potential and all the hype that went with it, Chilton's baseball career was confined to the minor leagues.

11. James Harrison, "Four Hits Plus Vance Subdue Giants, 3–2," *New York Times*, July 8, 1927. In the highly competitive world of New York journalism, sportswriters were not only colorful but partisan and not shy about offering their opinions as to what happened on the field.

12. Kieran, "Sports of the Times," *New York Times*, Aug. 25, 1927.

13. "Speed and Curves Receive Credit for Vance's Comeback as Hurler," *New York Times*, Aug. 2, 1927.

14. Scott Feisthumel, "Batting a Thousand," *Utica* (N.Y.) *Life & Times*, Oct. 25, 2001. The Walford Sporting Goods advertisement appeared in the *New York Times* on March 31, 1928. Walford's offered baseball shoes for $2.95 and up and tennis rackets on sale for $2.65 instead of the regular price of $3.75.

Chapter IX

1. Though the Pirates had won the pennant in two out of the last three years, this was the second time in two years they had problems between players and managers. In 1926, Fred Clarke, a former manager and now a vice president, spent time in the dugout overseeing the work of manager Bill McKechnie. Players expressed their displeasure to owner Barney Dreyfuss, who interpreted their complaints as insubordination. Several players were released or found new homes, such as Max Carey coming over to the Robins.

2. Cuyler sat out the 1927 World's Series under Donie Bush but played in two with the Chicago Cubs, in 1929 and in 1932. He was elected to the Hall of Fame in 1968.

3. Graham, *The Brooklyn Dodgers*, pp. 116–117.

4. Accounts of the salary negotiations were contained in John Drebinger's stories in the *New York Times* on March 4 and

March 6, 1928. While Vance was the highest paid pitcher in the National League, Herb Pennock of the Yankees was the highest paid hurler in all of baseball with his annual salary of $22,000.

5. *New York Times*, Feb. 27, 1928.

6. Sportswriters frequently used historical references to punctuate the drama of what was happening on athletic fields. Horatius, according to historical legends of ancient Rome, single-handedly defended a bridge leading into Rome that was being seized by Etruscan warriors. The account of the ballgame appeared in the *New York Times* on May 15, 1928.

7. "Speed and Curves Receive Credit for Vance's Comeback as Hurler," *New York Times*, Aug. 2, 1927. When Dazzy was rattling off the names of all the cities in his minor league travelogue, he neglected to mention St. Cloud and Hastings in the Nebraska State League, where his professional career began.

8. "Phillies and Robins Divide Twin Bill," *New York Times*, June 30, 1928.

9. George Moriarty, "New Delivery Style is Used by Ted Lyons," *Atlanta Constitution*, July 12, 1928.

10. Graham, *The Brooklyn Dodgers*, pp. 114–115.

11. The story was published in the *Washington Post* on Dec. 11, 1928. The contractions and misspellings (such as "Mistah" and "Noo York") are obvious attempts to imitate the way the writer thought black people talked. The story carried no byline.

12. Rice's column, "The Sport Light," appeared in the *Atlanta Constitution* on Jan. 6, 1929.

13. James S. Collins, "Almost the Naked Truth," New York World News Service, Feb. 1, 1929.

14. Westbrook Pegler wrote a column that was syndicated by the *Chicago Daily Tribune* Press Service and published in newspapers throughout the country. The author found this column, under the headline, "What Does the Name Matter If the Team Is a Flop?" published in the *Chicago Daily Tribune* on May 7, 1929, and the same column published in the *Washington Post* on the same day under the

headline, "The Port of Missing Men Found in Brooklyn."

15. McCarthy wasn't the only one to complain about Vance's shirt. Nothing was done immediately but eventually a rule was put in place banning any deformities in uniforms that would distract a batter. It could have been called "the Dazzy Vance Rule" because it was the Brooklyn pitcher's uniform that prompted the change.

16. Dazzy reflected on what he considered myths about his uniform sleeve in a June 1951 article in the *Sporting News.*

17. *Ibid.*

18. "Vance to Be Traded, Says Robins Pilot," *Chicago Daily Tribune*, Aug. 11, 1929.

19. "Vance Forgets His Primary Training," *Brooklyn Eagle*, July 25, 1929.

20. "Vance Trade Unlikely," *Washington Post*, Aug. 25, 1929.

21. Roscoe McGowen, "Freak Homer Beats Robins By 3 to 2," *New York Times*, Sept. 13, 1929.

Chapter X

1. Graham, *The Brooklyn Dodgers*, pp. 118–120.

2. Kieran, "Sports of the Times," *New York Times*, Feb. 6, 1930.

3. Westbrook Pegler, "Nobody's Business," *Chicago Daily Tribune*, June 15, 1930.

4. Robbie was referring to the 1929 World's Series in which the A's beat the Cubs four games to one and got the jump on them by winning the first two games. That was the series in which the Cubs had an 8–0 lead in the fourth game and seemed assured of tying the series at two games apiece. But the A's scored 10 runs in the seventh inning, won that game 10–8 and then took game five to win the World's Series.

5. Thurston threw eight shutouts in a nine-year career that included stints with the St. Louis Browns, Chicago White Sox, Washington Senators and Brooklyn. In 1924, he won 20 games for the White Sox and led the American League in complete games with 28. For Brooklyn, he won six games in 1930, none bigger than the shutout of the Cardinals on July 22.

6. Fred Lieb, *The St. Louis Cardinals* (New York: G.P. Putnam's Sons, 1947) p. 145.

7. Pegler, "Cardinals Beat Robins 1–0 in Tenth Inning," *Chicago Daily Tribune*, Sept. 17, 1930.

8. "I'd Hate to Pitch Nowadays," *Saturday Evening Post*, Aug. 20, 1955. In this article, written by Vance with Furman Bisher, Dazzy bemoans the fact that it has become a hitters game and that relief pitching has become a specialty. In his day, he said, starters were expected to finish what they started. "Brooklyn was made up of four or five starters and four or five other guys who weren't good enough to take a turn," he wrote.

9. The resurgence of Burleigh Grimes must have surprised Uncle Robbie and must have flustered him as well. Robinson prided himself in getting the most out of aging pitchers, thinking their experience and longevity was worth something. That was one of the reasons he had stuck with Dazzy Vance even though Dazzy confounded him sometimes with what appeared to be a lackadaisical effort. When the chips were down, Robbie wanted Dazzy on the mound. But after Grimes had his second straight losing season with the Robins in 1926, Robbie dispatched him to the Giants where he was 19–8 in 1927. He led the National League in wins with his 25–14 record for Pittsburgh in 1928, was 17–7 with the Pirates in 1929 and was 16–11 in a season split between Boston and St. Louis in 1930 — but he had a 13–6 record with the Cardinals. The well-traveled Grimes with the Cardinals and the Cubs in the next three seasons, appeared in the World's Series with St. Louis in 1903 and 1931 and with the Cubs in 1932. His 270 career victories earned him a berth in the Hall of Fame — and 107 of the wins came after he left the Robins.

10. Joseph Cardello, "Dazzy Vance in 1930 — One of the Game's 10 Best Seasons," *Baseball Research Journal*, The Society for American Baseball Research, 1996.

Chapter XI

1. "Dazzlin' Dazzy: Pitching Great Was Area's First Baseball Hero," *Citrus County Chronicle*, April 24, 1994.
2. "Homosassa Area Honors Dazzy With Ballfield Dedication," *Ocala Star-Banner*, July 30, 1978.
3. *Citrus County Chronicle*, April 24, 1994.
4. The author is indebted to Gene Vance, great-nephew of Dazzy Vance, for providing information about the Dazzy Vance family.
5. *Tampa Daily Times*, Feb. 25, 1933.
6. *Citrus County Chronicle*, April 24, 1994.
7. *Ibid.*
8. *Ocala Star-Banner*, July 30, 1978.
9. Some accounts of Mitchell's pitching are more charitable than others, not mentioning that Ruth took three strikes without lifting the bat off his shoulder and that Gehrig obviously timed his swing to miss each pitch. Tony Lazzeri, who followed Gehrig, walked on four pitches. When Mitchell played on the House of David, a barnstorming team of a religious sect, she was a teammate of Grover Cleveland Alexander, once one of the greatest pitchers in all of baseball.
10. "Here and There in Sports, *New York Times*, July 23, 1933.

Chapter XII

1. "Vance Would Train With Dodgers," *Washington Post*, Feb. 24, 1931.
2. "Old Uncle Wilbert Saves Another Baseball Player," *Chicago Daily Tribune*, March 12, 1931.
3. Pea Ridge Day is one of the more tragic figures in baseball history. He appeared in three games with the St. Louis Cardinals in 1924 and got into 17 games with them in 1925. Cincinnati picked him up in 1926 where he appeared in four games with no record. He toiled in the minor leagues for the next four years when the Robins signed him in 1931. Robbie used him in 22 games, two as a starter and he compiled a 2–2 record. But he was plagued with arm problems and found himself back in the minor leagues the next two years. He arranged to have surgery to repair his arm and he told friends the operation cost him $10,000. But Day discovered that the surgery did nothing to bring back the hop he once had on his fastball. In fact, from a baseball standpoint, the operation was a failure. Day went into fits of depression and on March 21, 1934, took his own life by slitting his throat with a hunting knife. Among his survivors was his five-week-old child.
4. The word "homo" was a play on words, a reference to Dazzy being a dignitary in Homosassa, Florida, and was not referring to sexual orientation, the connotation the word has in today's society.
5. The story about Pea Ridge Day and the characterizations of Herman, Vance, Lopez and Robinson were included in John Kieran's "Sports of the Times" column in the *New York Times* on April 14, 1931.
6. Kieran, "Dashing Around the Bases," Sports of the Times, *New York Times*, June 25, 1931.
7. Pegler, "Battle of 2 Old Nice Guys May Cost Brooklyn's Fans Manager and Much Mirth," *Washington Post*, Aug. 27, 1931.
8. Kieran, "The Brooklyn Manager, Hail and Farewell," Sports of the Times, *New York Times*, Oct. 25, 1931.

Chapter XIII

1. "Don't Go Out Nights, Hack; You'll Catch a Cold — Carey," *Chicago Daily Tribune*, Feb. 1, 1932.
2. "Vance Refuses to Sign Contract at Salary Cut," *Washington Post*, Jan. 17, 1932.
3. Graham, *The Brooklyn Dodgers*, pp. 127–128.
4. Kieran, "The Man on the Pier," Sports of the Times, *New York Times*, March 19. 1932.
5. Graham, *The Brooklyn Dodgers*, p. 128.
6. The Associated Press story was published in newspapers across the country. The version used here appeared in the

Los Angeles Times on Oct. 19, 1932. Beck, the 27-game winner for Memphis, was inserted into the Dodgers starting rotation and led the National League in starts in 1933 with 35. But he lost 20 of the games he started and won only 12. He spent two years with Brooklyn before he was released. He resurfaced with the Phillies in 1939 and earned the nickname of "Boom Boom" because of the number of home runs he allowed. Regarding the other trade rumors, Berger remained with Boston but Herman was traded not to New York but to Chicago for Bob Smith, Rollie Hemsley, Johnny Moore and Lance Richbourg. Lindstrom wound up with Pittsburgh in a three-way trade involving New York and Philadelphia.

7. "Carey Here, Sees Dodgers Improved," *New York Times*, Feb. 5, 1933.

8. "Vance of Dodgers Sent to Cardinals," *New York Times*, Feb. 9, 1933.

9. "Dodgers Tell Why They Sent Vance to Cards," *Chicago Daily Tribune*, Feb. 23, 1933.

Chapter XIV

1. "Dean, Derringer Exchange Blows as Cards Beat Reds," *Los Angeles Times*, June 7, 1933.

2. "Vance Fans Nine in Taking Duel From Warneke," *Chicago Daily Tribune*, Sept. 4, 1933.

3. Dazzy was holding the attention of many writers on the spring afternoon in Tampa. The comments reprinted here are from John Kieran's "Sports of the Times" column, aptly headlined "Warming Up With the Dazzler" and published in the *New York Times* on March 17, 1934.

4. "Bunch Hits Off Vance to Win For Guy Bush," *Chicago Daily Tribune*, April 19, 1934. Vaughan incorrectly gave Dazzy's age as 41 instead of 43. Ballplayers often lied about their ages, particularly when they were young because teams were always looking for young players. In an interview years ago, Hank Sauer, the slugging outfielder for the Cubs in the 1950s, told the author he lied about his age when he was in the minors because if a major

league team saw two players with equal ability, and one was 20 and the other was 22, they'd take the 20-year-old every time. In Sauer's case, he corrected his age for the record so that he would start receiving his pension at the proper time.

5. Lee Allen, *The Cincinnati Reds* (New York: G.P. Putnam's Sons, 1948), pp 226–228.

6. Robinson's death was naturally reported in newspapers across the country. This account appeared in the *New York Times* on Aug. 9, 1934.

7. Leave it to Dazzy, the businessman, to think of the money on the eve of the World's Series. For the record, Cincinnati finished in last place, 42 games behind the Cardinals. Vance's comments were published in a "World Series Side Lights" column in the *Washington Post* on Oct. 3, 1934.

8. *Ibid.*

9. "Early Drive Enables Dodgers to Triumph," *New York Times*, April 15, 1935.

10. "Six-Run Attack Brings Victory to Brooklyn," *New York Times*, April 24, 1935.

11. "Cards Unleash Barrage to Down Dodgers Twice," *New York Times*, Aug. 24, 1935.

12. "Dodger Great Tells of Last Fling, Regret He Didn't Win 200 Games," *New York Journal-American*, Feb. 9, 1955. The passage of 20 years may have clouded Vance's memory — or made it more selective. He is referring to a game on June 28, 1935, in which he pitched 3 1/3 innings in relief. Mancuso didn't hit a double. He hit a single and went to second when leftfielder Danny Taylor bobbled the ball. (It might as well have been a double from a pitcher's point of view). He was correct in remembering that Joe Moore singled home the tying run. The selective memory part of it is that none of that would have mattered if Dazzy hadn't given up a home run to Hank Lieber to start that inning, a fact he neglected to mention. Brooklyn lost 11–7 in 10 innings with Ray Benge, in relief of Vance, taking the loss. While Vance said it was his last chance to win his 198th game, the record shows he appeared in several more games before he was released.

13. Again, the passage of 20 years may have played tricks on the Dazzler's memory. It would be difficult to make a case for a game on May 15 "doing me in," as he said, considering that he appeared in games through the middle of August — and won three. His disdain for Stengel's handling of pitchers remained for most of the rest of his life. He made specific reference to the day he chased the fungoes for two hours and then pitched eight innings in a 1955 article in the *Saturday Evening Post*. At that time, Stengel was regarded as one of baseball's greatest managers as his New York Yankees teams of that era were the best in baseball.

Chapter XV

1. "Fans, Don't Sob; Vance is Happy," *Brooklyn Eagle*, Sept. 18, 1935.
2. *Ibid.*
3. *Ibid.*
4. "Daz Lauded as in Old Dodger Days— Runs Homosassa Hotel," *New York Post*, Dec. 22, 1936.
5. "Homosassa   Hermit — Dazzy Vance Leads Life of Reilly," *New York Journal-American*, March 24, 1937.
6. "Vance, Out of Baseball for Good, Fishing Fan," *Brooklyn Times-Union*, March 18, 1937.
7. Arthur Daley recounted the story of the rats and the ferret in his column in the *New York Times* on Feb. 21, 1961, shortly after Vance's death.
8. The anecdotes are from the Mercer, McCullough and Cassidy columns previously cited.
9. Kieran, "All in the Open," Sports of the Times, *New York Times*, June 5, 1941.
10. The author is indebted to Dazzy's grand-nephew, Gary Vance, for his insights concerning the Vance home in Homosassa.
11. "Dazzy Vance is Shadow of Old Self," *New York Journal-American*, Feb. 23, 1939.
12. "Memories Walk on Lonesome Street," *New York Times*, April 6, 1939.
13. "Former Dodger Hates to Leave Here," *Brooklyn Eagle*, Aug. 28, 1947.
14. "Knows How Columbus Felt, says HFer Vance," *The Sporting News*, Feb. 1, 1955.
15. "Brooklyn Pitches Big Day for Vance," *New York Times*, Jan. 31, 1955
16. It was not unusual to see Dazzy arriving at a train station. His great-nephew, Gary Vance, said Dazzy had an aversion to flying. "I don't know whether he ever flew anytime in his life," said Gary. The photo with Podres is interesting because of what the young lefthander would accomplish later that year. The Dodgers won the National League pennant in 1955 and then beat the Yankees in the World Series. Podres won two games, including the seventh and deciding one. So, for a time in 1955, Vance and Podres, though of different generations, were the most popular pitchers in Brooklyn history.
17. "Baseball Hall of Fame Series— 48," *The Sporting News*, Aug. 24, 1973. Ken Smith, baseball historian and director of the Baseball Hall of Fame is believed to be the last writer to have interviewed Vance before his death. His story was published on Jan. 18, 1961, two days shy of a month before Dazzy died. The quotation cited here is not from that article but from a piece Smith wrote 12 years later, reminiscing about that last interview.
18. "Florida Unimproved," *The New York Times*, Nov. 25, 1951. Warner captures the essence of the environment in which Dazzy chose to live. Warner's story begins, "To the visitor who wishes to see Florida as it was before subdivisions were created and landscaping carried out, this is an excellent spot to visit...."
19. "Dazzlin' Dazzy," *Citrus County Chronicle*, April 24, 1994.

Bibliography

"Absent Control Is No Handicap As Dazzy Vance Blanks Locals," *Atlanta Constitution,* April 20, 1921.

"Again a Dazzler," *New York Sun,* July 6, 1927.

"Alexander and Vance Had Too Much Stuff for Babe Pinelli," *Washington Post,* Feb. 8, 1953.

Alexander, Charles C. *John McGraw.* New York: Viking, 1988.

Allen, Lee. *The Cincinnati Reds.* New York: G.P. Putnam's Sons, 1948.

"American's Oldsters Win 12–5," *Chicago Daily Tribune,* Jan. 20, 1957.

"At the End of a Long Trail," *Atlanta Constitution,* Jan. 7, 1924.

"Babe Herman Recalls His Zany Days With Dodgers in Brooklyn," *Los Angeles Times,* Jan. 26, 1971.

"Baseball Hall of Fame Series— 48," *Sporting News,* Aug. 24, 1973.

"Baseball Notables in City for Dinner," *New York Times,* Jan. 30, 1955.

"Battle of 2 Old Nice Guys May Cost Brooklyn Fans, Manager and Much Mirth," *Washington Post,* Aug. 27, 1931.

"Batters Kept Loose as Dazzy Vance Aimed at Their Shins," *Pittsburgh Press,* Feb. 17, 1961.

"Batting A Thousand," *Utica Life & Times,* Oct. 25, 2001.

"Bench Hits Off Vance to Win for Guy Bush, *Chicago Daily Tribune,* April 19, 1934.

"Brooklyn Honors Vance, First Hall of Fame Dodger," *Brooklyn Eagle,* Feb. 1, 1955.

"Brooklyn Pitches Big Day for Vance," *New York Times,* Feb. 1, 1955.

"Brooklyn's Colorful Dazzy Vance Dies," *Washington Post,* Feb. 17, 1961.

"Cardinals Beat Robins 1–0 in 10th Inning," *Chicago Daily Tribune,* Sept. 17, 1930.

"Cardinals to Hand Dazzy Vance Along to Giants, St. Louis Hears," *The Sporting News,* Feb. 16, 1933.

"Cards Sell Dazzy Vance to Reds," *New York Herald Tribune,* Feb. 7, 1924.

"Cards Silent on Vance," *New York Times,* Jan. 14, 1934.

"Cards Unleash Barrage to Down Dodgers Twice," *New York Times,* Aug. 24, 1935.

"Carey Here, Sees Dodgers Improved," *New York Times,* Feb. 5, 1933.

"Citrus' Baseball Superstar," *Ocala Star Banner,* Aug. 14, 1977.

Corum, Bill. *Off and Running.* New York: Holt, 1959.

"Cubs Downed 9–5 and 3–2 by Dodgers," *Washington Post,* Aug. 15, 1935.

"Cubs Rout Vance, Take Sixth in a Row," *New York Times,* April 25, 1934.

"Daffiness Boys Are Legend in Flatbush," *Chicago Tribune,* Jan. 10, 1967.

"Daz Escapes from Farm," *New York Journal-American,* Feb. 7, 1955.

"Daz Lauded as in Old Dodger Days," *New York Post,* Dec. 22, 1936.

"Daz's Big Pitch— Confidence," *New York Daily Mirror,* Feb. 18, 1961.

"Dazzlin' Dazzy: Pitching Great Was Area's First Baseball Hero," *Citrus County Chronicle*, April 24, 1994.

"Dazzling Lecture Delivery," *New York Times*, March 12, 1936.

"Dazzy and Joe Get Good News on the Road," *Chicago Daily Tribune*, Jan. 27, 1955.

"Dazzy Vance," *New York Journal American*, Feb. 17, 1961.

"Dazzy Vance Blanks Crackers in Fast Game," *Atlanta Constitution*, May 15, 1918.

"Dazzy Vance Gets That $25,000," *The Sporting News*, March 21, 1929.

"Dazzy Vance, Hall of Fame Pitching Star, Dies at 69," *The Sporting News*, Feb. 18, 1961.

"Dazzy Vance Has Long, Hard Claim to Fame," *New York Herald-Tribune*, Nov. 18, 1922.

"Dazzy Vance in Hospital," *New York Times*, Nov. 11, 1938.

"Dazzy Vance in 1930," *Baseball Research Journal*, 1996.

"Dazzy Vance Is Chosen Star of National League," *New York Times*, Dec. 2, 1924.

"Dazzy Vance Is Shadow of Old Self," *New York Journal-American*, Feb. 23, 1939.

"Dazzy Vance Led N.L. Pitchers in Earned Runs for Third Time," *The Sporting News*, Jan. 1, 1931.

"Dazzy Vance Started Late But Blazed His Way to Hall of Fame," *Los Angeles Times*, Feb. 20, 1961.

"Dazzy Vance: The Pitching Sensation of 1923," *Baseball*, 1924.

"Dazzy Vance the Second Joins Atlanta," *Atlanta Constitution*, July 9, 1927.

"Dazzy Vance Traded for Catcher Dewie," *Atlanta Constitution*, Aug. 16, 1920.

"Dazzy Vance Wins Pneumonia Battle," *Citrus County Chronicle*, Nov. 17, 1938.

"Dazzy Was a Dazzler," *Chicago Daily News*, Jan. 28, 1955.

"Dean Beats Robins in Debut as Giant," *New York Times*, April 18, 1924.

"Dean, Derringer Exchange Blows as Cards Beat Reds," *Los Angeles Times*, June 7, 1933.

"Dodgers Call Up Dazzy Vance for Exhibition," *Chicago Daily Tribune*, July 21, 1951.

"Dodger Great Tells of Last Fling, Regret He Didn't Win 200 Games," *New York Journal-American*, Feb. 9, 1955.

"Don't Go Out Nights, Hack; You'll Catch a Cold," *Chicago Daily Tribune*, Feb. 1, 1932.

"Early Drive Enables Dodgers to Triumph," *New York Times*, April 15, 1935.

"Fans Don't Sob, Vance is Happy," *Brooklyn Eagle*, Sept. 18, 1935.

"Florida Unimproved," *New York Times*, Nov. 15, 1951.

"Former Dodger Hates to Leave Here," *Brooklyn Eagle*, Aug. 27, 1947.

"Four Hits Plus Vance Subdue Giants, 3–2," *New York Times*, July 8, 1927.

"Freak Homer Beats Robins by 3–2," *New York Times*, Sept. 13, 1929.

Frick, Ford. *Games, Asterisks and People*. New York: Crown, 1973.

Frisch, Frank. *Frank Frisch: The Fordham Flash*. Garden City, N.Y.: Doubleday, 1962.

"Giants Beaten 3–2 as Neis Hits Homer, *New York Times*, April 26, 1924.

"Giants Pound Vance and Defeat Robins," *New York Times*, April 13, 1922.

"Giants Rout Vance for 10th Straight," *Chicago Daily Tribune*, June 25, 1924.

"Giants Tie Robins in 9th, Win in 11th," *New York Times*, May 3, 1923.

"Girl Pitcher's First Task Will Be to Face Babe Ruth," *Washington Post*, March 27, 1931.

Graham, Frank. *The Brooklyn Dodgers*. New York: G.P. Putnam's Sons, 1945.

"Graham's Corner," *New York Journal-American*, Feb. 17, 1961.

"Here and There in Sports," *New York Times,* July 23, 1933.

"Homosassa Area Honors Dazzy with Ball Field Dedication," *Ocala Star-Banner*, July 30, 1978.

"Homosassa Hermit — Dazzy Vance Leads Life of Reilly," *New York Journal-American*, March 24, 1937.

"Honus Wagner's Own Baseball Story," *Atlanta Constitution*, Feb. 13, 1916.

"I'd Hate to Pitch Nowadays," *Saturday Evening Post*, Aug. 20, 1955.

"In the Wake of the News," *Chicago Daily Tribune*, March 29, 1938; July 25, 1940; July 20, 1955; Aug. 23, 1955; Feb. 18, 1961.

Kavanagh, Jack. *Ol' Pete: The Grover Cleveland Alexander Story*. South Bend, IN: Diamond, 1996.

Kieran, John. "Sports of the Times," *New York Times*, March 26, 1927, Aug. 25, 1927, Feb. 6, 1930, April 14, 1931, June 25, 1931, Oct. 25, 1931, March 19, 1932, Feb. 8, 1934, March 17, 1934, March 3, 1937, July 4, 1938, Jan.16, 1941, June 5, 1941, Aug. 24, 1941, July 9, 1942, Jan. 21, 1951, June 18, 1951, Oct. 11, 1953, Jan. 24, 1954, April 22, 1954, Aug. 19, 1954, Jan. 11, 1955, Feb. 1, 1955, May 18, 1959, June 3, 1959, Feb. 19, 1961, Feb. 21, 1961.

"Knows How Columbus Felt, says HFer Vance," *Sporting News*, Feb. 1, 1955.

"Late-Blooming Vance Beloved in Brooklyn," *Minneapolis Morning Tribune*, Feb. 17, 1961.

Lieb, Fred. *The St. Louis Cardinals*. New York: G.P. Putnam's Sons, 1947.

"A Little Bit of Everything," *Washington Post*, Feb. 12, 1924.

"McGraw Puts Ban on Golf for Season," *New York Times*, March 4, 1924.

"Memories Walk on Lonesome Street," *New York Times*, April 6, 1939.

"Murray Robinson Says," *New York Journal-American*, Feb. 19, 1961.

"New Delivery Style is Used by Ted Lyons," *Atlanta Constitution*, July 12, 1928.

"No Hits Off Vance But Phils Get Run," *New York Times*, Sept. 13, 1925.

"Nobody Like Dazzy Vance As Hornsby Had to Admit," *Brooklyn Eagle*, Feb. 20, 1961.

"Nobody's Business," *Chicago Daily Tribune*, June 15, 1930.

"O'Farrell Does Not Claim Flag But Predicts Improved Reds," *Washington Post*, March 27, 1934.

"Old Timers Get Stadium Ovation," *New York Times*, Jan. 31, 1955.

"Old Uncle Wilbert Saves Another Ballplayer," *Chicago Daily Tribune*, March 12, 1931.

"Petulant Rhino Considered Less Dangerous Than Dazzy," *Atlanta Constitution*, March 24, 1925.

"Phillies and Robins Divide Twin Bill," *New York Times*, June 30, 1928.

"Pitching of Vance Helps Robins Win," *New York Times*, May 5, 1922.

Rice, Grantland. "Sport Light," *Atlanta Constitution*, Jan. 6, 1929.

Ritter, Lawrence. *The Glory of Their Times*. New York: Vintage Books, 1966.

"Robins Ace Forced to Contend With Sore Arm for Five Years," *New York Journal-American*, Aug. 24, 1924.

"Robins Beat Braves, Clinching Second Place," *New York Times*, Sept. 28, 1924.

"Robins Beat Cards as Vance Fans 17," *New York Times*, July 20, 1925.

"Robins Bunch Hits and Defeat Pirates," *New York Times*, June 6, 1924.

"Robins Humbled by Giants in Opener," *New York Times*, April 20, 1922.

"Robins in Form, Win Two in Day," *New York Times*, Aug. 15, 1926.

"Robins' Onslaught Repulses Pirates," *New York Times*, June 12, 1927.

"Robins Save Vance with Rally in Ninth," *New York Times*, June 10, 1924.

"A Secret Daz Kept for 40 Years," *Brooklyn Eagle*, Aug. 7, 1952.

"Shortstop Needed to Make Dodgers Factors This Year," *Washington Post*, April 2, 1924.

"Six-Run Attack Brings Victory to Brooklyn," *New York Times*, April 24, 1935.

"Speed and Curves Receive Credit for Vance's Comeback as Hurler," *New York Times*, Aug. 2, 1927.

"Stengel Calls Vance One of the Great Ones," *Washington Post*, Feb. 17, 1961.

"The Story of Three Men on a Base," *Chicago Daily Tribune*, Jan. 29, 1951.

"Strikeout Ace to Get Record Salary While Rivals Claim Victory," *Brooklyn Eagle*, March 15, 1929.

"Strikeout King Conquers Jinx," *New York Journal-American*, Jan. 15, 1927.

"Surplus Yankees Go On Their Way," *New York Times*, Nov. 1, 1920.

"Talking It Over," *Chicago Daily Tribune*, Sept. 6, 1935; Oct. 29, 1935.

"This Morning," *Washington Post*, March 17, 1940; March 31, 1957.

"Tigers Jolt Yankees in Double-Header," *New York Times*, July 17, 1918.

"Twenty-Seven Men Face Vance and Get Only One Hit," *New York Times*, Sept. 8, 1925.

"Two More Robins Join Florida Squad," *New York Times*, Feb. 26, 1924.

"Uses His Fast One on Robby," *The Sporting News*, March 21, 1929.

"Vance Beats Reds for 10th Victory," *New York Times*, June 20, 1924.

"Vance Dies at 69; Was Dodger Star," *Chicago Daily Tribune*, Feb. 17, 1961.

"Vance Famed for Strikeouts," *Des Moines Register*, April 7, 1952.

"Vance Fans 9 in Taking Dual from Warneke," *Chicago Daily Tribune*, Sept. 4, 1933.

"Vance Finally Signs Three-Year Contract with Brooklyn Club," *New York Herald Tribune*, March 11, 1925.

"Vance Forgets His Primary Training," *Brooklyn Eagle*, July 25, 1929.

"Vance Goes to Cardinals," *New York Times*, June 26. 1934.

"Vance, Herman Notable for Their Absence," *Brooklyn Eagle*, Jan. 8, 1931.

"Vance Holds Reds to Only One Hit," *New York Times*, June 18, 1923.

"Vance Led League with Ten in a Row," *New York Times*, Jan. 28, 1924.

"Vance of Dodgers Sent to Cardinals," *New York Times*, Feb. 9, 1933.

"Vance, Out of Baseball for Good, Fishing Fan," *Brooklyn Times-Union*, March 18, 1937.

"Vance Put on Market; Robby Will Be the Salesman," *The Sporting News*, Aug. 19, 1929.

"Vance Refuses to Sign Contract at Salary Cut," *Washington Post*, Jan. 17, 1932.

"Vance Superman," *New York Post*, Dec. 22, 1936.

"Vance Tames Cubs and Robins Win," *New York Times*, May 13, 1924.

"Vance to Be Traded Says Robins Pilot," *Chicago Daily Tribune*, Aug. 11, 1929.

"Vance Traces Start to His Boyhood Days," *St. Louis Star-Chronicle*, 1924.

"Vance Trade Unlikely," *Washington Post*, Aug. 25, 1929.

"Vance Would Train with Dodgers," *Washington Post*, Feb. 24, 1931.

"Vance's 2.09 Earned Run Average Behind Weak Team Great Feat," *New York Herald Tribune*, Sept. 29, 1928.

"Veterans Make Brooklyn a Mystery Team in Race," *Chicago Daily Tribune*, March 18, 1924.

"World Series Side Lights," *Washington Post*, Oct. 3, 1934.

"Yankees Going South," *New York Times*, Feb. 19, 1916.

Index